The

Organisation

The Ethical Organisation

Robert Campbell
and
Alan Kitson

Second Edition

palgrave
macmillan

First published 1996
Reprinted five times

This edition published 2008 by
PALGRAVE MACMILLAN
Houndmills, Basingstoke, Hampshire RG21 6XS and
175 Fifth Avenue, New York, N.Y. 10010
Companies and representatives throughout the world

PALGRAVE MACMILLAN is the global academic imprint of the Palgrave Macmillan division of St. Martin's Press, LLC and of Palgrave Macmillan Ltd. Macmillan® is a registered trademark in the United States, United Kingdom and other countries. Palgrave is a registered trademark in the European Union and other countries.

ISBN-13: 978–0–333–99421–4
ISBN-10: 0–333–99421–3

This book is printed on paper suitable for recycling and made from fully managed and sustained forest sources. Logging, pulping and manufacturing processes are expected to conform to the environmental regulations of the country of origin.

A catalogue record for this book is available from the British Library.

A catalog record for this book is available from the Library of Congress.

10   9   8   7   6   5   4   3   2   1
17   16   15   14   13   12   11   10   09   08

Printed and bound in China

Contents

List of Figures, Tables, Case Studies, Examples, Appendixes and Scenarios

Figures

Tables

Case studies

Examples

Appendixes

Scenarios

Acknowledgement

The authors and publishers would like to thank Blackwell Publishers for permission to quote material previously published in the journal *Corporate Governance: An International Review* (1997) 5 (2): 52–9. Every effort has been made to contact all the copyright-holders, but if any have been inadvertently omitted the publishers will be pleased to make the necessary arrangement as soon as possible.

For Linda, with my love
A.K.

For Lynn and Laura, with my love, and
in memory of Jack and Janet
R.C.

Part I

Ethics and Organisations

Introduction

The first edition of this book was well received. In this edition, we have sought to strengthen further the focus on an active interrelation between theory and practice. We have introduced new material on leadership, corporate social responsibility, and information technology and the Internet. We have changed the structure so that there is an even closer relationship between theoretical aspects and practice, and we have introduced a new case study, with thanks to Dr Richard Warren of Manchester Metropolitan University. We have also taken this opportunity simply to tidy up some loose ends.

A problem in writing on business ethics is the risk of falling into one or another of two traps: of concentrating on theoretical (philosophical) material without grounding that material sufficiently in the real issues to which it should apply; or else of taking an overly pragmatic approach which ignores or minimises the theoretical difficulties such approaches should raise. We have tried to avoid both of these traps by placing at the heart of the book a sequence of case studies and sharply focused surveys of areas of management practice and surrounding them with grounded discussion of the theoretical material that is designed to supply both introduction and commentary. We hope we have, thereby, achieved an appropriate balance between theorising about business ethics and describing actual ethical problems.

It is not just a matter of balance, of course: theory needs to be integrated with practice, and that presupposes a methodology to achieve it. We have adopted a position that owes a good deal to John Rawls (1972: 20f.). A given ethical theory will have implications (obviously) about what is right and what wrong, and these implications may or may not square with our moral intuitions ('gut feelings'). It would be naive to suppose that the first attempt to formulate a theory must be correct. But neither can we assume that our pre-theoretical moral feelings are defensible just as they stand. Rawls suggests that we should go through a process of reflective consideration as to how to adjust both our feelings and our theory until a stable balance is struck between them. He calls this position 'reflective equilibrium'. We do not claim to have achieved this here. But we do believe that the book provides material that will enable readers to achieve a 'reflective equilibrium' between their own instinctive reactions to the cases and vignettes we describe and a more considered, theoretically informed judgement. It is hopeless to suppose that theories can be formulated (or worse, taken off the philosophical shelf) in advance of considering the nature of the actual cases or problems to which they are meant to apply. But neither is it sensible to believe that simply working through cases, however thoroughly and assiduously, is enough to provide sufficient insight to generate realistic and principled responses to them. There is a halfway house that, in our view, is as bad as – or worse than – either of these. This is to apply a limited number of simplified theoretical insights (usually loosely based on Kantianism and utilitarianism) and mechanically derive some stock conclusions, which are often inconsistent with each other and which yield no insight into either the nature of the problems or of the merits and shortcomings of the theories themselves.

Quite apart from anything else, all of these ignore the question of how case studies are selected and formulated. What makes something a problem that is worth our attention? How much information is needed to convey what makes a situation problematic? What is important and significant in a case study and what inessential and incidental? Clearly, without some kind of theoretical 'take' on an issue, none of these questions can be answered and examples, problems and case studies cannot even be put together. The belief that a pretheoretical position is possible usually means that the most conservative view has prevailed and that, in itself, is something that ought to be questioned. Nonetheless, consideration of actual cases may lead one to wish to adjust the initial theoretical 'take' and then to reconsider the case in the light of that next move. Ultimately, what is being aimed at is a set of mutual adjustments that achieves the best possible 'fit' between example and theory.

Theory needs to be informed by actual cases in another sense, too. We need to be clear about what kinds of cases really are morally problematic for practitioners and not merely rely on theory to tell us what ought to be difficulties. We do not want to invent problems that are hardly ever confronted in practice but which are theoretically interesting; neither do we want to swamp the reader with cases structured only by the most superficial or naive theoretical underpinnings. It has been our aim throughout to avoid both of these undesirable outcomes.

Finally, we hope that this volume will make a contribution through its stress on the importance of organisations to the study of business ethics. Whilst it is true that organisations are made up of people and that much depends on whether those people are equipped to make ethical decisions, to consider only those people and their decisions is to leave out something that is so important that, in its absence, the rest hardly makes any sense. Not only are organisations increasingly important influences on our lives, most of us, for a significant portion of our lives, work within an organisation of one kind or another. Our ability to live an ethical life is profoundly affected by the ethics of the organisations with which we deal and within which we operate. For this reason, we have chosen to focus on the extent to which it is possible for an organisation to be ethical and the impact that will have on the actions of those who work for it.

CHAPTER 1

The Ethical Organisation

After reading this chapter you will:

- Be able to identify a range of criteria used to describe ethical organisations

- Understand some of the fundamental concepts underlying those criteria

- Be able to analyse claims made by organisations and place those claims within a general context.

1.1 Introduction

People, with very few exceptions,[1] are moral entities. In other words, their actions are governed by rules, explicit or implicit, that can be subjected to ethical appraisal. We might praise them for being courageous, charitable, just, sensitive or magnanimous, or we might condemn their foolishness, envy or deviousness. We might neither praise nor blame, but wonder, instead, whether they really knew what they were doing or were, perhaps, coerced or pressured, or in some other way not fully responsible for what they seemed to have done. This language of moral evaluation does not only apply to adult human beings, but that is its primary and most typical use. Children might be selfish or act unfairly, but we accept that they only gradually acquire full moral responsibility for their actions. Animals, too, may be courageous or altruistic, but we may suspect a degree of anthropomorphism in extending moral language too far in their direction. The moral status of animals is a matter of debate, but no one thinks butterflies can have or lack charity or that jackdaws are dishonest. The rest of the world lies outside the moral realm altogether, except, perhaps, for our moral responsibilities towards it. Rocks and stones and trees do not have moral responsibilities.

At one end of the spectrum, then, there are adult, rational human beings with the full panoply of moral rights, duties, virtues and vices; at the other are inanimate physical objects to which moral language is entirely inappropriate. In the middle of the spectrum are small children and some animals (to whom some moral categories may be applied). Where on this spectrum do organisations belong?

One answer is that organisations – which in this context means clubs, societies, incorporated bodies, companies and so on – belong with the rocks and stones and trees on the non-moral end. To that, it is usually quickly added that, of course, such entities are made up of people and those people are moral agents, but the organisations as such are not. It would, therefore, be as absurd to require an organisation to act justly or to behave charitably as it would to expect the sea to be responsible in deciding which bits of the coastline to erode or a tree as to which passers-by it dropped its dead branches on.

A second answer is that organisations may well be agents that it makes sense to praise or blame for their actions, though, perhaps, not agents in exactly the same way that human beings are. Nonetheless, it is not a good idea to lay social, moral or political obligations on organisations; they are not very effective or efficient (or, sometimes, they are inappropriate) entities for carrying them out. A bank should operate according to financial principles, and not impose its political or social values on the community. Major concerns should not seek to remedy social problems through their hiring and firing policies, because they are not very good at it. In any case, attempting to do so will detract from their main mission – making a profit – out of which some genuine social benefit might eventually accrue.

A third answer is that some (though not all) organisations have sufficient structural complexity to be agents whom it makes sense to call to account for their actions and the consequences of those actions. It may not be possible for such organisations to be responsible in the way that people can be, but they can be responsible in a way that is appropriate to organisations. Being profitable is a virtue of business organisations, but it is not the only virtue. We can expect organisations to be socially responsible because that is part of the contract out of which they were created.

We want to argue that the third answer seems to us to be the most plausible and defensible of the three, but first we need to explain what is wrong with the other two.

1.2   Organisations are not agents

Margaret Thatcher once famously asserted that 'there is no such thing as "society"', there are only individuals'. The argument that organisations cannot have moral or social responsibilities seems, sometimes, to take as its premise a similar assertion, that 'there are no such things as organisations, there are only individuals'. Such an assertion cannot be as simple as it seems, or else it would have to be taken as affirming what is obviously false: that Marks & Spencer, Crédit Lyonnais, the Catholic Church, the United Nations and Greenpeace and similar organisations all over the world do not, in fact, exist and the illusion that they do is one suffered by millions of people. Clearly any argument resting on such a foundation could be easily rejected.

Instead, we must read the premise as asserting something more sophisticated; namely that organisations are made up out of people and that they have no real existence of their own apart from the people out of which they are constituted. This is like saying that rainbows do not (really) exist. It is not that if you think you have seen one you are mistaken, but that rainbows are made up out of the sunlight refracted through raindrops and that, were it not for the existence of raindrops and sunlight, there would not be rainbows. And what that is saying is that rainbows are not material objects, though they are an effect caused by physical objects (raindrops) in certain circumstances.

There may be people (as there certainly were in the past) that think that rainbows are material objects, at the bottom of which (could you get there) you would find a pot of gold. To such people the previous paragraph would be news. To the rest of us, the statement that rainbows are not real either tells us nothing we did not know before (read as telling us that rainbows are caused by raindrops) or else it is obviously false (read as telling us that rainbows are illusions).

Similarly, if the assertion that organisations are not real is saying no more than that the existence of organisations depends on people, then it is telling us nothing we did not already know. And, equally, if it is saying that organisations are illusions, then it is false. But perhaps we do need to be reminded that organisations are made up of people because we are inclined to attribute to organisations qualities that, properly, are properties of the people who make up those organisations rather than of the organisations themselves. If we are inclined to think that a rainbow is a material object, then we may be puzzled as to why we cannot get closer to it in order to see it more clearly. If we are reminded that a rainbow is just the sun refracted through raindrops as seen from a particular position, then the puzzlement vanishes. We can get closer to the raindrops but, once we do so, we are no longer seeing them from the right position for the rainbow to appear. It is not the rainbow that has a particular spatial location, but the raindrops.

Milton Friedman (1970) assumed that, when we talk about the social responsibilities of business, we are making just such a mistake. Businesses are not the kinds of things that can have responsibilities 'Only people can have responsibilities.' Friedman did not attempt to defend this, except by saying that a corporation is an artificial person (and, in this sense, may have artificial responsibilities). By this, he seems to imply that, just as artificial cream is not really cream, an artificial person is not really a person and artificial responsibilities are not real ones. But though artificial cream is not real cream, it is, in its own way, real enough. Incorporated organisations may not be real persons, only legal ones, but they are really organisations, and so the question of whether they can have duties, responsibilities, obligations, intentions, purposes and so on has been left untouched. Indeed, on the face of it, the idea that organisations cannot have responsibilities seems obviously false once actual examples are considered. Even Friedman thinks that governments have responsibilities (the responsibility, amongst others, to leave businesses alone to make money and not to impose social obligations on them). And the fact that other institutions – such as law courts, professional bodies, pension funds and so on – also have responsibilities seems unarguable.

This last fact is what makes the argument advanced by Danley (1993) rather curious. It does not deny that organisations are real, but that they are, like rocks and stones and trees, entities that are not capable of assuming responsibilities because they cannot form intentions. He explains the fact mentioned above – that some organisations seem, on the face of it, to have genuine responsibilities – by agreeing with Friedman that to talk in this way is simply a shorthand way of saying that certain individuals within those organisations have responsibilities. His argument is a severely positivist one that assumes that we cannot make a sensible distinction between the way in which an organisation ought to function and the way in which it actually does; between, that is, the decisions taken that are actually decisions of the corporation, and those that are decisions of its wayward members, acting outside the scope of their authority. The reason why this is a problem is that most organisations act in accordance with a corporate structure that is both much more complicated than, and also quite different from, the official organisational chart that hangs outside the CEO's office or in the reception area.

Thus, argues Danley, we must accept either that most decisions are not decisions of the organisation, as such, at all (because they are not in accordance with the officially publicised decision-making procedure), or else that all decisions made by any member of the organisation are decisions of the organisation (in which case we can no longer distinguish between decisions that are and those that are not decisions of the organisation).

As with many philosophically generated dilemmas, this one is quite bogus. Just because the officially produced organisational chart is both naive and over-simple, it does not follow that there are no rules at all that determine what counts as following the proper procedures. Official grammars of English (or, indeed, any natural language) are also both naive and over-simple, but it does not follow that there are no implicit rules at all that people follow and that anything (and hence nothing) can count as a correctly formed English sentence. Without rules, however informal and imperfectly characterised, there could be no such thing as the English language. Equally, without procedures and protocols – even if these are not what people would actually say they were, if asked – there could be no organisation as such, merely an anarchic mass of people.

This matters because it follows that many (though admittedly not all) kinds of organisations do have the complexity of internal structure that would permit us to say that they can take decisions and perform actions that are not either the decisions and actions of any one member, or an aggregate of the decisions and actions of all. This fact will be familiar to anyone who has served on committees (or boards of management, tribunals, juries, or anything of that kind): decisions are taken and acted on that are not the decisions or actions that any individual member would have chosen or predicted. Whether this is something that counts for or against committees is another issue. Nor is it relevant that, of course, sometimes an individual member will succeed in securing the committee's agreement to his or her own personal wishes, or that it is seldom the case (though it can happen) that a body makes a decision that none of its members, individually, would agree to. The point is not that, without its members acting and deciding, there could be no body that could act and take decisions. A committee is not some kind of magical machine that can operate without people. And the people involved will, of course, be responsible for the decision arrived at. The point is, rather, that a procedure exists that, if followed correctly, will result in a decision that is corporate or collective rather than individual; the responsibility for it will be collective or corporate rather than individual too.

1.3 Limited liability

If we have established that the idea of collective responsibility makes sense and that organisations can have responsibilities just as people do, we have still to establish that organisations either can or should have ethical responsibilities. Friedman (1970) and Friedman and Friedman (1980) argued (as does Hayek (1982) and, arguably,[2] Adam Smith (1976) did before him) that it is not prudent, even if it is possible, to require business organisations to take on responsibilities beyond those of making money and acting within the law.

The argument for this view comes in a number of forms, but common to all of them is the idea that the collective good is an unspecifiable and unknowable value. Individuals have differing conceptions of the good, and it is better to allow each to attempt to realise their own version of the good in their own way than to enforce some preferred version on everyone. There are two reasons for this. One is that, because individuals are different, there will be genuine differences in what is good for each and the attempt to sum over those individual goods is fruitless and, probably, also harmful. The other is that there is no clear formula for establishing what the good is and, so, any attempt to do so is prone to error. If individuals are left to determine what is good for them by themselves, then the scope of any error is restricted to that individual who has, in any case, a considerably greater incentive to correct it, or, indeed, to get it right in the first place, than has any third party.

Organisations, then, should 'stick to the knitting'[3] and do what they do best. In the case of business organisations, this is to turn a profit by trading in the market place. They should not, still less should they be obliged to, attempt to impose their view of what is socially good on the rest of us. They are not especially qualified to determine what that good is and, if they are wrong, we bear the consequences. And, because society is composed of individuals, that good is going to be so variable, so complicated and so diverse that they are extremely unlikely to get it right.

The idea that business organisations are, because they are essentially money-making enterprises, best to stick to making money and, also, that they should not be obliged to strive to do anything else, is undoubtedly appealing in its simplicity. There is also an economic argument that allegedly proves that, in a market of perfect competition, they can do nothing else, for any effort directed elsewhere than at profit must be a cost to the company. This cost can only be met by a decrease in profit or by degradation in the quality of the company's product: in a perfectly competitive market, a business that took this road would be forced out by competitors who chose not to bear this additional cost and could, therefore, increase their profits or sell a higher-quality product.

1.4 Society, markets and law

The idea of a perfectly competitive market is, however, an unrealisable ideal to which actual markets may only approximate. It requires that participants be small and anonymous, and that entry to and exit from the market be rapid and costless. The reason for this is that the larger and better known a company is, and the greater its investment in the market, then the more the market is distorted towards monopoly. Advocates of free-market economics find this point troublesome because it implies regulation of the market of a kind they would normally deplore simply in order to retain the free-market whose benefits they are advocating. Friedman glossed over this point in a single sentence when he remarked that the responsibility of a corporate executive 'is to conduct the business in accordance with [the] desires [of his employers], which generally will be to make as much money as possible while conforming to the base rules of society, *both those embodied in law and those embodied in ethical custom*' (our emphasis).

What, we believe, he had in mind here is that certain core legal and moral values are essential if business and trade within the market is to be possible. These would include promise-keeping, financial probity, honesty, integrity and reliability. They would also require the avoidance of price-fixing, cartels and other monopolistic tendencies. This is because, unless a business paid its bills and met its orders, it could not continue to trade and, if it began to dominate the market, then that market, to that extent, would no longer be a free one. But once this is spelled out it would seem that Friedman has conceded the case that corporations can and should be ethically responsible. The only way to avoid this conclusion is to draw a dubious distinction between positive and negative duties; between those things one should refrain from doing and those things one ought to do. An organisation can be required not to do harm. It ought not, in addition, be required to do good. This is partly because it is governments through the political process that are the appropriate organs for determining what social good is. It is also partly because doing good involves costs that it is not appropriate for a business organisation to have to bear if it is to remain in a competitive position within the market place.

Several highly questionable assumptions are involved in this argument. One is that positive duties have costs whereas negative duties are cost-free. But to refrain from exploiting or creating a monopoly market is certainly not cost-free, whereas anti-discriminatory hiring and promoting policies may well, after a certain initial investment, bear fruit in the form of a more highly qualified, better-motivated work force. A second assumption is that refraining from doing harm is readily distinguishable from doing good. But, clearly, to refrain from harming someone is to benefit them, whereas to fail to benefit someone when one is able to do so, is to harm them. A third assumption is that to require organisations to act in a socially responsible way is to render them less competitive and, thereby, to injure the market that creates the wealth in the first place. But it is not clear that this is any different, in principle, from the requirement, which Friedman himself accepts, that businesses 'conform to the base rules of society'.

It is true that, in a perfectly competitive market, free riders[4] can benefit from dishonesty and honest traders will be disadvantaged by it. This process can continue until the supply of honest traders runs out and the market is totally corrupted. (At which point it will, presumably, disintegrate, along with a substantial portion of the fabric of civil society.) Thus, a perfectly competitive market must be maintained by legal and/or social regulation that imposes on all those obligations that honest traders impose on themselves. It is, therefore, in the interests of those who do not need to be regulated that they be regulated. That creates a level playing field in which free riders are compelled to quit or else compete on equal terms. In other words, society creates a market it is prepared to live with, and there is no reason why it should be prepared to live with a market in which only minimal standards of honesty and decency prevail, rather than one that is able to take on a higher degree of responsibility towards the society that created it and the environment in which it operates and from which it benefits.

The question is not whether organisation can or should have ethical and social responsibilities. We believe that we have shown this to be the case. Indeed, it would seem that even Friedman has conceded this point, though he might well have thought that his position can avoid its implications. The question is, rather, that since organisations do and must have such responsibilities then, whether and where a line can be drawn around what they can do and what we would wish them to do (or not do). What are the characteristics of a properly ethical organisation?

1.5   Characteristics of ethical organisations

How can it be known, either by organisational members or by external others, that a particular organisation is ethical? Given the enormous size and complexity of some business organisations, to what extent does it make any kind of sense to ask the question? How are the claims of an increasing number of businesses seeking to establish themselves as ethical in the minds of customers and others to be assessed?

It is not necessarily the case that the most admired companies are also the most ethical. For example, every year chief executives of large companies are asked to identify the most admired companies in their sectors and the most admired generally. The reasons given for admiration show a wide range. In 2000, General Electric was voted as the most admired company overall. It was admired for its leadership and management and for the way it has increased the value of its shares. On the other hand, Microsoft and Sony (second and third respectively) were admired for their vision and innovation. Coca Cola was highly rated, as fourth, for its product portfolio and its sense of ethical and social responsibility. IBM, fifth, was admired for its constant improvement and its marketing and advertising. Toyota came sixth and was admired for its focus on consumers. In only one of these cases was ethical standards considered to be a factor in generating the admiration of a company's peers. It is doubtful that Coca Cola would have rated so highly without its excellent product portfolio – it would not have been fourth purely on the basis of its sense of ethical and social responsibility (Skapinker 2000).

However, this is a survey of company chief executives. Their admiration for each other is clearly influenced by the factors that drive and reward their business performance. It may be unsurprising then that a range of factors emerges from this survey and that ethical business behaviour is not necessarily paramount.

There is some evidence to indicate that members of the public, customers and other stakeholders do place greater emphasis on business ethics and corporate social responsibility when deciding whether or not particular firms are admirable or, at least, worthy of support. KPMG's survey (1999) indicates that members of the public rate philanthropy as a significant feature of corporate behaviour.

The behaviour of businesses and other organisations is increasingly under scrutiny. There has been a significant growth in interest in corporate social responsibility during the last 10 years and the emergence of a range of indices for measuring social responsibility as the basis for investment in companies' shares, as well as the growth of international standards for social responsibility auditing. An increasing number of organisations see advantages to their corporate reputations coming from their willingness to report annually a range of aspects of their behaviour. As Adrian Godfrey, a partner with Ernst & Young, puts it 'Investors, employees, customers, suppliers, joint venture partners, community groups, NGOs, government bodies, the media ... Each of these groups has an opinion on your company – what you're good at, what you're not, what sort of people work for you, how well you treat them and how well they treat others.'

So, organisations do have reputations and those reputations are the consequence of a wide range of judgements being made by a wide range of people and, for some of those people, it is the ethical behaviour of the organisation that lays at the base of their judgement about the organisation. What are these criteria that are used by widely disparate groups to assess the ethical behaviour of organisations?

Assessing the ethical dimensions of organisational behaviour is a complex task. The criteria chosen as the basis for assessment are critical. There are various approaches adopted by the many different organisations engaged in this assessment activity. Examples 1.1, 1.2, 1.3 and 1.4 present various sets of criteria, each set indicating a particular approach for assessing the ethical dimensions at work in a business.

EXAMPLE 1.1

Council for Economic Priorities

The Council for Economic Priorities, a New York based organisation, provides awards – the Corporate Conscience Award – to companies that meet a broad range of criteria. Its criteria are classified under the broad headings of:

- Environment

- Women

- Minorities

- Charitable giving

- Family

- Workplace issues

- Disclosure.

A company's grades are determined by using company questionnaires and data from non-governmental organizations. In addition, CEP researchers use the *Dow Jones News Retrieval*, monthly publications (such as *Business Weekly* and *The Economist*), daily publications (such as the *New York Times* and the *Wall Street Journal*), company lists (Fortune 1000 and S&P 500), and product data from consumer reports.

Each of the headings is broken down into more detailed criteria and use is made of a wealth of published information about the company's performance.

EXAMPLE 1.2

Ethical Junction

Ethical Junction, by way of contrast, requires only that businesses wishing to subscribe to its services should operate in accordance with the following seven principles:

- Active demonstration of care for the environment

- Support for fair trade practices

- Avoidance of practices causing long-term damage for short-term gain

- Operation of non-exploitative employment practices

- Challenging of all forms of discrimination

- Acting in a socially responsible manner

- Support for the development of ethical organisations and business.

The Ethical Junction does not assess in detail, the degree to which any particular organisation fulfils its statement of principles. Nor do they undertake any comparative analysis of companies who are accepted for subscription. They direct those requiring an in-depth analysis to research organisations in the ethical field, such as EIRIS or CEP.

EXAMPLE 1.3

GoodCorporation

The GoodCorporation network in the UK was established by the Institute of Business Ethics. It was set up to provide organisations with a standard of corporate social responsibility (CSR). By developing a network of GoodCorporations, it hopes to encourage and promote CSR, particularly in new sectors and businesses. It is their belief that CSR is at the heart of good business practice and they hope that it will spread to a much wider group of businesses and organisations.

The GoodCorporation defines CSR as meaning:

- Fair treatment of employees, customers, suppliers, the community

- Protection of the environment and being fair to shareholders or

- Suppliers of finance.

The verification process uses a standardised reporting format. This involves checking at four levels:

- That policies are in place

- That a system exists to implement these policies

- That records are available to show that the system works

- That stakeholders (such as employees) actually agree that the system works and is fair.

This process is applied annually to all members of the network.

EXAMPLE 1.4

Caux Round Table

The Caux Round Table of business leaders from Europe, Japan and the United States is committed to energizing the role of business and industry as a vital force for innovative global change.

The Round Table was founded in 1986 by Frederik Philips (former President of Philips Electronics) and Olivier Giscard d'Estaing (Vice-Chairman of INSEAD) as a means of reducing escalating trade tensions. It is concerned with the development of constructive economic and social relationships between the participants' countries, and with their urgent joint responsibilities toward the rest of the world.

The Caux Round Table believes that the world business community should play an important role in improving economic and social conditions. It aims to express a world standard against which business behaviour can be measured. It seeks to begin a process that identifies shared values, reconciles differing values and, thereby, develops a shared perspective on business behaviour acceptable to and honoured by all.

These principles are rooted in two basic ethical ideals: *kyosei* and human dignity. The Japanese concept of *kyosei* means living and working together for the common good, enabling cooperation and mutual prosperity to coexist with healthy and fair competition. 'Human dignity' refers to the sacredness or value of each person as an end, not simply as a mean to the fulfilment of others' purposes or even majority prescription.

There are seven general principles proposed by the Caux Round Table. These can be summarised as:

Principle 1   Businesses should share the wealth they have created with their employees, customers and shareholders; they should honour their obligations to their suppliers and competitors in a spirit of honesty and fairness; they should be responsible citizens of the local, national, regional and global communities in which they operate.

Principle 2   Businesses established in foreign countries to develop, produce or sell should also contribute to the social advancement of those countries by creating productive employment and helping to raise the purchasing power of their citizens. Businesses also should contribute to human rights, education, welfare and vitalization of the countries in which they operate.

Principle 3   While accepting the legitimacy of trade secrets, businesses should recognise that sincerity, candour, truthfulness, the keeping of promises, and transparency contribute not only to their own credibility and stability, but also to the smoothness and efficiency of business transactions, particularly on the international level.

Principle 4   Businesses should respect international and domestic rules. In addition, they should recognise that some behaviour, although legal, might still have adverse consequences.

Principle 5   Businesses should support the multilateral trade systems of the GATT/World Trade Organization and similar international agreements.

Principle 6   A business should protect and, where possible, improve the environment; promote sustainable development; and prevent the wasteful use of natural resources.

Principle 7   A business should not participate in or condone bribery, money laundering or other corrupt practices: indeed, it should seek cooperation with others to eliminate them. It should not trade in arms or other materials used for terrorist activities, drug traffic or other organized crime.

There then follows a detailed statement about how each stakeholder in the business should be treated. Stakeholders identified are employees, suppliers, investors, shareholders, competitors, the environment and communities.

Each of the four approaches outlined uses a different set of criteria (with some common elements) as the basis for assessment of ethical business. The Council for Economic Priorities focuses on making prestigious awards to businesses that meet their exacting criteria, and businesses can win awards in each of the seven areas identified for examination. The Ethical Junction exists as a kind of broker for ethical business and aims to put ethical businesses in touch with each other so that they can trade with each other. The aim is to expand the amount of business-to-business trade between ethical businesses. Registering with the Ethical Junction does not require any exacting tests to be passed. It is enough for the business to want to do business with ethical businesses. The GoodCorporation has developed an approach based around the stakeholder concept: it does not make awards but lays down rigorous standards that businesses wanting to use the badge 'GoodCorporation' have to meet. The Caux Round Table focuses on the global responsibilities of global businesses and operates at a very high level in political and economic terms. Its principles underlay what it sees as an ethical business system but they could be used by a business as guides to operating ethically.

But where do the basic concepts underlying these different approaches originate?

The search for the characteristics of ethical organisations can be based on three different approaches. These approaches are not mutually exclusive. Each of them offers useful insights. First, there is the approach that stems from a desire to build a model or theory of corporate moral excellence from a basis of first principles. Second, there is the approach that is based on stakeholder theory. Third, there is the approach that stems from a concern about issues of corporate governance.

This chapter goes on to examine each approach and outlines an emergent paradigm that draws its dynamic from seeking to build upon them to create a more holistic model.

1.6 Theories of corporate moral excellence

The notion of corporate or organisational culture is well established in the field of organisation theory and behaviour. Although there are some significant divergences of view about the features and origins of corporate culture, there is widespread agreement amongst analysts that organisational culture significantly affects behaviour in organisations.

Fundamental to any corporate culture are the values embedded within the corporation. Deal and Kennedy (1982) express this view forcefully when they write 'Values are the bedrock of any corporate culture.' They assert that values produce a sense of direction for employees and help to guide and control their day-to-day behaviour.

One useful distinction between corporate values is that between espoused values and values in practice. Espoused values are those found in company mission statements, codes of ethics or credos. They state what the company stands for and describe the ethical perspective of those who are responsible for leading and directing the company. They are intended to indicate to employees, customers, competitors, suppliers and others the type of behaviour and approach that is acceptable to the company.

These espoused values may be very different from 'values in practice'. For example, a company statement may contain a sentence that says 'We regard our employees as our most valued asset.' If this is the case in practice, then one might expect to see clearly considered and effective policies and procedures in relation to the appointment, induction, training and development, remuneration and other rewards of employees. If these do not exist, then the contrast between espoused values and values in practice may be clear. If the company practices are seen as unfair and discriminatory or repressive and outdated, then its employees will need no one to point out to them the differences between espoused values and values in practice. No one would regard the publicly stated espoused values as, in themselves, an indication of an ethical company. There would be a reasonable expectation that espoused values would be followed through in practice.

Michael Hoffman (1986) builds upon the concept of corporate culture in order to develop a powerful theory of corporate moral excellence. Hoffman holds the view that corporate culture has three main elements. First, there are the basic values, attitudes and beliefs of the organisation. Second, there are the organisational goals, policies, structures and strategies shaped by those basic values, attitudes and beliefs. Third, there is the organisational 'way of doing things'. These are the everyday, accepted and unchallenged processes and procedures. Almost hidden from view within these everyday forms of behaviour are the basic values, attitudes and beliefs of the organisation.

However, Hoffman asserts that within organisations it is individuals who are responsible for creating goals, criticising and evaluating the corporate culture and instigating and implementing change. He states that the morally excellent corporation is one that discovers the healthy reciprocity between its culture and the autonomy of its individuals. This reciprocity is a necessary, but not sufficient, condition for corporate moral excellence. It is also necessary for the corporate culture to be a moral corporate culture.

This means that the espoused values and values in practice should be ethically acceptable. Although not directly concerned with issues of business ethics, the work of Peters and Waterman (1982) supports this view. They studied successful companies that had achieved excellence in their fields and concluded that, amongst other characteristics, excellent companies were clear on what they stood for and took the process of shaping value very seriously. They doubted whether it was possible to be an excellent company without clarity on values and without having the right type of values. Morally excellent organisations, therefore, have, according both to Hoffman and to Peters and Waterman, cultures based on ethical values.

How can an organisation ensure that its ethical values are reflected in its corporate culture? How can it ensure that its basic ethical beliefs are reflected and carried through in its goals, policies, structures and strategies, and in its everyday ways of behaviour? Goodpaster (1983a) offers an approach based on four steps. First, there is the need to look for ethical issues or situations that raise ethical questions. Second, rational principles are applied to produce ethical strategies and procedures. Third, there is a need to coordinate the ethical strategies and procedures with other demands, interests and constraints. Fourth, there is the implementation of the agreed ethical strategies and procedures. This produces action or 'good deeds' and involves integration within the everyday way of doing things in the organisation.

However, Goodpaster takes the view that such an approach could be dangerous to individual moral autonomy if it takes place within a corporate culture that is too strong or prescriptive. Excellent organisations are driven by a few key values and give space to individuals to use their initiative to support those values. Morally excellent organisations, according to the approach exemplified by Hoffman and Goodpaster, are characterised by ethical values and clarity about those values. They also have good communications systems to aid the process of clarification and implementation, room for rational disagreement and protest, avenues of withdrawal for anti-pathetic individuals and minimised bureaucracy and control.

However, according to Sinclair (1993) the prevailing approach to corporate ethical behaviour holds that creating a unitary cohesive culture around core moral values is the solution to enhancing ethical behaviour. Strong cultures are characterised by being shared by all employees, being deeply felt, being capable of determining behaviour and being consistent across the organisation. However, he argues that strong cultures present dangers. They can be simply a managerial ideology designed to serve the interests of those who exercise power within the organisation. They can run counter to the long-term performance needs of the organisation by blinding organisational members to the need for change. They can undermine ethical conduct by removing dissent and rational debate of issues.

Having identified the dangers of a powerful, uniform organisational culture, he goes on to identify the benefits of sub-cultural conflict within organisations. A sub-culture within an organisation can be defined as a subset of the organisation's members that identifies itself as a distinct group and routinely acts on the basis of collective understandings unique to that group. The prevailing approach described above sees sub-cultures as likely to undermine the dominant, unitary corporate culture. Sinclair argues that sub-cultural conflict can actually be beneficial to the organisation. It could enhance commitment to organisational goals if sub-cultural goals can be assimilated into the organisational purpose. It can help to prevent 'groupthink'. It can improve the overall performance of the organisation if its members have diverse norms and styles, and it can help to prevent disasters by encouraging a critical approach to organisational management. Sub-cultural conflict can also stimulate ethical behaviour by preventing insulated or blinkered thinking on the part of the organisation's managers. However, sub-cultural conflict presents dangers to ethical behaviour. This is because it might develop into anarchy with no shared values across the organisation and a lack of perceived responsibility to the organisation as a whole.

These approaches to corporate moral excellence begin with models of ethical behaviour that offer rich insights into organisational life and often produce very practical approaches to the development of ethical behaviour within organisations. Having established, on the basis of principles or theory, the likely features of an ethical organisation, the next step is to consider ways in which such characteristics can be developed, embedded and encouraged within actual organisations. There is considerable experience in the United States in the implementation of corporate ethics programmes and a great deal of guidance is given to managers about how to go about creating more ethical organisations. There are four major features of such advice and guidance, which rest upon a pre-determined model of ethical organisations similar to those outlined above.

First, the need for an ethics audit – this is an exercise in self-assessment by the organisation, usually in response to a series of prepared questions dealing with major aspects of behaviour and operations within the organisation. Clutterbuck et al. (1992) identify three levels of audit. These are, first, the policy level; second, the level of systems and standards; and, third, the level of recording and analysing performance.

Second is the need for publicly stated expectations about employee behaviour. There has been a proliferation of company codes of ethics in both European and US business over the last 20 years.

Third is the need for organisational structures to support ethical behaviour. For some organisations, this has meant the creation of ethics committees with, sometimes, very wide-ranging powers. In others, it has meant the provision of confidential hotlines for whistleblowers.

Fourth is the need for ethical behaviour to be supported by the reward systems within organisations. Employees soon notice the difference between espoused values and values in practice. The ways in which an organisation responds to ethical or unethical behaviour are extremely potent influences on employees' perceptions and behaviour.

1.7 Ethics and stakeholder theory

A different approach to the problem of defining and developing ethical behaviour in organisations is provided by stakeholder theory. According to this approach, paying attention to the needs and rights of all the stakeholders of a business is a useful way of developing ethically responsible behaviour by managers. An ethical organisation is seen as one in which obligations to stakeholders figure prominently in the decision-making of managers within the organisation.

Stakeholder theory has a long tradition. John Donaldson (1992) writes that the term 'stakeholder' was created by Robert K. Merton in the 1950s and has enjoyed a vogue in recent years. Goodpaster, on the other hand, states that the term appears to have been invented in the early 1960s as a deliberate play on the word 'stockholder', which is the American equivalent of the British 'shareholder'.

The Stanford Research Institute, in 1963, defined the stakeholder concept as including those groups without whose support an organisation would cease to exist. Its list of stakeholders originally included shareowners, employees, customers, suppliers, lenders and society. It was argued that unless business executives understood the needs and concerns of these stakeholder groups, they would be unable to secure the support necessary for the continued survival of the firm. Freeman (1984) widens the definition to 'any group or individual who can affect or is affected by the achievement of the organisation's objectives'.

Company law in Britain enshrines the view that the interests of shareholders of public companies take precedence over any other interests in the company. Companies are managed by those appointed by the Board of Directors, who are themselves elected by shareholders, to ensure that shareholders enjoy the largest possible return on their investment; the managers act as agents for the shareholders, who are their principals. Of course, this bald assertion is not always the reality. James Burnham, writing in the 1930s, alerted others to the trend that he labelled 'the managerial revolution', and there have been many examples of boards of directors being taken to task by shareholders when they appear to have prioritised interests other than those of the shareholders – recent examples being those of Tiphook and Queens Moat Houses.

The primacy of the shareholder is, however, being challenged in the UK through a fundamental review of company law. Launched in 1998 by the Department for Trade and Industry, this review is developing an inclusive approach to directors' duties and responsibilities. They are increasingly seen as having a duty to consider all the interrelationships on which the company depends and to take a long-term view when making decisions. The long-term interests of shareholders are seen as requiring directors to take account of the interests of other stakeholders. A new legal requirement is being proposed, an operating and financial review (OFR), which will require the directors of a company to 'provide an account of the company's key relationships with employees, customers, suppliers and others on which its success depends' (DTI 2000). This review of company law is heavily influenced by stakeholder theory and, in particular, by the model developed by the Royal Society for the Encouragement of the Arts, Manufacture and Commerce – the Tomorrow's Company model.

The Tomorrow's Company model seeks to develop an inclusive approach to the leadership, management and development of businesses. By 'inclusive' is meant an approach that identifies values and builds upon the contribution to the success of the company from its various stakeholders. It argues that, to be successful in the newly emerging economy of tomorrow, businesses need to work collaboratively, both internally and externally. This has implications for how the business treats its employees, its suppliers, its customers, the environment and community; how it measures its performance by incorporating measures other than simply financial ones; how it uses and shares information; and how the business is led (RSA 1995).

Stakeholder theory is an attempt to broaden the perception that there is one dominant interest – that of the shareholder – in public companies. It challenges the view that the primary, or even sole, purpose of a company is to maximise the return to shareholders. It does not directly challenge the Friedmannite view that businesses exist only to maximise profits. This is because a firm may aim to maximise its profits without necessarily maximising the return to shareholders. Conversely, a firm may maximise the return to shareholders without necessarily maximising its profits. Indeed, within the concerns of theorists of the 'managerial revolution' tradition is a concern that managers often ensure maximum returns to themselves rather than to shareholders and that this is often done on the basis of business objectives that are not focused on the maximisation of profits. Growth and market share are often the predominant objectives of managers. This may or may not lead to a maximisation of profits.

In challenging the predominant view, as enshrined in the legal codes of many societies, that the interests of shareholders have primacy, stakeholder theory introduces the notion that there are a variety of stakeholders in any business. The decisions of managers and Boards of Directors have an impact on many different groups, communities and individuals. Stakeholder theory asserts that companies have responsibilities and obligations beyond those to the shareholders.

But what kind of responsibility do organisations have to their stakeholders? Hosmer (1991) identifies five levels of managerial responsibilities: ethical, conceptual, technical, functional and operational. Ethical responsibilities include the distribution of benefits and the allocation of costs or harms created by the firm. Hosmer argues that, if these functions are performed well, the benefits and harms will be distributed in a way that stakeholders will see as right, proper and just. Ethical principles should be used to distribute benefits and allocate costs or harms because the decisions subsequently made will be seen by stakeholders as ethical. They will be more acceptable to stakeholders and ensure the continuing support of stakeholders.

However, there are significant differences within the tradition of stakeholder theory. The major differences revolve around the question 'How far do the responsibilities of companies extend?'

We have already looked at the Friedmannite view, which holds that the role of business is to make profits and its only responsibility is to the shareholder (pp. 5–8). This view rejects the notion that there are any other stakeholders in business. Those who wish to argue that businesses do have wider social responsibilities express a very different view. For example, in Britain, the work of New Consumer, a public interest research organisation, identifies a broad range of issues and stakeholders when describing the activities of many of Britain's major companies. Adams et al. (1991), writing on behalf of New Consumer, seek to evaluate company performance along dimensions such as disclosure of information, employment issues, pay, benefits and conditions, industrial democracy, equal opportunities, community involvement, environment, other countries, respect for life, political involvement, respect for people, oppressive regimes, military sales and marketing policy. There is an underlying assumption here that businesses have a very wide range of responsibilities and that a very wide range of groups, including shareholders, have a stake in the business because they are affected by the actions of the business.

Between the Friedmannite and New Consumer approaches, there lies a considerable range. Raven (1994) draws a distinction between a narrow definition of stakeholders and a wider definition. The narrow definition would include the following groups as stakeholders: employees, shareholders, customers, suppliers, creditors and the local community. The wider definition would add the following: social activists, public interest groups, trade associations, local government, international organisations and society in general.

Some approaches include 'competitors' as stakeholders. This may seem rather strange at first sight, but is worth exploring a little. There are many examples, particularly in the small business sector, of mutual interdependence between firms operating within the same industry. If a small garage, for example, is presented with a repair job that requires specialist equipment, it may be able to borrow the equipment from its 'competitor' around the corner. If it cannot cope with the repair, it may recommend another of its 'competitors' to the customer. Collaboration with competitors is not unknown in big business. When several European companies combine their efforts to produce Airbus or the channel tunnel, it could be argued that they become stakeholders, not only in that particular project but also in each other's future success. It is also the case that in entering into trade associations that are designed to protect and further the interests of businesses within a particular industry, competing businesses are acting on the assumption that their future success as individual businesses is intimately connected with the success of the industry – that is, with the success of their competitors.

Stakeholder theory presents managers in business and other organisations with a significant challenge. Managing a business knowing that your primary responsibility is to the shareholders might not be easy, but at least it is likely to be a much less complex task than managing a business within the context of multiple claims from multiple stakeholders.

A significant challenge to the claim that stakeholder analysis is a way of introducing ethics into managerial decision-making comes from Goodpaster (1983a). He argues that managers may carry out an analysis of stakeholder reactions to decisions for reasons that have little to do with ethics. They might be concerned that stakeholder reaction could impede the achievement of strategic objectives and that the effects of decisions on relatively powerless stakeholders might be ignored or discounted. Expanding the list of stakeholders who are taken into account may be a form of enlightened self-interest but Goodpaster doubts that it is really a way of introducing ethical values into business decision-making.

Goodpaster also casts doubt on what he calls the 'multi-fiduciary view' of stakeholder analysis. This view argues that managers do not have only a single fiduciary duty to shareholders. They have multiple fiduciary duties to all stake-holders. If shareholders are the principals and managers act as their agents – which is a relationship that forms the basis of much of company law – then a major objection to the multi-fiduciary view is that the obligations of managers to shareholders takes precedence over all other obligations. The multi-fiduciary view imposes a neutrality on managers. They are required to be neutral regarding the competing interests of stakeholders and to produce decisions that, effectively, balance their competing claims. This neutrality undermines their moral respon-sibility, as agents, to act in the best interests of their principals, the shareholders.

The solution to this problem, for Goodpaster, lies in the argument that prin-cipals cannot expect of their agents behaviour that would be inconsistent with the reasonable ethical expectations of the community. The ethical challenges faced by managers are the same as those faced by other people. Goodpaster (ibid.) states 'The foundation of ethics in management ... lies in understand-ing that the conscience of the corporation is a logical and moral extension of the consciences of its principals. It is not an expansion of the list of principals'. Stakeholder analysis may assist managers in their strategic planning but it will not, of itself, introduce ethical considerations into their decision-making.

1.8 Ethics and corporate governance

Theories of corporate governance offer a further perspective on the characteris-tics of the ethical organisation. In his book *Management and Machiavelli* (1967), Anthony Jay draws a parallel between the large, modern public corporation and the independent or semi-independent states of the past. He feels that theories of government offer a way of fully understanding the behaviour of these large corporations. For Jay, management can only be properly studied as a branch of government.

Theories of government make use of concepts such as accountability, author-ity, power, consent, responsibility, policy-making and administration. They are concerned to produce guidance about the best forms of government and the appropriateness of procedures of decision-making and execution. Classical the-ories of management (see, for example, Brech 1953) saw management as a process incorporating planning, control, organisation, delegation, responsibility, and authority and accountability. They were concerned to improve the manage-ment of the modern large corporation and drew heavily on concepts developed in the study of government.

The connection between ethical behaviour and political or governmental pro-cesses are well established in the field of political philosophy. Aristotle, for example, saw a close link between his ethical theory and his political theory. He begins his discussion of ethics with the statement that every craft and every enquiry, and similarly every action and project, seems to aim at some good. He concludes that the good has been well defined as that at which everything aims. His discussion of ethics is followed by his treatment of politics. According to MacIntyre (1977), 'The *Ethics* shows us what forms and style of life are necessary to happiness, the *Politics* what particular form of constitution, what set of institutions, are necessary to make this form of life possible and to safeguard it.'

One can expect theories of government applied to the large corporation to be closely linked to a concern about ethical behaviour. Such theories tend to be labelled as theories of corporate governance. The use of the word 'governance' is partly based on fad or fashion but it emphasises the focus on the 'act, manner, function of government' (*Oxford English Dictionary*).

Before going on to examine some of the more significant aspects of corporate governance, it is important to note that, for Aristotle and other major political theorists, the formal mechanisms of government were produced and sustained by human action and could, therefore, be changed by human action. There was nothing inevitable or necessary about particular forms of government. Also, the existence of a particular form of government was no guarantee of human happiness. People in positions of power and influence, within any system, needed to behave in ways that produced happiness, and this behaviour was shaped by their intentions which were, in turn, shaped by their values and beliefs.

The values and beliefs of those engaged in the processes of corporate governance are as significant in influencing their behaviour as are the formal procedures. Clearly, some procedures are more likely to produce ethical behaviour than others, and discussions of problems in corporate governance do need to focus on issues of procedure, powers and responsibilities in a formal sense. However, the existence of formal procedures will not, of themselves produce ethical behaviour.

Much of the literature on corporate governance is a response to problems of compliance, by businesses, with their obligations to their shareholders. Cannon (1992), for example, defines corporate governance as:

> the sum of those activities which make up the internal regulation of the business in compliance with the obligations placed on the firm by legislation, ownership and control. It incorporates the trusteeship of assets, their management and their deployment.

This perspective on corporate governance sees senior managers as accountable, for the use of the firm's assets, to the owners of the business. The managers are stewards or trustees acting as agents on behalf of the owners of the assets. Cannon draws attention to the relationship between the poor performance of several large corporations and the increasing clamour during the late 1980s and the 1990s from shareholders who wished to able to exert more control over those with responsibility for managing their companies.

This approach is based on the pursuit of the self-interest of the owners of the business. They are concerned to protect their investment and to enhance their income levels from share dividends. If their managers had performed well – in the sense of ensuring at least stable levels of income for shareholders – then concerns about corporate governance issues would be less likely to be raised.

This does not seem to be a very promising basis for the development of an ethical organisation. The argument is that changing the style and methods of corporate governance is justifiable because it will result in enhanced income for shareholders; therefore, one ought to be concerned about corporate governance and try to produce models of corporate governance reflecting this justification. Such an approach might produce ethical behaviour, or at least encourage it, but not intentionally. The intention is to produce enhanced income for shareholders through enhanced corporate performance.

A second perspective on corporate governance derives from a concern with the excessive pay increases that directors received in the 1990s, the perks and conditions of senior executives and the golden handshakes received by executives leaving their organisations. The relationship between company performance and executive pay is perceived as having broken down. Despite relatively poor market performance, the pay of senior executives has outstripped that of middle and junior managers and of other employees. Many scandals have been reported in the media. For example, in 2001, Airtours (a major UK tour operator) dismissed 2,800 employees and sacked the director of a failing division. The director received almost £1 million as compensation for losing his job. This was a contractual requirement on the company. The director's contract, agreed when he entered the company, entitled him to this payment. Edmond Warner, writing in *The Guardian*, states 'If there is a scandal, it is not that failed executives receive more than they deserve, it is that a system exists that straps such golden parachutes to their backs before they are asked to demonstrate their worth.'

This concern has developed within the private sector, and is particularly powerful in the newly privatised areas. It has also spread to the public sector. For example, the decision, in 1994, of the Council of the University of Huddersfield, England, to offer a package amounting to over £500,000 to its retiring Vice-Chancellor was a subject of parliamentary investigation and, as a result, changes to the instruments and articles of government of the 'new' universities have been made. In this case, the Vice-Chancellor was retiring early following a bitter dispute over the representation of staff, students and the local community on the university's governing council. This dispute resulted in an overwhelming vote of no confidence in the governing council by the staff of the university.

In Britain, concern about corporate governance in the private sector led to the production of what became known as the Cadbury Report. In 1991, the Financial Reporting Council, the London Stock Exchange and the accountancy professional bodies established a committee, chaired by Sir Adrian Cadbury, to examine the financial aspects of corporate governance.

The particular reasons for the establishment of the committee were based upon a concern about the lack of confidence in financial reporting and in the value of audits. These concerns were heightened by several failures of major public companies, whose financial statements gave no forewarning of their true state of affairs. Interest in the work of the committee extended beyond what might have been expected from such a technical and fairly narrow brief, and the work of the committee became a focus for a wide debate about issues of corporate governance in general.

The committee's report, published in 1992, presented a voluntary Code of Best Practice, which is aimed at the boards of listed companies based in the UK. It argued for adequate disclosure of financial information and for checks and balances within the governance structure of companies. Their view was that disclosure of financial information was necessary to ensure that all those with a legitimate interest in a company have the financial information they need in order to exercise their rights and responsibilities towards it. They argued that openness by companies is the basis of public confidence in the corporate system.

The proposals in relation to checks and balances within the structure of a company were based on the view that they assist the directors in fulfilling their duty to act always in the interests of the company and guard against undue concentrations of power. These proposals included a recommendation that there should be a clear division of responsibilities at the head of a company between the Chairman of the Board of Directors and the Chief Executive of the company. These roles should not be combined in one person. Recommendations to strengthen the role of the non-executive directors were made. These included having a formal process for their selection, that they should be independent of the management of the company, and that they should not have business interests that conflict with those of the company.

The report also proposed that the non-executive directors should form a remuneration committee to decide on the remuneration package of executives and that full details of remuneration packages should be disclosed in the annual reports of companies. The establishment of an audit committee was also proposed. This should have at least three non-executive directors. This was designed to bring greater objectivity into the auditing process and ensure greater public confidence in the published, and audited, accounts of public companies.

In June 1993, the London Stock Exchange introduced an obligation on listed companies to state, in their annual reports, whether they comply with the Code of Best Practice and to give reasons for any area of non-compliance. This Stock Exchange requirement does not mean that companies must comply with the Cadbury Report's recommendations. It requires only that companies make a statement about compliance. The committee took the view that it was in the best interests of companies to comply with the code, as this would enhance their market standing. They also argued that non-compliance might lead to greater statutory control in the future. If companies could not be seen to comply with a voluntary code, the threat was that the government would feel obliged to introduce legislation to enforce compliance.

The Cadbury Committee's recommendations on corporate governance were followed by further reports on executive remuneration and responsibilities for disclosure of information to shareholders – the Greenbury Report (1995), the Hampel Report (1998), the Combined Code (Financial Services Authority 1998) and the Turnbull Report (1999) All of these reports sought to build on the work of Cadbury and develop further guidance for companies listed on the London Stock Exchange. Their influence, however, spread beyond the private sector. In particular, the Turnbull Report's approach to the identification and management of risk has had a significant influence on a wide range of organisations in both the public and private sectors. For example, the Higher Education Funding Council in England now requires all the universities and colleges to which it provides funds to conduct a detailed analysis of risks and identify how those risks will be managed. The Turnbull Report classifies risks under the headings of legal, health and safety, and environmental, reputation and business probity issues.

In 2003, the list of reports on corporate governance was added to by the publication of the Higgs Report. This built upon and extended the recommendations of previous reports. It recommended that half of the membership of the board of public limited companies should comprise non-executive directors. It re-affirmed the recommendation of previous reports that the role of chairman and chief executive should be split, but went further in suggesting that the chairman should not previously have been the chief executive. It aimed to strengthen the voice of non-executive directors by recommending that they should meet without the chairman and executive officers present, and that one of them should be chosen to listen to shareholders on a regular and formal basis. It went further in defining the responsibilities of non-executive directors in relation to strategy, performance, risk and people, and that they should be limited to two three-year terms of office. In the light of difficulties in finding appropriately qualified and experienced non-executive directors, the Higgs Report recommended that a group of senior business people should be set up to identify people from outside the business world.

Compliance with the codes and reports published since Cadbury is still not a legal requirement. Companies can decide whether or not to comply with 'best practice' identified in the various reports. If they decide not to comply, they must then be willing to take the consequences. The main consequence will be a reduction of trust in the company, and the long-term effect this will have on the company's reputation and business success. If they chose not to comply, they must state where non-compliance has occurred and explain their reasons. However, the new Financial Services Authority is empowered to levy fines on companies for breaches of the Stock Exchanges rules and the Stock Exchange rules now incorporate the principles developed through this series of reports.

Theories of corporate governance focus attention on the policy and decision-making structures of large companies. They stem from a concern with the rights of shareholders and place responsibilities on directors and senior executives. They emphasise the need for openness in decision-making and for a clear demonstration that the company is being governed in accordance with perceived business virtues.

Judgements about undesirable business practices are usually based on a notion of business virtues. Clearly, perceptions of virtuous behaviour differ over time and place. Equally clearly, perceptions that some forms of business behaviour are unacceptable are based on a model or theory that indicates what is acceptable. These views arise from, and exert great influence within, the relevant community. Only if the labellers have a standard by which to judge can actions and behaviour be labelled excessive or unacceptable. The concerns about excessive secrecy in annual company reports, about a lack of suitable checks and balances within company decision-making structures, about the excessive power of the one person who combines the roles of chief executive and chairman of the board of directors are all based on some commonly held standards that apply at the time the judgements are being made. These standards are based on what are seen as business virtues.

If an organisation follows the requirements of a code of best practice in relation to corporate governance, is it likely to be an ethical organisation? A board of a UK company may decide to follow fully the Cadbury Committee's recommendations, but it does not follow that the company is an ethical organisation. It may still produce shoddy or dangerous goods, pollute the environment, impose adverse conditions on its workforce or tell lies in its advertising. However, the following of a code such as that found in the Cadbury Report is more likely than not to lead to a corporate governance regime with greater openness of information, less likelihood of domination by one or a few people, and fewer excesses in the remuneration packages of senior executives.

1.9 A holistic paradigm

Each of the three major perspectives outlined above can be compared with the others on the basis of three elements. These are values, structures and processes.

This comparison is represented in Table 1.1.

In relation to values, there is no fundamental conflict between the three approaches. The 'moral excellence' approach does not, per se, identify what values lead to moral excellence. It stipulates that the values of organisations should be clear, that they must be ethical and that the culture based on those values should not oppress organisational members but rather should recognise the importance of the autonomy of moral actors. The ethicality or otherwise of such values (or the content of such values) is a judgement that can be based only on the business community's values, or business virtues. The 'stakeholder' approach places value on the satisfaction of the needs of a range of stakeholders. By implication, the managers of organisations should reflect values such as fairness, equity, openness and honesty. The values regarded as important by the 'corporate governance' approach are derived from a view of the everyday business virtues that make business life possible. These include openness and honesty in dealings, and compliance with what is regarded, within the business community, as good business practice.

Each approach has something to say about organisational structure. 'Moral excellence' approaches identify the need for the creation of structures that reinforce the organisation's values as expressed in its mission statement, code of ethics or other ethical statement. The 'stakeholder' approach specifies the need for structures that are representative of the different stakeholders. The 'corporate governance' approaches emphasise the need for internal checks and balances, so that power does not become concentrated and the need for the 'general interest' to be represented effectively through non-executive directors.

In relation to processes, the 'moral excellence' approach identifies the need for ethical audits, the production of codes of ethics/conduct, and the need for reward systems to be oriented towards encouraging ethical behaviour.

Table 1.1   Comparison of major business perspectives

	Excellence	*Stakeholder*	*Governance*
VALUES	Values must be clear Values must be 'ethical' Culture should not be too strong, individual autonomy is important	Central value is the commitment to satisfy the needs of stakeholders	State control or regulation of business should be avoided Central importance of business virtues (e.g. temperance, honesty, trust) Reporting on activity should be transparent and voluntary codes should be complied with
STRUCTURE	Structure should be specifically aimed at reinforcing ethical statements/codes/ Mission Emphasis on formal roles and procedures (ethics officers/committees, hotlines, whistle-blowing avenues)	Structures should represent the interests of stakeholders, representative structure for stakeholders Management seen as a neutral balancer of competing interests	Board of directors needs checks and balances on power Separation of powers between Chief Executive and Chair of the Board Role of non-executive director seen as providing balance and an external view on the corporation's activities
TYPICAL PROCESS	Ethical audits using national or international standards Codes of behaviour are produced to clarify the core values of the business and to shape behaviour by influencing expectations Systems are revised to orient towards ethical behaviour	Strong emphasis on strategic planning as a process for reflecting the interests of a range of stakeholders	Strong focus on processes of reporting on the firm's conduct and achievements with an emphasis on the need for comprehensive, honest and transparent reporting to the wider business community

The 'stakeholder' perspective emphasises the strategic planning process as central to the ethicality and success of the organisation. A strategic planning process that does not incorporate the needs/views of the various stakeholders is likely to be unsuccessful, and could be unethically dominated by one group pushing its own interests to the detriment of others. The 'corporate governance' approach focuses on reporting processes, particularly financial reporting and its truthfulness.

There are, at least, two possible conceptualisations of the relationship between values, process and structure that can be derived from an examination of the

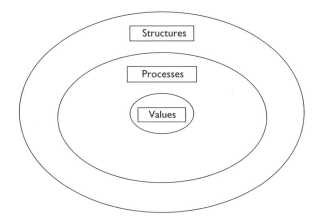

Figure 1.1 Concentric circle approach

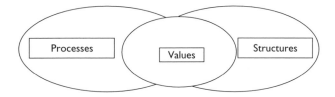

Figure 1.2 Differential overlap approach

three approaches. The first is a concentric circles approach and the second is a
differential overlap approach.

The concentric circle approach (see Figure 1.1) implies that values are central to any ethical organisation. Indeed, some would argue (see Campbell and
Tawadey 1992) that values are central to any organisation. Values are articulated
and implemented through processes that require an organisational structure for
their delivery.

The differential overlap approach (see Figure 1.2) places values at the organisational centre, but implies that not all organisational structures and processes
are driven by organisational values. Some processes and structures may exist for
reasons other than the consummation of the organisation's central values.

1.10 The ethical organisation

What does this examination of the three perspectives tell us about the possible
characteristics of ethical organisations?

The concentric circles approach implies that an ethical organisation is one
in which there is an almost perfect match between the organisation's values,
its internal processes and structures. Organisations wishing to become ethical
would need, in accordance with this model, to clarify their values, ensure that
their values change to ethical ones if necessary, and implement a thorough review
of their internal processes and structures. Changes in environmental factors or
internal changes – such as a change in leadership, or the opening up of new

centres of operation, or mergers and acquisitions – would require the exercise to be done again, and again, and again.

An organisation that tried to develop itself on the basis of utilising organising concepts from more than one of the three perspectives outlined above might find itself in some difficulty. Each of the three approaches suggests a different pathway to the ethical Holy Grail.

The differential overlap model offers a more realistic scenario. The centrality of values is accepted. However, the need for absolute clarity is less pressing and, to some extent, there can be a borrowing from each perspective, or the importation of aspects of the other two into a dominant perspective. The extent to which organisations derive their values from a variety of perspectives is an empirical one worthy of further research. But it seems to be intuitively plausible to argue that many (if not all) organisations of a certain size do, in fact, take an eclectic attitude to value sources.

Value change, from whatever source, can be more readily adopted within organisations that do not feel the need for root and branch change every time there is a (significant) change in values. This is more likely to be possible in organisations that do not attempt to ensure that all of their processes and structures are derived uni-dimensionally from a clear value statement.

However, even if values are not totally clear, it must be the case, for an ethical organisation, that significant features of organisational processes and structures are shaped by the particular value set of the organisation. Absolute clarity might not be desirable or possible. Some organisations will find it easier than others to ensure a total reflection of a clear set of values within their structures and processes. Such organisations might be less able to respond readily to change. They might also have a tendency to veer towards some kind of moral absolutism. Those organisations that adopt a more pluralist approach might be less able to define their values clearly, might have elements of their processes and structures that are not much influenced by a concern for ethical values, and might be more susceptible to accusations of unethical conduct. But an incremental, less driven approach might be more likely to produce an organisation with greater flexibility, more willingness to change practice, less convinced about its own moral superiority, and more willing to admit mistakes when they happen.

1.11   Dimensions of ethicality

Through an examination of the three perspectives and an acceptance that the differential overlap model is likely to be more consonant with reality than the concentric circles model, it is possible to draw up a set of dimensions along which to place the degree of ethicality of organisations.

An organisation would be ethical if it:

- Wanted to be ethical, preferably, but not necessarily, for non-instrumental reasons

- Were as clear as possible about its values, without an unquestioning acceptance of them

- Has a culture which reflects these values, without being so dominant as to stifle dissent;

- Had processes that reflect its values, but were ready to change them as circumstances change

- Took into account the needs/views of stakeholders in its strategic thinking, without simply trading off one stakeholder's need/view against those of another

- Fully, accurately and honestly reported on its activities in ways suited to the needs of its different stakeholders

- Had internal checks on power, so that too much power is not accumulated into the hands of a single person or small group

- Had a fair system of remuneration and division of the spoils of success.

Each organisation needs to refine these characteristics further for its own purposes. For some organisations, at a particular time in their history and with a particular conjunction of circumstances, some of these characteristics will be more important than others. This approach to identifying ethical organisations is not very far from that used by the judges in the Business Ethics Magazine's report, in its November/December 1995 issue, on its search for ethical corporations in the USA. All three winners were said to demonstrate a commitment to ethics and social responsibility, integrity and fairness, concrete beneficial outcomes from an ethical approach, steadfastness in remaining ethical during difficulties. Each winner individually excelled at either implementing an ongoing ethics programme, or environmentalism, or community involvement, or employee relations or diversity. This was not a search for perfection. As Dale Kurschner put it, 'Every company, just like every individual, has character flaws. It's how we deal with them that reveals our values.'

QUESTIONS AND TASKS

1 Write down your own personal list of the criteria you would choose to assess the ethical standing of an organisation. How does your list of criteria differ from the list at the end of this chapter?

2 By using the Internet and other research sources, find out about one of the following organisations: Coca Cola, British American Tobacco, The Body Shop, Sainsburys, British Petroleum. From what you have discovered, rate your chosen organisation against your personal ethical criteria.

3 Now review your personal criteria and make any adjustments to them that you would feel to be appropriate.

4 Keep your revised list and refer back to it as you proceed through the rest of this book.

Part II

Case Studies

Introduction

The case studies in the following chapters are classic stories of companies in trouble of one kind or another. We have preferred not to use particularly topical or contemporary cases. This is because, although there is something to be said for immediate currency, it is outweighed, in our view, by the difficulty that the facts are not yet definitively agreed – or perhaps not even all in – thereby making it is impossible to come to a comprehensive and properly informed judgement. The case studies therefore range from the 1960s to the year 2000. They present you with themes and issues that continue to confront contemporary business practice. The case of Queens Moat Houses, for example, is clearly comparable with that of Enron.

The case studies are intended to present well-grounded material to which you may return or upon which you may reflect during the later parts of the book. You will find lengthy and detailed examinations of actual events and problems that offer a rich background from which to draw and against which to test understanding of the models and theories introduced later.

These case studies are not vignettes, neither are they short, stylised stories of incidents or brief résumés of ethical difficulties. They provide considerable detailed contextual material and they are complex. Vignettes, of which there are several in later chapters, provide an opportunity to focus sharply on issues and to identify dilemmas. Complex and detailed case studies present a different challenge. There is the need to clarify the issues, to relate them to the body of information, and to place oneself within the culture and structure of the organisation. We have therefore chosen to present cases that are now, to a large extent, settled, in the sense that there is little prospect of further information emerging that might radically alter our perception of what is going on.

Part II begins with a discussion of the role and value of case studies, together with a consideration of the different ways in which they can be approached.

The Turner & Newall asbestos case study is based on material prepared by Richard Warren and he has kindly agreed to its use here. This case study presents issues of distributive justice and the procedures that are needed to ensure that the demands of distributive justice are met.

The case of Virgin Atlantic and British Airways, in describing a complex set of events, alerts us to the impact of organisational structure, culture and circumstances on behaviour.

The case of Queens Moat Houses provides opportunities to review the relationship between shareholders and directors within the context of business regulation and control.

The case study dealing with the UK-based Co-operative Bank examines the impact of the Bank's Ethical Policy on a significant group of managers within the Bank.

CHAPTER 2

The Use of Cases in the Study of Business Ethics

After reading this chapter you will:

- Have a good understanding of the different approaches to case study analysis

- Be able to identify an approach to case study analysis that you personally favour

- Be aware that issues of business ethics are often complex, intriguing and demanding.

2.1 Introduction

Business and management education has the purpose of improving business practice. Many other claims are made for it but none is as intuitively or philosophically appealing as this. Employers and practitioners might sometimes take the view that business and management education exists to serve their needs for competent employees who can carry out the tasks necessary for successful operation. Therefore, education should aim to provide people with the requisite skills and appropriate attitudes as well as knowledge of business practice. Others take the view that an education should enrich the mind and develop critical faculties and, therefore, a good understanding of critical theory is central to the process of business education, and skills and attitudes can be acquired during the early stages of employment.

We take neither of these positions. Our view is that both business education and business practice are enriched by the synergy of theory and practice. The best practice is theoretically informed. It is based on a clear and firm grasp of concepts and principles. These are not developed as independent, free-standing intellectual products. They are developed within the context of theory. Good theory reflects a sound grasp of practice. Just as it is the case that theory can often be challenged on the basis of non-compliance with reality, so business practice can be criticised because it is not in accordance with best practice. The notion of best practice is that of practice that is theoretically informed. Case studies can help students of business ethics to refine theory by referring to the application of theory to instances and by illustrating the deficiencies of or inadequacies of theory.

One argument against the use of cases might be that, since ethical issues are essentially irresolvable dilemmas, there is little point in trying to resolve them. On the contrary, we believe that an introduction to ethical reasoning will help you to analyse situations and cases rationally. Furthermore, even if some dilemmas are not totally resolvable, they may be partially resolvable. Dilemmas may also be avoided or minimised in their force by skilful management. The use of cases can help to sensitise current and future managers to the situations likely to lead to ethical dilemmas and to ways in which they might avoid, minimise or otherwise cope with such situations.

2.2   Aims of the case study approach

Mathews et al. (1994) identify three purposes for the study of cases in business and management education. The first is to develop the sort of understanding, independent thinking, judgement and communication that are needed in the business world. It is the stubborn facts embedded within a chunk of reality that require us to face up to the thorny issues experienced by business people. Second, the study of cases develops confidence in the exercise of judgement and the willingness to give regard to other viewpoints. Third, analysing cases in ethics helps to develop moral judgement. Cases in business ethics are usually difficult to resolve and require a moral understanding on the part of the analyst.

The cases presented in the next four chapters are intended to help you to develop confidence and skill in the analysis of complex issues in business ethics. In analysing these cases, you will develop the ability to recognise the complexities of ethical issues in business and to form your own conclusions. The cases are intended for classroom discussion and it is in the process of challenging others' conclusions and defending your own that you will be able to refine your ideas and produce more sustainable conclusions. Beyond this, you will also develop greater sensitivity to others' views and greater awareness of the different perspectives that can be brought to bear on ethical problems in business.

2.3   Approaches to the analysis of cases

There is no one best way of analysing cases. There is, however, a well-established and widely used approach. This is often labelled the 'rational' approach. This approach to analysis owes much to the belief-systematic and positivistic explanations of organisational behaviour. It is a powerful, explanatory approach, derived substantially from Benthamite utilitarianism. Jeremy Bentham's 'hedonistic calculus' (1789) was based on the view that the consequences of any social, economic or political action could be divided into costs or benefits, and that it was possible to calculate with some precision the balance of cost and benefit for any such action. It has been developed into the dominant, almost unquestioned method of problem solving within business.

The rational approach consists of the following five steps:

- Identifying the problem
- Generating alternative solutions

- Evaluating the alternatives, using cost-benefit approaches
- Selecting the solution
- Implementing the chosen solution.

Each step can require detailed investigation and some very hard thinking, and the process may become iterative – that is, the analyst may need to think again about an earlier stage as a result of the work carried out in later stages. It may also be the case that instead of seeking to identify and implement the optimal solution, the analyst may be satisfied with a sub-optimal solution. This may be due to pressures of time, lack of analytical capacity, the inability to obtain all the necessary information, or basic human faults such as laziness or lack of interest (see Simon 1947).

An alternative, less widely used but equally powerful approach, is Aristotelian in origin. Malloy and Lang (1993) present this method as a 'transrational' approach. The transrational approach to analysis is more comprehensive than the merely rational. In *Metaphysics* (1947), Aristotle explores the causes of things in existence. He proposes that things exist because of the First Principle and Four Causes. The First Principle is the cause of all causes or the prime mover – Aristotle's equivalent of the Judeo-Christian God. The Four Causes are the material cause, the formal cause, the efficient cause and the final cause. The material cause is that from which something is made. The formal cause is that into which something is made. The efficient cause is that by which something is made. The final cause is that for the sake of which something is made.

The Prime Mover in relation to business organisations is the person who creates the organisation. The final cause for an organisation could be described as its *raison d' être* – it is the organisation's philosophy or ideology. It can be seen in mission statements and ethical policies. The formal cause is the organisation's culture or its way of doing what it does. The culture is shaped by the climate of the organisation and this is a product of the leadership process. Leadership is, therefore, the efficient cause of the organisation. The material cause of the organisation is its membership.

Malloy and Lang offer the following questions, based upon the Four Causes, as an aid to case analysis:

Final cause

1 What is the stated purpose of the organisation?

2 What is the unstated purpose of the organisation?

3 What are the organisation's official goals?

4 What are the organisation's operative goals?

5 Is there a stated organisational philosophy?

6 Is there an unstated organisational philosophy?

7 How do employees, management, clientele and society perceive the organisation's purpose, goals and philosophy?

Efficient cause

1 What is the style of leadership?

2 What is the perceived style of leadership within the organisation? By superiors? By subordinates?

3 What is the preferred style of leadership in the organisation? By superiors? By subordinates?

Formal cause

1 How does the organisation socialise new members?

2 What are the organisation's rituals, myths, unique language and slogans?

3 What are the explicit standards of organisational behaviour?

Material cause

1 How do employees perceive the organisation?

2 What is the employees' value orientation towards work?

Malloy and Lang claim that their approach to the analysis of managerial dilemmas is holistic in nature, and they contrast this with the limited perspective on organisational reality provide by the rational approach.

A third approach to the analysis of cases is provided by Goodpaster (1983b). He begins by describing several frameworks for analysis of ethical issues. First, he distinguishes between issues relating to the external environment of the organisation as a whole and those relating to the internal environment. Within the context of the external environment, the manager sees the organisation as a moral agent in the wider society. The internal environment is to be managed with a view to maintaining the freedom and well-being of the organisation's members. He goes on to distinguish between descriptive ethics, normative ethics and metaethics. Descriptive ethics is aimed at an empirical or neutral description of the values of individuals and groups. Normative ethics seeks to develop and defend judgements of right and wrong, good and bad, virtue and vice. Metaethics is concerned with examining questions about the meaning and provability of ethical judgements, or of comparing one ethical theory with another.

He then divides approaches to ethics into three categories. These are utilitarianism, contractarianism and pluralism. The first asks, 'What action or policy maximises the ratio of benefits to costs?' The second asks, 'What action or policy most fairly respects rights?' The third asks, 'What action or policy reflects the stronger duty?' Goodpaster, on the basis of these frameworks, then offers a list of questions that may be asked in relation to a case study. They are:

1 Are there ethical issues involved in this case? Centrally or peripherally? Is a decision required?

2 If there are ethical issues involved, do they relate to the external environment or the internal environment? Or are both involved? How? What precisely are the ethical issues involved in each category?

3 From a descriptive ethical perspective, what appear to be the critical ethical assumptions or values shown by the persons or organisations in the case?

4 From the point of view of maximising utility for those affected, what is the best course of action? What facts in the case support this conclusion?

5 From the point of view of fairness or individual rights, what is the best course of action? Again, what facts support this conclusion?

6 From the point of view of setting priorities among duties and obligations, what should be done? Why?

7 Do the three avenues (utilitarianism, contractarianism and pluralism) converge on a course of action or do they diverge?

8 If they diverge, which avenue should override?

9 Are there ethically relevant considerations in the case that are not captured by any of the three avenues? What are they?

10 What is the decision or action plan?

The three approaches to the analysis of cases all offer useful guidance. We suggest that, for cases designed to encourage identification of and deliberation about ethical issues, the approaches of Malloy and Lang or Goodpaster may be more helpful than the rational approach.

2.4 Ethical theories

In considering the case histories, you may find it helpful to have a very brief introduction to the major ethical theories and some consideration of their strengths and weaknesses. There are a great many theories about what it is right or best to do, but ultimately only three basic types: consequentialism, absolutism and virtue theories. The first two focus on actions or choices or situations. Consequentialism says that what matters morally and what has to be judged are the good and bad consequences of an action and how they balance out. If the bad outweighs the good then the action is wrong; and if the good outweighs the bad, then it is right. Absolutism says that some things are right and wrong whatever the consequences. Virtue theory says that the right thing to do is what a good person would do and a good person is someone with the qualities that are needed (for example, courage or compassion) to live a good and successful life.

If you were considering the morality of the use of torture, then a consequentialist would say that torture – in order to gain vital information, say – can be justified so long as having that information prevented more pain and harm than the torture would itself cause. An absolutist would say that if torture is wrong (and most absolutists would agree that it was), then it is wrong absolutely, whatever good might come from it. A virtue theorist would ask: 'Is this some-thing a good person (that is, someone who is habitually kind, considerate and compassionate) would do?' If not, then it is not the right thing to do.

Each of these basic types comes in a variety of forms. For example, there can be significant disagreement about what virtues are necessary to live well: how important is honour, for example, or forgiveness. Although absolutists agree that some things are just wrong, they do not agree about which things, neither do they agree about what to do when, for example, those things conflict. Suppose an absolutist is committed to the sanctity of human life. What is such a person to do when a pregnant woman with cancer needs, in order to survive, chemotherapy that would kill the foetus she is carrying? Killing people is absolutely wrong, but here you have to kill someone. And consequentialists differ both in what consequences are to be sought after (though usually it is human happiness meas-ured in one way or another) and in how to discount bad consequences against good ones. So, rather than try to cover everything, we will look at one version of each of the three types; but these are mainstream versions, not unusual or eccentric ones.

2.4.1   Consequentialism: Utilitarianism

Utilitarianism says that, when we have a choice, the right thing to do is that which brings about the 'greatest happiness of the greatest number'. Nothing is wrong that does this, and nothing is right that fails to do it. The first, most obvious, difficulty with this is the problem of determining what counts as happiness. Bentham (1789) dealt with that by equating happiness with simple pleasure or the avoidance of pain. Mill (1861) complicated the issue by distinguishing different kinds and degrees of happiness. Modern economists tend to look either to preference satisfaction or economic gain (which, given the model of 'rational economic man' comes to the same thing, but see, also, Sen 1987). But, for our purposes, we can simply state that utilitarianism advocates the view that to act morally is to attempt to secure the most good for the most people, and stay agnostic about what that good might actually be.

So, for every action, we should choose that which will, or which seems most likely to, bring about the maximum good for the maximum number of people. This gives rise to some important problems. First, it may be that stopping to work out what the possible actions and consequences are, and trying to estimate their relative costs and benefits, will actually affect your ability to do the best thing. Suppose I come across someone apparently drowning in a river. If I were a good utilitarian, then I could well be working out what best to do while they drowned. In many situations *not* calculating consequences may well bring about the best results. Second, it is often pointed out that good utilitarians are, at best, unpredictable and, at worst, unreliable. They cannot, for example, be trusted to keep their promises or tell the truth, show loyalty or uphold justice because they will only do any of these things when, it seems to them, doing so will bring about the best consequences (which it sometimes will not, of course). But if you cannot trust or rely on a utilitarian, then people will tend not to work with them. And since most things rely on people working together to make them happen, utilitarians will probably not bring about the best consequences that they were hoping for. In other words, there are a great many situations in which utilitarianism, as a moral theory, is self-defeating. However, as an instrument of public policy, it can be very useful. It is never a bad idea to try and do the best for everyone, and it is always better if that is based on the kind of cost benefit analysis that utilitarianism advocates. It is simply that, once we know what the costs and the benefits are, utilitarianism is often not very good at telling us what to do next.

2.4.2 Absolutism: Kantianism

One reaction to this problem is Kant's. He maintained that there was a moral law that required you to do your duty. Your duty is to do what you would expect anyone else to do in the situation in which you find yourself.[1] You cannot, in other words, allow yourself to pick and choose which bills you will settle this month (if any) unless you would also be happy for those who owe you money to do exactly the same. Kant's assumption is that you would not. But there is more than just an assumption involved here. The kind of reason you might give for defaulting on your payments might be that it suited you to. Logically, you then must allow that 'suiting me' must also be a sufficient reason for *anyone* to default (or else it could not be a reason for you to do so). But business simply could not be conducted – would cease to exist, as such – if people only paid bills when it suited them to and everyone was completely happy about that. So, paying bills on time, even when it hurts, is simply being consistent about tying together reasons, excuses and actions. Hence, telling the truth and keeping your promises are also part of your duty, because you could not survive in a society in which no one ever told the truth or kept a promise.

The problem with Kantianism is not his stress on duty or the moral law; it is his absolutism. For example, suppose the security guard in a woman's refuge answers the door to a psychotic and violent man who has physically abused and seriously injured his wife on a number of occasions. The man asks if his wife is staying there. She is. Even if silence would indicate that the woman was nearby, Kant would maintain that the guard must either tell the truth or say nothing. Even in this situation he cannot try and mislead or lie to the abuser. It is hard to see that this is, actually, morally correct. Though it provides a useful corrective to utilitarianism's rather unpredictable attitude to what ought to be, Kantianism does so at the cost of being inflexible and, possibly, psychologically unrealistic.

2.4.3 Virtue theory: Aristotelianism

Both utilitarianism and Kantianism assume that the nature and character of the agent – the person actually making the decision – is not important. Nor is the environment in which the choice is to be made – the expectations of others, the culture of the organisation, the reaction of the general public and so on. They also assume that what we are looking for is a rule or a procedure that will resolve any moral difficulties. This cannot work because life and people are much too complicated and individual for a general rule ever to apply properly. We do use general rules, of course, and one way of approaching a moral problem is to generalise it in order to try and achieve a rough fit with some rule ('do not tell lies', 'treat people with respect', 'practice what you preach', and so on). But the fit will only ever be a rough one, and doing as much as we can with these general rules will always still leave many things open. No matter how detailed or explicit moral rules are, judgement is always required to decide how they fit the individual case. Aristotle maintained that moral judgement is formed by training, experience and general knowledge of the world. There is moral training and education, experience of actual situations, and knowledge about how things and people in the world generally work.

Just as a carpenter learns how to make furniture that not only looks right but also does the job, partly from theory but mainly from the experience of making furniture, so we learn what the right thing to do is, partly from our moral education but mainly from the experience of doing it. There is no specific faculty we could call moral judgement. It is just our judgement (wisdom, good sense) applied to moral problems and dilemmas.

Judgement is a virtue. Virtues are not rules; rather they are personal characteristics, tendencies to behave in one kind of way rather than another. Initially, they are acquired by training and education, but the mature person will learn to scrutinise and adjust his or her behaviour on the basis of experience of the world and the exercise of reason. We do not and cannot, however, make every decision a fresh start and, as it were, rebuild ourselves from scratch. We often simply do not have time; more importantly, many virtues will not do their job unless they are quite deeply engrained. If temptations were easily resisted, they would not be temptations.

As examples of virtues, Aristotle lists, amongst others: courage, temperance, liberality, a sense of self-worth, gentleness, modesty, justice and wisdom. These are qualities he felt were necessary to live well, to prosper and to flourish. We might dispute whether they are all equally necessary, or whether, to succeed in modern business, we might not have to add one or two others ('firmness of purpose' perhaps, or 'persistence'). However, that some such list would describe the kind of person (or organisation) one would have to be to survive, prosper and sleep soundly at nights is probably beyond dispute. Such qualities are exhibited in action, in how you behave; and, if you wish to know what they imply for a particular situation, you must look at how a virtuous person behaves (or imagine how they would behave) in that situation. There is no theoretical way of reading off from the nature of virtue what the right thing to do is. The right thing is what a virtuous person does[2].

2.4.4 Judgement and case studies

There is a lesson here – and also, perhaps, an explanation – for all the volumes produced on how to succeed in business that have tried to produce a recipe or a series of rules for business success.[3] Such books never work, in the sense that there are always successes that do not conform to the rules and failures that do. Success in business is a matter of a certain amount of luck, but also of skills and expertise and judgement acquired through practice and experience, and it cannot be reduced to a set of rules that anyone could follow mechanically without that practice and experience. Not everyone is equally good at it; we value the expertise and judgement of those who are. The same is true of morality. How is expertise and judgement, whether in business or morality, to be acquired? By training and education, certainly, but also, and most importantly, by experience and practice supplemented by reflection. This is why the case study approach is so valued in business education. It supplies real examples in their full complexity and difficulty, but does so in a situation where there is space to reflect on one's judgement about them. And this is exactly the reason why case studies are also important in educating moral judgement.

It is not that rules and reasons have no place in morality any more than that they have no place in business. But they can only take us so far and, once that point is reached, then wisdom, experience, imagination, flair, practical intelligence – good judgement acquired by experience in practice – must take over. All, in fact, are needed, for without the rules and the reasons, judgement has very little to go on. But without judgement, rules and reasons go nowhere.

QUESTIONS AND TASKS

1 Which of the different approaches described above do you personally favour? Write down your reasons for your choice and compare them with another person's choice. Do you now want to change your choice?

2 Write a case study based on a real situation. You can base this on your own experience or on published material that you can obtain from newspapers, magazines, the Internet or broadcast media.

CHAPTER 3

Turner & Newall: The Case of the Asbestos Industry

After reading this chapter you will:

- Be aware of a range of ethical issues: secrecy, duties of care, distributive justice, informed consent, corporate punishment and corporate responsibility

- Be aware that people in business are confronted by a complex of social and political issues, even in routine activities

- Understand the underlying values and ideas that have shaped the actors' perceptions of the situation and institutional structures of the organisation, and the fact that managers often have to choose between ambiguous and conflicting courses of action.

3.1 Introduction

By the 1920s it was very clear that asbestos was causing this dust disease of the lungs called asbestosis and nobody new better than Turner & Newall, because the first big scientific report was done on their workforce in the Rochdale factory and that found about a third of their workforce had got asbestosis (Waite 1993a).

The expenditure which may arise from such possible future claims cannot be determined and, in the absence of any reasonable basis for making such provision, no provision is made (T&N Annual Report and Accounts 1994).

It is widely acknowledged that the impetus for the setting up of a series of reviews on corporate governance and company law, starting with the Cadbury Committee in the UK, was the series of corporate scandals that became public in the last two decades of the twentieth century, culminating in the Enron and World Com scandals in the USA. And, whilst hard cases do not always help in making good laws, they can sometimes prompt us into reflective action to consider what arrangements might prevent these problems from occurring in the future. This chapter seeks to describe and examine a hard case that poses business ethics questions regarding distributive justice and the appropriate form of procedure that will satisfy its demands. The hard case in question is that of Turner & Newall, later T&N Plc, and its handling of its asbestos liabilities. This case raises many ethical issues (secrecy, duties of care, distributive justice, informed consent, and corporate responsibility) that can only be touched upon in this brief examination, which is mainly focused upon the issue of corporate responsibility arising from this firm's predicament.

The case will be discussed as follows:

- The facts as they are now known will be presented concerning the asbestos risks and damage liabilities of T&N

- T&N's policy in dealing with this issue will be outlined

- The moral inadequacies of their response will be highlighted; then a contrast will be drawn with the strategy adopted in the USA by the Johns-Manville Corporation

- An alternative solution (the 'Goyder Sanction') will be proposed and its wider lessons for corporate governance considered.

3.2 The facts of the case

Asbestos is derived from the Greek word meaning incombustible. Today, it is the generic name given to the hydrated silicate mineral that is resistant to fire, rot and rust, and yet is light, strong and fibrous and can be used in a wide variety of ways from woven fabrics to additives in cement. At the end of the nineteenth century, in the new machine age, the demand for asbestos began to grow enormously after large deposits of the mineral were discovered in Canada in the 1870s. By 1930, annual production of asbestos was 339,000 tons per year; in 1950 1.2 million tons were produced worldwide (Jeremy 1995). Asbestos was used in the manufacture of motor vehicles, ships, electrical and power generating equipment and, extensively, in the building industry. Henry Ward Johns, which eventually became the Johns-Manville Corporation in 1901, was the first firm to process and manufacture asbestos products in the USA. In Britain, the leading firm in asbestos production became Turner & Newall, formed in 1920 by merging four other firms: Turner Brothers Asbestos, The Washington Chemical Company, Newalls Insulation and J.W. Roberts. Turner & Newall was floated on the London Stock Exchange in 1925 and soon after acquired Ferodo Ltd, a brake linings manufacturer, making Turner & Newall the largest vertically integrated asbestos based business in the UK. In 1926, it had 5,000 employees and, in 1961, 40,000 employees, half in the UK and half abroad. Its sales turnover grew consistently and was over £300 m in 1958, the company being consistently profitable up until the early 1980s. In some years, it returned its shareholders a 16 per cent yield on their investment (Jeremy 1995).

Medical historians have shown that both the Greeks and Romans had noticed that asbestos was a health hazard because slaves who wove it into cloth tended to develop a sickness of the lungs (Brodeur 1972). However, modern acknowledgement of its dangers dates from 1900 when, in Charing Cross Hospital in London, a post-mortem on a 30-year-old asbestos-textile worker revealed that there were 'spicules of asbestos in the lung tissues' and that his occupation might have contributed to his death (Brodeur 1972: 11). A diagnosis of 'asbestos poisoning' was made by Dr Scott Joss in Rochdale in 1922 on a woman asbestos-textile worker and, at her death in 1924, the pathologist Dr Cooke testified that the 'mineral particles in the lungs originated from asbestos and were, beyond reasonable doubt, the primary cause of the fibrosis of the lungs and therefore of death' (Jeremy 1995: 256). His findings were published in the *British Medical Journal* in 1924 and in 1927. Today, it is widely accepted that the inhalation of asbestos can be the cause of several diseases: asbestosis is a chronic disease of the lungs and results in shortness of breath, similar to emphysema; mesothelioma is a cancer of the chest or abdominal lining; and lung cancer.

3.3   Turner & Newall's reaction to the asbestos hazard

Professor David Jeremy and Dr Geoffrey Tweedale have chronicled the corporate attitudes to the unfolding health hazards at Turner & Newall and offer some explanations for where these responses originated and how they began to change (Jeremy 1995; Tweedale 2000). Initially, in public and in court, Turner & Newall repudiated the term 'asbestos poisoning'. They denied that the disease was caused by asbestos and that there was any risk to the public, acknowledging that there was perhaps only a limited risk for some workers. In the early stages of the asbestos crisis from 1927 to the 1950s, Jeremy characterises Turner & Newall's directors' response strategy in the following terms: that 'the doctors' opinions and judgements should be challenged; that the interests of the company, as understood by the board, were paramount; and that the appropriate defensive tactics were denial, a legalistic view of the situation, and litigation' (Jeremy 1995: 258). Although Turner & Newall accepted and complied with government safety regulations, they were often grudging in their acceptance of their necessity, and tried to negotiate delays and restrictions on their implementation. And when forced to tighten up on conditions in its UK factories, failed to do likewise in its overseas operations in Zimbabwe (Waite 1993b). Jeremy notes that the Turner family, who dominated the company, came from the respectable religious background of the United Methodist Church and that they took their 'responsibilities on accumulating capital and wealth seriously' (Jeremy 1995: 262). Their hostile initial response to the news of the asbestos threat also needs to be seen in relation to the relative health hazards in the cotton trade, which were also a source of concern. Perhaps their first thought was that asbestos was no worse than this, and so should be handled in the same piecemeal fashion. In short, Jeremy characterises the early response of Turner & Newall as one of self-deception in order to preserve the profitability of a thriving industry, and that 'commitment to their faith and paternalism precluded the possibility that the springs of their wealth were poisoned (Jeremy 1995: 264).

From the 1960s onwards, as the dangers and incidence of asbestos-related deaths became better known and widespread, the company's stance began to shift from that of outright denial towards that of risk assessment and damage limitation. Improvements in safety were put into its factories, knowledge of the dangers propagated more widely, and claims for worker compensation assessed and some damages conceded. What had been a few dozen claimants in the pre-war years now began to go into thousands, and estimates of the future number of claims began to run to the order of hundreds of thousands, if not millions, as exposure to asbestos fibres was so widespread in society. Increasingly, medical evidence showed that a limited amount of exposure is sufficient to bring on the onset of the disease in some people. In the UK, medical research suggests asbestos-related disease killed about 3,000 people in 1995, and is likely to peak at 5,000 to 10,000 deaths a year in 2020 (*The Times Higher Education Supplement* 1995). In the USA, it is estimated that some 4.5 million workers in shipyards alone have been exposed to harmful concentrations of asbestos (US Dept. Health, Education and Welfare 1978). The problem for the victims is knowing against whom to make the claim for compensation, for nobody wants to accept responsibility for such a widespread and devastating tragedy. Claims are being made against the manufacturers (such as Turner & Newall – from 1987 renamed T&N), against the distributors, the contractors, the insurance companies; by former workers, people who worked with asbestos in other occupations and by people who lived in the vicinity of its factories. Chase Manhattan Bank sued T&N for £117 m over asbestos contamination of its New York headquarters building. In October 1995, T&N was ordered to pay compensation for environmental contamination outside its factory in Armley in Leeds to women who contracted mesothelioma when playing as children near the factory.

In the future, claims against T&N are set to rise, but the policy of only making limited provision to pay compensation encourages observers to think that T&N's defensive and legalistic strategy towards the victims of asbestos will have to be maintained indefinitely. In 1998, T&N were taken over by the Federal Mogul Company of the USA. But claims against the legacy of T&N and the other asbestos companies are set to continue, despite the insurance arrangements (£1.19 bn) put in place to try to cap the liability from these claims. In fact, Federal Mogul has now filed for Chapter 11 bankruptcy protection because it is facing ever-rising asbestos claims (173,000 personal injury claims were pending in 2000, and its latest estimate of probable liabilities is $1.6 bn payable over the next 12 years). The shareholders of Federal Mogul might well ponder the announcement from the Chairman of T&N, Sir Colin Hope, at the time of the takeover, just before his board received a £3 m severance package: 'I believe that for all practical purposes we are now asbestos-free' (*Financial Times*, 28 November 1996). The collapse of the asbestos companies, together with the increasing failure of their insurance providers (such as Chester Street Insurance), could mean that asbestos victims will go uncompensated and be left to the mercy of the welfare state.

In regard to T&N's overseas operations, John Waite, of BBC Radio 4's *Face The Facts* programme, claimed that, 'The documents we obtained from the T&N archive make it clear that certainly until late 1980s and not withstanding earlier pledges, the companies subsidiaries failed to protect workers in India and Africa in the same way the law compelled them to do in the UK' (Waite 1993b). It would appear, then, that T&N operated a double standard in its business conduct: double standards are often accepted in some quarters of the business community by those who take a strictly legalistic view of corporate responsibility but, from the moral point of view, this policy has horrified and appalled many observers of corporate conduct. Perhaps this is a case where the process of corporate governance needs to be put under the spotlight and ethical questions asked; some new procedures might be needed if companies are to continue to remain legitimate institutions in society.

3.4 T&N – an ethical analysis

The best interpretation that can be given to T&N's response in this case is a utilitarian one: the continuation of the company for the sake of its shareholders and communities was felt to outweigh the damage done to what was initially only a minority of asbestos victims. When the balance of the utility calculation began to change in favour of the victims, T&N's response became grudging and legalistic, lacking in both compassion and imagination. In essence, T&N's utilitarian response was to do too little, too late. This analysis will attempt to interpret the facts of the case from the perspective of the virtuous bystander who is concerned with the demands of justice and the lessons that need to be learned about corporate governance and responsibility. One of the key points to bear in mind is that the asbestos problem emerged in an unfolding way and that, with hindsight, it is easy to criticise the failure of T&N executives to act decisively when, in the early stages of the problem, their knowledge horizons were short. The important lessons of this examination of the case revolve around the dangers of blind loyalty to the company as an institution, and the importance of having the courage to take the decision to go against this for the greater good. A virtue theory interpretation of the T&N response recognises that the character and background of the executives was of upright, Christian gentlemen, who were concerned about the welfare of the communities in which they had established their factories; but that the virtue of loyalty to shareholders and the company was allowed to override that of the demands of justice owed towards stakeholders. The demands of justice in this case, it will be argued, were overriding and needed to be carefully considered.

What are the demands of justice in the asbestos case?

Did T&N executives consider the justice of their actions and did they show compassion towards those they had injured? Let us consider how an impartial spectator would judge T&N's response to the asbestos tragedy. As employers in their communities, they treated their employees much like any other: the mining and textile industries have always had practices that were harmful to health but, under the legal duty of care, improvements in safety standards have reduced the damage done to employees over the years. These risks were often openly acknowledged and were widely understood by employees who, in the face of these dangers, sought to ensure that the employers paid wages that reflected the conditions. The asbestos industry was similar to the coal industry in generating claims for respiratory injuries; however, the difference between the two industries is the degree of openness about the risks that were involved and the degree of informed consent to the dangers that employees and others could be said to have accepted. The moral wrong in the asbestos case arises from the secrecy T&N maintained with regard to the hazardous nature of the asbestos mineral in its products. This knowledge was kept from the workers, customers and the local community until forced out of the company by other parties. This secrecy, perhaps exercised for paternalistic reasons, was a corrupting influence on the executive and their abuse of power went undetected; those responsible were not held accountable for many years. As Sissela Bok has remarked:

> For all individuals, secrecy carries some risks of corruption and irrationality; if they dispose of greater than ordinary power over others, and if this power is exercised in secret, with no accountability to those whom it affects, the invitation to abuse is great. (Bok 1983: 106)

Perhaps, in this situation, the phenomena of 'group-think' can be seen to have been at work on men who were otherwise respectable individuals. This is where members of a group are, at times, willing to take larger risks than each member would have taken individually. In this way, both the individual's sense of personal responsibility for joint decisions and their personal judgement become careless, and collectively they exhibit all the signs of reckless behaviour.

The secrecy practised by T&N would seem to be on a par with lying to its employees and customers because they were not given the facts of the danger to which asbestos exposed them, and so they could not be presumed to have exercised informed consent to such risks. T&N's secrecy does not seem to be justifiable – that is, according to the test of justification put forward by Bok in this kind of situation (Bok 1983). For the secret to be justified, one would need to answer three questions:

1 Were there other courses of action that could achieve the aims T&N was hoping to achieve without the deception?

   Surely the interests of the company would have been better served by an earlier acknowledgement of the problem and earlier research into the possible substitutes for asbestos, if the truth had been made public much sooner. Protection and regulations could have been introduced earlier, and workers and customers could have been given some indication of the risks to their health if they undertook this sort of work.

2 Could the company have set forth the moral reasons thought to excuse or justify the secrecy and the counter arguments against greater openness? For example, the loss of a vital product used in many safety applications; the loss of employment in the communities where the factories were located; and the need to prevent panic amongst those already exposed to asbestos dust.

   The testing out of these reasons and arguments is not something that should have been confined to the board room of T&N, it is important that Bok's third test of public reasonableness is applied to these arguments.

3 Could the T&N board have obtained a response to their stance from outside the company to test the acceptability of its actions against public opinion?

In all likelihood public opinion would have become increasingly unfavourable as the evidence of the hazardous nature of asbestos began to accumulate rapidly. But at least the call to restrict its use to vital safety protection in some industrial applications and the need for more research on its implications for human health would have been strengthened. In this way the community would have been asked to share in, and to some extent, consent to some of the risks involved, and also could have begun to prepare for the changes needed to run the asbestos industry down. Moreover, the shareholders of T&N, by being kept in the dark about the risks of this investment, did not have the opportunity of withdrawing their investments or the opportunity to censure the company executives for their deceitful actions. Consequently, the shareholders, in the early years, profited at the expense of the victims exposed to asbestos, and were therefore, albeit unwittingly, party to grave injustices. The failure of T&N to disclose the truth constitutes an injustice on two grounds: the requirement for a fair distribution of rewards in business has been abused and the workers' moral autonomy has been violated. These two injustices will be examined in more detail below.

Distributive justice in business is about making sure that organisational rewards are proportional to the contributions made to organisational ends. Workers in T&N were paid the going rate for their jobs in the local labour market, but with the harmful nature and conditions of this work being largely unacknowledged. Had workers been informed of the risks to health, it is likely that the supply of labour to the firm would have been reduced and higher rates of pay offered to attract workers who were willing to face the hazards involved. Indeed, the beneficial effect of high wages for dangerous work would have made the product more expensive and so would have encouraged the early search for substitutes, and partly prevented its widespread use in much of the building trade. The consequence of T&N's secrecy is that the market was deprived of vital information which economic actors would have been able to evaluate and factor into their calculations. If this secret had been exposed across the asbestos industry as a whole, a smaller workforce would have been highly paid, declining shareholder profits would have reduced levels of investment and so have encouraged the search for substitutes for asbestos much earlier, and then customers and community would have had reduced contact with asbestos in many of its uses. The paying out of compensation claims under strict criteria of liability does not compensate the victims adequately because they did not get the chance to enjoy these rewards while living, and it ignores the question of whether they would have consented to accept the hazards in the first place.

Informed consent is an important aspect of justice because to treat others as merely a means to an end and to ignore their moral agency and well-being is wrong. In medicine, respect for patients is shown by asking them to consent to surgery before it is performed and by informing them of its implications and uncertainties. In employment, whilst the employer has a duty of care towards the employee under the law, it is assumed that the employee tacitly accepts the risks inherent in some jobs that essentially involve dangerous work; for example, deep-sea divers or steeplejacks. 'Informed consent' simply means consent that is real; that is to say, consent that is unforced, given by someone capable of consenting and aware of all the relevant facts. For Beauchamp and Childress, it consists of a number of components: disclosure, understanding, voluntariness, competence and consent (Beauchamp and Childress 1989). T&N failed to disclose the nature of the asbestos risks fully to its workers until very late in the day, when limited protective measures were introduced. Customers of T&N and their workers using asbestos were often ignorant about the nature of the danger and the degree of protection required. Ignorance of the full extent of the hazard means that the component of voluntariness was not respected by T&N, and so the consent they assumed others had given under the contracts of employment and supply did not, in fact exist. Moreover, it is debatable whether employees and customers had the competence to give the consent required. Legally and morally in our society, the competence to engage in harmful activities is restricted to mature consenting adults. But even then, some contracts to engage in harmful activity or to exchange bodily harm or mutilation for money are illegal in our society. Slavery and the selling of body parts are said to be examples of blocked exchanges where even mature consenting adults are not allowed to make this kind of exchange contract. This has been explained by the theory of blocked exchanges developed by Michael Walzer (1983), who argues that it is important to recognise that in different aspects of life different principles of distribution are appropriate to prevent unjust dominations. Separating these spheres or blocking certain exchanges limits the power any one person can acquire; for example, money should not be able to buy political office, criminal justice, friendship or human beings. Whilst we can sell our labour power to an employer, we are not allowed to sell our bodies into slavery. Nor should employees be able to consent to working with substances that are harmful to their health without forewarning and being provided with the appropriate protection and safe systems of work. Working in an unprotected fashion with asbestos was similar to asking a person to handle nuclear waste with their bare hands. Asbestos workers who are asked to exchange health for wages under an employment contract should be protected from such a blocked exchange, which is unjust in moral terms. Those who are seeking to make such an exchange should be regarded as not having the competence to make such contracts. As regards those who have suffered harm from asbestos dust in the surrounding communities of the factories, they were certainly never in a contractual relationship with T&N and, consequently, have been exposed to the graver injustice of having their moral rights and well-being ignored altogether by the firm.

It would appear that from the preceding analysis that T&N have behaved unjustly towards a range of stakeholders so how should these wrongs be redressed? Many observers think that the law in the UK has been cumbersome and weak in upholding the rights of the asbestos victims against the legal might of T&N, and now Federal Mogul; and so justice, in the moral sense, has not been seen to be done. Perhaps we can learn something from the experiences of the Johns-Manville Corporation in the USA.

3.5   Johns-Manville and the asbestos crisis

A similar company to T&N in the USA, Johns-Manville, took a very similar line against its many claimants for compensation. They strenuously denied the allegations of negligence brought by former employees and handlers of asbestos, and used the defence of contributory negligence and ignorance of the risks involved. But in the Borel case in 1969, brought by the widow of a deceased asbestos worker, Johns-Manville were found to be negligent in the precautions taken to protect the worker and substantial damages were awarded to the plaintiff (Borel v Fibreboard Paper Products Corporation 1973). Between 1969 and 1982, the firm was the defendant in over 20,000 cases and paid out over $50 m in compensation payments. Then, in 1982, when faced with a potential of 52,000 suits that could cost the firm over $2 bn (nearly twice the company's net worth), the directors decided to apply for reorganisation under Chapter 11 of the Federal Bankruptcy Act. Chapter 11 did not stop the processing of claims already registered with the courts but it did prevent all future claims, forcing the claimant to look to the bankruptcy court for relief and to take their place in line behind secured creditors. Naturally, the claimants and the public were angered and outraged, but were not able to do very much about it. Meanwhile, Johns-Manville wanted to transfer its operating assets to a new company, diversify its activities out of asbestos and use some of its cash flow to pay off the debts of the old company. The asbestos victims contested this course of action in court, as they felt that this was going to deprive future claimants of their right to claim compensation. After protracted litigation, the company agreed to set up a separate trust fund to deal with claims relating to asbestos disease, but stipulated that the fund would not be part of the company. The trust would be funded by a bond of $1.65 bn to be paid in instalments of cash and company shares. After a four-year period, the trust fund could use its voting rights on its shares to take over the company. During the period of reorganisation, it was estimated that 2,000 of the personal injury plaintiffs died without receiving any compensation (Bucholtz 1989). At least, however, the trust fund can in future take over the company and liquidate it if it runs out of money to pay future claims. Losing control of the company, and doubling the number of claimants suing the company, was not the result that many in the financial community were looking for. Their hope was that Chapter 11 bankruptcy would provide a quick fix to the stream of claimants and, after setting aside some money to pay compensation, the company would be able to resume its operations unencumbered by future liabilities. So, an uneasy compromise was struck and, whilst the lawyers had a field day, a form of retributive justice was arrived at. The shareholders lost control of their company and property to some extent, but a wide range of claimants can now be assured of getting some compensation for their injuries. In terms of corporate governance, this was a clumsy and pragmatic approach towards finding an acceptable solution. Clearly, there are lessons to be learnt here for the T&N case in the UK and our practices of corporate governance in general. Perhaps we can build upon the Johns-Manville experience and develop stronger procedures for dealing with these situations in other similar cases.

3.6 An alternative solution: The Goyder Sanction

The following section is necessarily speculative, because in reality it would appear that Federal Mogul has settled the matter to the satisfaction of its shareholders and many business commentators. Perhaps the appropriate response in this case would have been for the company to express its own sense of shame and guilt. After all, the old proverb says 'Where there is no shame, there is no honour'. However, in T&N's company communications, a sense of shame or guilt is not much in evidence (Tombs 1995). If T&N were ashamed, they would want to keep in touch with the asbestos victims and seek to offer more generous help. Instead, they have cut and run by capping their liabilities and selling off their asbestos responsibilities. Some sections of the media have tried to expose the executives of T&N as the unacceptable face of capitalism on a par with the likes of Robert Maxwell, but little good seems to have come of it in terms of T&N's stance on social accountability: this outcome may even have been accepted by the British government because T&N's chairman was knighted in the 1996 New Years honours list for his services to the motor components manufacturing industry. But it is unlikely that this case will be put to rest because our increasing knowledge of the social impact of corporate activities on the environment is a major concern in the debate about improving corporate governance in business.

Consequently, if social accountability is not taken up on a voluntary basis, then it can only be upheld if new and imaginative legal mechanisms are introduced to enforce retributive corporate punishment. Corporate social accountability is about recognising that companies have non-fiduciary obligations to their stakeholders and that these cannot be ignored, even in a crisis. As a legal inducement to improving corporate governance practices and social accountability, an 'enforced trust' legal procedure is outlined as an alternative solution. This procedure will be named the 'Goyder Sanction' after the pioneering efforts of George Goyder (1961) in his book *The Responsible Company* to bring about a change in company law such that the directors of the firm are institutionalised as trustees on behalf of the stakeholders of the business.

In the T&N case, the shareholders and the executive have profited from the injustices done to others. The workers, customers and communities who have suffered from being in contact with asbestos need to be fully compensated for the damage done – and not only in financial terms; knowing that other companies will not be allowed to do the same again will help too. The business ethicist Peter French (1984) has suggested that in this situation, when a fine seems inadequate and the company cannot be sent to prison, corporations be shamed by subjecting them to adverse publicity that threatens their prestige, image and social standing. He calls this punishment the 'Hester Prynne Sanction', after the heroine in Nathaniel Hawthorne's novel *The Scarlet Letter*. Hester Prynne committed adultery and was punished by the magistrates of Boston by having to stand on the pillory platform for three hours, and then was ordered to wear a large letter 'A' on her gowns when in public for the rest of her life. The punishment was meant to mark a transgression and bring shame on her before the community. French thinks this is an appropriate sanction to apply to the irresponsible corporation as a non-monetary means for the government to use in these circumstances.

After all, if reputation and esteem are such valuable corporate assets, then the denigration of corporate prestige will come as a hard blow for the managers and shareholders. The government sanction would consist of running advertising campaigns that would publicise the corporation's wrongdoing in its own markets and through its designated media. This shaming sanction would be paid for by the errant company and be produced by commercial advertising agencies contracted to government authorities. This form of punishment may be both redistributive and retributive at the same time, and, therefore, French argues, satisfy more fully the demands of justice.

However, the 'Hester Prynne Sanction' is unlikely to be effective in this case because of T&N's disinvestment out of asbestos, and the subsequent change in company investments and ownership. Merely to bankrupt the company would not be enough and could be counter productive, as we have seen in the Johns-Manville case, because it would not provide for those who wish to make claims in the future. Moreover, the Johns-Manville case was very cumbersome in moving towards a just settlement. But the loss of company status and a transformation of the assets into a mutual status organisation would seem to be an appropriate punishment in such cases. This entails the shareholders losing their property rights to help with compensation claims, but this should be for a limited period of time. The general proposal here is that companies who have seriously failed to discharge their corporate responsibilities should be obliged to change their status under the Companies Acts and undergo conversion into a mutual trust for the benefit of those they have harmed. In T&N's case, it would be transformed into a trust to be run as a going concern, trying by means of safer forms of investment to make profits which will be paid out to future suffers from asbestos-related damage on more generous claims criteria than are presently the case, the mutual trust being jointly administered by representatives of claimants, shareholders and workers. Until all future claims are settled, the company should remain as a trust and shareholders' rights be superseded in favour of the damaged persons. After all claims have been settled, then the trust can be converted back into a company and returned to its shareholders and their property rights resumed.

The 'Goyder Sanction' should become an option in the Companies Acts of all countries to be used in other cases of this sort where substantial injustices have occurred and company power has been abused. Perhaps this would be an appropriate punishment for some firms in the tobacco industry, or those companies breaching codes of conduct in the selling of infant formula milk in developing countries. The purpose of the proposed 'Goyder Sanction' is not only to provide mechanisms of compensation to victims, but also to provide a salutary example to the corporate world of how irresponsible practices will be punished, thereby providing another spur towards higher standards of corporate governance. Good corporate governance requires leaders who exercise wisdom and are able to balance the demands of loyalty and prudence to the company against those of justice towards its stakeholders. In the absence of a sense of shame and guilt when a corporation falls below these standards, good corporate governance also requires a strong regulatory framework to ensure that these responsibilities will be enforced by legal duress if needs be.

QUESTIONS AND TASKS

1 Is the use of bankruptcy law by asbestos companies an adequate way to deal with the liabilities that arise in toxic pollution incidents?

2 How should responsibility for the liability and damage done to workers and consumers be divided amongst the various stakeholders (shareholders, company board, management, workers, trade unions, medical professionals, government, media, and so on) in this situation?

3 Evaluate the practicality of the 'Goyder sanction'. Can you think of other mechanisms of redress that would be more appropriate and more just?

4 Should the management of a company be held to be personally responsible when they act in the interests of their company? How is a company to be punished?

5 What responsibility do exporting governments and companies have towards other countries that import asbestos manufacturing plants and asbestos products?

CHAPTER 4

Virgin Atlantic and British Airways

After reading this chapter you will:

- Understand the significance of organisational leadership styles in relation to ethical behaviour

- Understand the impact of factors specific to an industry on ethical behaviour in that industry.

4.1 Introduction

In January 1993, British Airways (BA) ended a libel case brought against them by Richard Branson's company, Virgin Atlantic, by apologising unreservedly for any 'injury caused to the reputation and feelings of Richard Branson and Virgin Atlantic', and particularly for questioning the good faith and integrity of Mr Branson. The judge ordered BA to pay legal costs (approximately £3,000,000) and Mr Branson was awarded £610,000 in damages.

This case was widely seen as a humiliating climb down for BA, especially for Lord King, the Chairman of the board, and Sir Colin Marshall, Chief Executive of the company. BA was labelled as a company that would stoop to any level of dirty trickery to get rid of competition. The shock waves from this case will reverberate around the halls of big business and government for some time.

The case involves several strands of interest to students of business ethics. The clash between BA's carefully crafted image as the world's favourite airline and its publicly pronounced customer culture and its actions in this case is one such theme. The avoidance of responsibility by senior executives and board members is another. The logic of free-market competition and its effects on business behaviour is a third. The consequence of unethical behaviour is a fourth.

This case study examines the background to the case, the details of BA's behaviour and the consequences that flowed from the discovery of unethical business behaviour.

4.2 Background

Competition between airline companies is fierce. Much of the competitive action revolves around pricing, flexibility of flight arrangements, customer convenience, and quality of service at airports and on the plane. There is another side to the battle between airlines of which most air-travellers are not aware. This relates to slots. A slot represents the right of an airline to take off or land at a given airport. Slots can be 'arrival' or 'departure' slots. They are allocated by the hour, so that a slot in the 0800 hour might be from 0800 to 0855.

Each airport has an airport coordinator responsible for allocating slots. This can be either an individual or a group or committee consisting of airline representatives. Airlines make seasonal submissions to the coordinator at each airport that they wish to use. This is a submission for a whole season – summer (April to October) or winter (November to March). Clearly, with the greater the congestion at an airport and the greater the demand for slots, the role of the coordinator becomes more difficult. Airlines compete for the most lucrative slots and the process of slot allocation can be crucial for the success or failure of the competitive strategies of individual airlines. From one season to the next, airlines are able to rely on their historical allocation. Any planned growth in activity requires new slots. Slot planning is affected by some unpredictability in the environment. This might consist of announcements about enhanced runway capacity by the British Airports Authority (as happened in 1992) or changes in the Traffic Distribution Rules by the Department of Transport (as happened in 1991, enabling 17 new airlines to operate in and out of Heathrow).

Virgin Atlantic had long campaigned to be allowed more slots (that is, take-off and landing times). Their long-standing ambition had been to fly to the world's 12 largest cities from Heathrow. In 1993, Virgin had 3,000 slots per year and had been offered a further 1000 slots. This gave Virgin a 1 per cent share of total available slots. This can be compared with 5 per cent for Lufthansa, which was Heathrow's third largest carrier.[1] The relative sizes of the two protagonists in this case were remarkably disparate. At that time, Virgin Atlantic employed 2,400 people, whereas BA employed 48,450; Virgin had 8 aircraft, BA had 227; Virgin carried approximately 1 million passengers a year, BA carried 25 million; Virgin made a loss of £3 million in 1991, BA made over £300 million profit; BA had a turnover approximately 14 times greater than that of Virgin.[2]

The Virgin Atlantic case was the latest in a series of controversial cases involving British Airways and smaller competitors. In 1985, Freddie Laker alleged that BA had conspired with a group of other airlines to put Laker out of business and to remove the threat created by the novel and popular Skytrain operation, which made air travel more convenient for the regular traveller. The case against BA was settled out of court with significant payments being made to the Laker organisation, its creditors, pension fund and staff.

Sir Michael Bishop, the Chairman of British Midland, also considers his company to have been the victim of sharp practice by BA. British Midland had a small sister airline, Loganair. Sir Michael claims that Liam Strong (BA's then marketing director) made an approach to him during 1992. BA was interested in a joint venture serving the Scottish highlands and islands. They had some problems with their own service in this area and approached Sir Michael because of the Loganair connection. Loganair was involved in this area also. Sir Michael states that letters of confidentiality were drafted and for signature by both companies. These letters were designed to protect the commercial secrets of both organisations and to prevent either side using any confidential information to its advantage. Sir Michael signed his; BA management did not sign theirs. Sir Michael trusted them and proceeded with the exchange of information about passenger numbers and began negotiations. As the time approached to sign a final deal, Sir Colin Marshall, BA's Chief Executive, called the whole thing off.

Six months later, BA had established new flights from Manchester to Edinburgh – which happened to be Loganair's most profitable route. Sir Michael took the view that BA extracted useful commercial information from him and then withdrew from a possible agreement in order to take commercial advantage of the information that they had been given in confidence.[3]

BA is clearly the dominant player in the British civil aviation industry. It also makes strenuous attempts to maintain strong links with important political and governmental decision-makers. The House of Commons annually publishes a list of members' interests. This is a list, declared by MPs themselves, of any outside interest they have with external bodies, including trade unions, charitable organisations, pressure groups and businesses. It is common for MPs to indicate the financial aspects of any relationship that may exist. The list of members' interests published in early January 1993 indicated that BA appeared as a donor more often than any other company. At least 14 MPs received free flights or other benefits during 1992. Angela Rumbold, then Deputy Chairman of the Conservative Party, and Alan Haselhurst, a member of the House of Commons Select Committee on Transport, were among the beneficiaries.[4] Select Committees can exert some influence on government policy and the practices of the departments that they scrutinise. BA decided to stop making payments to the Conservative Party in 1991, after Mrs Thatcher was ousted as party leader. Two members of Parliament registered that they had received free flights from Virgin.

BA had been privatised in 1985. It had been prepared for privatisation by Sir John (now Lord) King and Colin (now Sir Colin) Marshall who launched a series of major training events and reorganisations within the business to enhance the quality of customer service.

There is considerable evidence to show that the changes brought about by BA management have led to a clear customer service focus. BA's Annual Report for 1991/92 (see Appendixes A4.1, A4.2 and A4.3) describes the company as being 'Committed to quality with every one of its 50,000 staff participating in its new customer service programme, "Winning with Customers"'. David Young,[5] in a report for the Ashridge Management Centre, indicates that employees generally recognise that considerable changes had taken place between 1983 and 1989. BA managers interviewed in 1988 saw the organisation as being more professional, customer-led, adapting, innovative and more purposive. This change was further underlined by customer reaction. The airline regularly won awards for good customer service voted by the customers themselves.

The BA mission statement[6] contains a series of value statements, which are meant to guide the operations of the company. The mission statement declares that the overall mission is 'To be the best and most successful company in the airline industry', and the goals that stem from this mission are:

- To be a safe and secure airline

- To deliver a strong and consistent financial performance

- To secure a leading share of air travel business worldwide with a significant presence in all major geographical markets

- To provide overall superior service and good value for money in every market segment in which we compete

- To excel in anticipating and quickly responding to customer needs and competitor activity

- To sustain a working environment that attracts, retains and develops committed employees who share in the success of the company

- To be a good neighbour concerned for the community and the environment.

In addition to introducing a strong customer culture within the company, Sir Colin Marshall also made fundamental changes to the management style within BA. The emphasis shifted from decision by committees and the avoidance of individual responsibility to an approach that stresses urgency, the need for individual managers to take decisions and to accept responsibility. There was also an expectation that managers would be visible. David Young described the style thus: 'At all levels it is clearly about "putting the customer first", the customer service focus established by Marshall back in 1983. At a management level it appears to be about getting things done, responding to the business challenges, and not standing on ceremony in doing it.'[7]

In discussing the reasons for BA's success in creating a sense of mission within the organisation, Young identified the following 'keys to this success':[8]

- The selection of simple and appropriate themes encouraging care for people and personal accountability

- A context of uncertainty to make change possible

- Consistent, persistent, courageous, visible and open leadership

- Focus on the practicalities

- Formal programmes that reinforced the messages of the new management style.

Sir Colin Marshall, according to a former BA manager Michael Levin, was recognised by the staff as a decent human being who projected caring, concern and moral probity, and Young asserted that this was an important factor in BA's success. Michael Levin reappears below.

4.3 The story

The activities of BA, which came to light as a result of the court case brought by Mr Branson, could be taken straight from any novel about big business. All it appears to lack is a sex theme. Searching through journalists' rubbish, phone tapping, people attending meetings with hidden microphones secreted about their person, attempts to hide trails and shuffle off responsibilities to others are all aspects of this bizarre case.

There are three main components to BA's campaign against Virgin Atlantic. First, there was the attack on Virgin's Atlantic operations. This consisted of persuading Virgin passengers at airports to switch to BA, cold-calling Virgin customers and alleged hacking into computers to discover sensitive commercial information. Second, there was a report on Virgin produced by Brian Basham, a Public Relations Consultant hired by BA. This cost BA £40,000 and was presented to the Chief Executive in the form of a slide show. Finally, there was 'Operation Covent Garden', which began in 1991 as a response to worries within BA that it had a mole in its midst.

The first campaign – the so-called 'switch-selling campaign' – was allegedly backed-up by hacking into Virgin's computers. Former BA employees reported on television in January 1992 that they had accessed Virgin's computerised reservations service. They had subsequently telephoned passengers to tell them that their flights had been cancelled and offered them flights with BA. This may have been in breach of the Data Protection Act, which seeks to establish certain basic principles about the fairness and legality with which personal information is obtained. The Computer Misuse Act 1990 makes it a crime to access other people's computers.

The second component consisted of the report produced by the external consultant. This component was known as 'Operation Barbara': estimates as to its costs vary from £40,000 to £50,000; that it was sanctioned by the Chief Executive, Sir Colin Marshall, does not seem to be in doubt. This report was selectively leaked to parts of the press and resulted in items appearing that were critical of Richard Branson personally, and made allegations about the weaknesses of Virgin as a company. The report was produced in April 1991 and authorization of the project was needed from the Chief Executive's office because it cost more than the Director of Public Relations, Mr David Burnside, was able to approve.

The report summarised financial, personal and operational aspects of Mr Branson's businesses. It identified popular misconceptions about Virgin, drew attention to Mr Branson's personal style of management and his highly experimental strategy. It also commented on the fact that he owns a nightclub about which there were allegations of crime, drug peddling and homosexuality. The report stated that this ownership 'seems to be high risk in terms of his all-important image'.[9]

The third component was known as 'Operation Covent Garden'. The court case made it clear that Mr Branson had not attempted to discredit BA or its business; however, BA executives became convinced during their attempts to undermine Virgin that Virgin was organising industrial espionage against BA. It was towards the end of 1991 that BA became worried about possible spying by

Virgin. Ian Johnson Associates were hired by Sir Colin Marshall and David Hyde, BA's head of security.[10] Such was the paranoia at this time that when Mr David Burnside, BA's Head of Public Relations, went for dinner with a mutual friend of Mr Branson, he was wired for sound and the conversation was recorded: staff from Ian Johnson's organisation were also keeping watch. This meeting had been arranged by the mutual friend so that Mr Burnside could meet with the person who had, indeed, been hired by an organisation other than Virgin to investigate Mr Burnside.

The report produced by Mr Johnson details phone tapping of BA's senior executives. An executive's car was broken into and details of BA's UK management were taken. Informants told BA senior staff that informants had been planted at one of their offices and that a secretary at headquarters was feeding information to Virgin. The report strung together a series of unconnected events to support a claim that Virgin was spying on BA. However, the report concluded that the investigators were not able to substantiate the claim. The report recommended that senior executives should be very cautious when using mobile telephones and fax machines, and when engaging in conversations that could be heard.[11] The court case showed conclusively that Virgin had not been investigating BA.

4.4 The consequences

The consequences flowing from the court case and judgement made can be categorised as follows:

- Consequences for BA as a business

- Consequences for individuals within BA

- Consequences for Virgin.

Clearly BA's image had been tarnished: press and other media coverage was generally unfavourable to BA. The then opposition spokesman on Transport, John Prescott, called for resignations from Lord King and Sir Colin Marshall for what he labelled their 'disreputable campaign of deceit, lies and illegal activities' (letter to John MacGregor, Minister of Transport). He refused to accept the attempt made by BA to dissociate the board from the actions taken. Following the court case, Mr Branson demanded a concrete expression of good faith from BA and negotiations began between the two companies focusing on slot allocation and financial compensation for Virgin.

On 27 January 1993, Mr Prescott wrote again to Mr MacGregor, protesting at the way in which BA was trading airline slots as part of the negotiations between BA and Virgin. His criticism was that such private deals should not be the way in which slot allocation is made and he urged the minister to intervene.

Other airlines watched with some apprehension as negotiations between BA and Virgin proceeded. These negotiations were seen as an attempt by BA to buy off Virgin and to encourage them not to take the threatened legal action against BA in the US courts. On 15 February 1993, Sir Michael Bishop, Chairman of British Midland, said 'It has to be nipped in the bud that BA has the power to pass over slots other than the ones that they own. If BA wants to settle their dispute with Virgin by trading slots they can only trade the ones they already have.'[12]

Further political pressure was brought to bear when Peter Mandelson, then MP for Hartlepool, urged the Transport Secretary to arrange for the Office of Fair Trading to investigate the 'commercial bullying and political manipulation' allegedly practised at British Airways.[13] The Data Protection Registrar, established by the Data Protection Act, began investigations into possibilities of breaches of the law by BA and asked for details of allegations and information from Virgin.

The outcome of the libel case was to have serious implications for BA's activities in the USA. Shortly after the court case, BA acquired a 19.9 per cent shareholding in US AIR, which is America's sixth largest carrier. On 1 February 1993, the three biggest US airlines formally lodged a petition with the US Department of Transportation in an attempt to overturn this arrangement. Previous bids by BA had been received with hostility by the US authorities, and the three US airlines were now arguing that the deal between BA and US Air was substantially the same as an earlier plan from which BA had been forced to withdraw.

Press coverage in Britain was been generally damning of BA. Jeremy Warner in *The Independent on Sunday* (17 January 1993) wrote of a company driven by deep paranoia operating a no-holds barred approach to business. Will Hutton writing in *The Guardian* (12 January 1993) said that 'Competition British Airways style seems to include personalised attacks, systematic campaigns of denigration and even abusing commercial privacy – not what the enterprise culture was supposed to be about.'

The boardroom changes that took place on 5 February 1993 were unsympathetically covered by the media with prime time news broadcasts showing an angry and somewhat harassed Lord King responding aggressively to loud press questioning. Further image and public relations difficulties for BA arose from the awards of the *Executive Travel* magazine. Its readers voted Virgin Atlantic 'Airline of the Year' and best transatlantic carrier, best business class, cabin staff, food and wine, in-flight entertainment and airport lounges.

Despite the generally unsympathetic media coverage, BA's customers showed no signs of deserting them as a result of the 'dirty tricks' case. *The Financial Times* reviewed customer reaction (22 January 1993) and found that factors other than BA's guilt in conducting 'dirty tricks' were foremost in travellers' minds. The quality of customer service on BA flights and its safety record were important factors in retaining customer loyalty. Even customers of Virgin stated that BA's behaviour would not stop them using BA in future.

Shareholders (see Appendix A4.2) were reported in the press to be alarmed at the extent of the 'dirty tricks' campaign and the prospects of Sir Colin Marshall taking over as Chairman and retaining his Chief Executive position, contrary to the recommendations of the Cadbury Committee. They were, however, unwilling to press Sir Colin too hard on this issue as he had let be known that he would resign if he were not made Chairman and they were impressed by his performance as Chief Executive.

Some shareholders were concerned that the board had not tried hard enough to get to the bottom of the case. BA's solicitors had conducted an investigation a year before and found nothing. Sir Michael Angus, Non-executive Deputy Chairman, emerged as a pivotal figure during January and February. He ordered a second full investigation, the report of which was highly critical of aspects of the 'dirty tricks' campaign. *The Financial Times* stated (21 January 1993) that this report 'confirmed that the campaign was carried out by a few individual employees and did not involve the highest levels of management'. Shortly after the court case was closed, BA published a new code of business conduct for its entire staff (see Appendix A4.4).

Calls for the resignations of Lord King and Sir Colin Marshall quickly followed in the wake of the outcome of the court case. BA insisted that no director was involved in the case. The claim by the company is that no director – including Lord King and Sir Colin – knew anything about the case, despite the fact that substantial sums were spent and the case lasted for almost a year. Richard Branson also claimed that a member of the board, Mr Michael Davies, who is also a friend of Mr Branson's father, was sent as an emissary from the board of BA to ask Virgin to drop their libel case. Mr Basham, the public relations consultant who produced the report on Virgin Atlantic that was selectively leaked to the press, signed a sworn statement insisting that everything he did was with the full approval of the board.[14]

It had been planned that Lord King would take up the position of President, an honorary position, during the summer of 1993 and that Sir Colin Marshall would take on the roles of Chairman and Chief Executive. There was much media speculation about boardroom manoeuvrings during January and February 1993. Finally, after strong intervention from non-executive directors on the BA board, Lord King became President on 5 February and Sir Colin became Executive Chairman. Robert Ayling was appointed as Group Managing Director.

Lord King's remuneration package as President was the subject of press articles. He was said to be receiving £200,000 per year, plus a contribution to his pension, a central London office and secretary, use of a limousine and chauffeur, free first class air travel for himself and his family, and free air travel for his staff. This could have amounted to £600,000 per year for life. Sir Colin became responsible for corporate strategy, finance, legal and company secretary affairs, safety, security, public relations, the environment, health and medical matters. Mr Ayling added to his previous portfolio of marketing and operations: responsibility for engineering, flight crews, information services and human resources.[15] The changes in the boardroom also resulted in Sir Michael Angus agreeing to give more time to his role as Deputy Chairman of the board. In addition, two further non-executive board members were to be appointed.

Mr Basham's public relations contract was not renewed. Mr Burnside resigned on the day the board changes were announced. Michael Levin, quoted above (p. 57), provides a curious postscript to the discussion of consequences for individuals in BA. *The Guardian* reported on 28 January 1993 that a New York lawyer had offered confidential papers collected by a former aide of

Sir Colin Marshall for auction. This former aide was Michael Levin, who had acted as a management consultant for BA between 1983 and 1989, when he was dismissed. He died in 1991. The contents of the papers have yet to be revealed.

Winning the case, and the positive publicity for Virgin Atlantic resulting from it, helped Virgin in its campaign to open up competition in the civil aviation industry. Mr Branson divided up the damages paid by BA amongst his workforce at Virgin Atlantic in an action that received widespread press coverage. In a letter to his staff, he wrote 'Thank you all for your help in our defence. After all, a Virgin's honour is her most prized possession.' Mr Branson indicated that he expected an expression of good faith from BA. He also put his case to the Secretary of State for Transport that more slots should be released at Heathrow generally. The official government view is that the court case and the slots issue are unconnected. Slots are agreed by an independent committee made up of the airlines. But clearly, the outcome of the case opened up possibilities for Virgin. It is, at the least, arguable that their current success in the airline business may have owed something to the mistakes that BA obviously made.

4.5 Postscript

Protracted negotiations between Virgin and BA aimed at settling the dispute between them came to halt on 19 March 1993. They had started in January, immediately after the court case. They focused on demands by Virgin for compensation from BA for business lost by Virgin during the 'dirty tricks' period. Mr Branson claimed that BA had insisted on demanding a commitment from Virgin not to refer again to the 'dirty tricks' campaign. He was prepared to accept the £9 million financial compensation but not to accept a clause in the draft agreement, which he claimed would 'gag' Virgin and restrict 'its ability to refer to the case in any further actions or to provide information to anyone else in a similar dispute.'[16]

BA's Group Managing Director, Mr Robert Ayling, said 'We have simply asked them not to rake over the events of the past. The fundamental point on which we cannot agree with Virgin is their requirement to reopen past events.'[17] BA published the controversial clause. It read: 'British Airways and Virgin Atlantic agree that they shall each use their best endeavours to discourage media coverage or comment about the past relationship between BA and VA and the matters covered by this agreement.'[18] Virgin instructed its lawyers to consider all the remedies available to it, including UK legislation concerning the misuse of computer information (the Data Protection Act and the Computer Misuse Act), US anti-trust laws and the competition rules of the Treaty of Rome through the European Commission.

The British government was said to be unhappy about the prolonged dispute. Adverse publicity, especially in American courts, could have damaged its position in discussions with the US government about aviation deregulation.[19]

███ QUESTIONS AND TASKS ███

Tasks I and 2 are suitable for small group discussion followed by the production of individual written responses.

1 Evaluate the actions of BA using any model of ethical behaviour with which you are familiar.

2 Describe and justify the strategy that you would advise BA to adopt if it wishes to see its new code of ethics fully implemented.

3 Write a 500-word speech that you would give to a group of BA junior managers who have expressed concern at BA's behaviour.

4 Write a letter to *The Financial Times* expressing your personal views about BA's behaviour.

███ APPENDIX A4.1 ███

BA Annual Report 1991–92: Chairman's statement

I BEGAN my annual report to you a year ago by describing the preceding 12 months as among the most volatile in the history of our industry. Times since then have been little, if any, easier. The effects of the Gulf War persisted well into the financial year ended 31 March 1992.

In fact, 1991 has been described as the most difficult year since records began. ICAO, the International Civil Aviation Organisation, has reported the first ever annual fall in international scheduled passenger traffic, down overall by *six* per cent, with IATA, the industry association, estimating combined losses on international scheduled services alone of some $4 billion.

Against this background, I think we may fairly describe British Airways' performance as highly creditable.

Profits are up 119 per cent to £285 million at the pre-tax level and turnover up six per cent, leading the Board to recommend a final dividend of 7.24 pence a share, against the 6.05 pence in each of the past two years. This would give dividends for the full year of 10.18 pence a share, a rise of 15 per cent.

To accomplish this, your company had to call upon its considerable store of talent, skill, ingenuity and sheer determination as never before. The World's Biggest Offer, our imaginative and bold promotion, which took off on 23 April last year, jump-started the world travel market after the slump caused by the Gulf War. Besides creating immense goodwill towards British Airways, this daring promotion attracted publicity worth tens of millions of pounds. More importantly, it ensured that we recovered from the downturn faster than our rivals. Meanwhile, we have had to contend with economic recession in our main markets, which has meant that a return to more normal trading conditions has not happened as speedily as we would have wished.

As expected, we have also faced increasingly tough competition, particularly at our Heathrow home base. Following changes in the Government's traffic distribution rules controlling access to the airport, the number of carriers competing with us there last summer increased by 17, to 87. They include some of the largest and most competitive airlines in the world. We have responded strongly, with a whole host of marketing initiatives and product enhancements. The result has been an increase in our market share at London.

Within the company, we have acted energetically in the past 12 months to reduce our costs, with the support of our employees and trade unions. The contraction in the size of our workforce has been achieved through early retirement, voluntary severance and the disposal of certain activities, with a consequent increase in productivity of almost 12 per cent.

We have made some important changes in the structure of our business. In order to liberate resources for the development of the airline, we sold the business formerly carried on by British Airways Engine Overhaul Limited to a subsidiary company of General Electric Company of the USA. We believe that the new owners, as engine manufacturers, will be able to invest further resources in the development of this excellent business, while allowing us to get on with what we do best. We also contracted out our property maintenance and parts of our security functions.

We have carried out in-depth reviews of our operations at Gatwick and in the UK regions, to ensure that these activities have the best opportunities to reach adequate levels of profitability.

We exceeded our initial targeted savings of £200 million in the initial phase of our three-year Gap Closure programme by £65 million. We are aiming to trim a further £150 million from our costs in the 1992–93 financial year.

What we shall not trim, however, is the quality of our customer service. In our determination to build on this principal underlying strength of British Airways, we recently launched 'Winning for Customers', the latest and most extensive in our series of customer service development initiatives. Every employee will take part in its corporate event, called 'Winners'. Our intention is that this programme should gain us as much of a competitive edge in the 1990s as did our original 'Putting People First' initiative in the 1980s.

There has been a great deal of media speculation in the past year regarding British Airways' globalisation plans. Although we remain committed to the concept of a global airline, and while we believe our long-term future may be bound up with worldwide alliances, we are still in a position of strength which many would envy. We will not act in haste and repent at leisure. Finding the right partner remains high on our agenda, but there is much else besides. Until the right deal presents itself, we will continue to operate a highly successful, profitable business achieving exceptional levels of customer satisfaction.

Growth prospects for this industry remain sound. British Airways is in a good position to take advantage of the opportunities afforded by the liberalisation of the industry, provided the playing field is level and 'competition' is not misinterpreted to mean 'substitution'. We are encouraged by the support of the UK's newly-elected Government for opening the skies of Europe and for examining the role of state subsidies enjoyed by some continental carriers – particularly as the United Kingdom holds the presidency of the European Community in the six months leading up to 1993 and the dawning of the single European market.

We now have our own first platform on the continent, with the establishment of the new German airline Deutsche BA, in which we hold a 49 per cent stake. We are also progressing the development of Air Russia, working with our partners in Russia.

The Company's Directors have for many years benefited from the counsel of Robert Ayling, in his capacity as Company Secretary, Legal Director and Director of Human Resources. Following his appointment as Director of Marketing and Operations, we were pleased to welcome him in December as a full member of the Board.

British Airways is now firmly on its flight path to recovery after the turbulence caused by the Gulf conflict and recession in many countries. We have demonstrated our ability to manage this business effectively during the most severe downturn it has experienced. In doing so, we have earned the admiration of the industry.

For this, the employees of your Company deserve a substantial vote of thanks, reflected by my Board's decision to increase the level of their profit sharing bonus from the formula driven 1.4 weeks to a full two weeks' basic pay. Their contribution in a trying, often unsettling and constantly challenging 12 months cannot be overstated.

Nonetheless, they and I are only too well aware that there is still much to achieve if we are to accomplish our mission of becoming the undisputed best and most successful company in the industry – to which we remain committed.

King

Lord King of Wartnaby

Chairman

Board members and executive management

Board members

LORD KING OF WARTNABY (74) *Chairman*
Chairman since 1981.
Chairman, Babcock International PLC since 1972; Director, Daily Telegraph plc; (B)

SIR COLIN MARSHALL (58) *Deputy Chairman and Chief Executive*
Chief Executive since 1983.
Director, Grand Metropolitan plc, IBM United Kingdom Holdings Limited, Midland Group plc and British Tourist Authority, (B)

SIR MICHAEL ANGUS (62) *Deputy Chairman and Chairman of the Audit and Remuneration Committees*
Deputy Chairman, Whitbread plc and National Westminster Bank plc; Director, Thorn EMI plc; President, Confederation of British Industry, (A, C)

ROBERT AYLING (45) *Director of Marketing and Operations*
Joined the Board of British Airways in December 1991 after his appointment as Director of Marketing and Operations in September. Joined the airline as Legal Director in 1985 and subsequently took on the duties of Company Secretary and, later, Director of Human Resources. Formerly Under Secretary at the Department of Trade.

DEREK STEVENS (53) *Chief Financial Officer*
Chief Financial Officer since 1989. Formerly Finance Director, TSB Group plc.

CAPTAIN COLIN BARNES (58) *Chairman of the Air Safety Review Committee*
Joined the Board of British Airways in 1991 after 36 years flying with the airline as a pilot, the last ten as Chief Pilot and the final five as Director of Flight Crew. (A, B)

MICHAEL DAVIES (57)
Chairman, Calor Group plc, Wiltshier plc and Perkins Foods plc; Deputy Chairman, TI Group plc. (A, B, C)

SIR FRANCIS KENNEDY, KCMG, CUE (66)
Special Advisor to Chairman and Board
Diplomatic Service, 1964–86. Director, Fluor Daniel Corpn and Smith and Nephew plc. (B)

THE HON. CHARLES H. PRICE II (61)
Former United States Ambassador to the UK; Chairman, Mercantile Bank of Kansas City; Director, Hanson Plc, Texaco Inc., Sprint Corporation and New York Times Company Inc. (A, B, C)

LORD WHITE OF HULL, KBE (69)
Chairman, Hanson Industries (A, C)

[The letters in brackets indicate membership of the following committees of the Board: (A) Audit Committee, (B) Air Safety Review Committee, (C) Remuneration Committee.]

Executive management

DAVID BURNSIDE (40) *Director of Public Affairs*
ALISTAIR CUMMING (57) *Director of Engineering*
DR MICHAEL DAVIES (54) *Director of Health Services*
TONY GALBRAITH (53) *Treasurer*
DAVID HOLMES (57) *Director of Government and Industry Affairs*
DAVID HYDE (55) *Director of Safety, Security and the Environment*
CAPTAIN JOCK LOWE (48) *Director of Flight Crew*
CLIVE MASON (48) *Director of Purchasing and Supply*
ROGER MAYNARD (49) *Director of Corporate Strategy*
GAIL REDWOOD (43) *Company Secretary*
MERVYN WALKER (33) *Legal Director*
JOHN WATSON (48) *Director of Human Resources and Information Management*

[Membership as at the time of publication.]

APPENDIX A4.2

BA Annual Report 1991–92: shareholder information and directors' interests

Shareholders

As at 15 May there were 265,819 shareholders; an analysis is given below.

Size of shareholding	Percentage of shareholders	Percentage of shares
1–1,000	95.59	9.11
1,001–5,000	3.77	2.70
5,001–10,000	0.24	0.61
10,001–50,000	0.18	1.57
50,001–100,000	0.05	1.43
100,001–250,000	0.07	4.47
250,001–500,000	0.05	6.36
500,001–750,000	0.01	2.99
750,001–1,000,000	0.01	3.06
Over 1,000,000	0.03	67.70
	100.00	100.00

Classification of shareholding	Percentage of shareholders	Percentage of shares
Individuals	98.33	12.21
Nominee companies	1.02	77.15
Insurance companies	0.03	3.72
Banks	0.14	1.52
Pension funds	0.02	0.90
Other corporate holders	0.46	4.50
	100.00	100.00

The following have holdings in the company in excess of 3 per cent of the total shares issued:

	Percentage of shareholding
Templeton Investment Management Limited	5.53
Fidelity Investments	4.52
Schroder Investment Management	3.96

Morgan Guaranty Trust Company of New York, the Company's ADR Depositary, has a non-beneficial interest in 17.68 per cent of the shares in the name of Guaranty Nominees Limited. British Airways is not aware of any other interest in its shares of 3 per cent or more.

Directors' interests
At 31 March 1992

| | British Airways Plc | | | | | | | British Airways Capital Ltd |
| | Ordinary shares subject to no restrictions | | Ordinary shares subject to restrictions | | Options executive and SAYE share schemes | | Options exercised during year | Convertible capital bonds | |
	31 March 1992	1 April 1991	31 March 1992	1 April 1991	31 March 1992	1 April 1991		31 March 1992	1 April 1991
Lord King	105,000	35,084	–	316	296,809	853,330	556,521	13,332	13,332
Sir Colin Marshall	25,836	25,520	–	316	485,436	710,155	224,719	11,304	11,304
Sir Michael Angus	3,000	3,000	744	–	–	–	–	1,333	1,333
R.J. Ayling**	4,459	3,485	3,403	1,718	215,261	334,224	187,938	–	–
D.M. Stevens	5,050	5,050	–	3,403	337,254	337,254	–	109	109
A.M. Davies	5,060	5060	4,723	–	–	–	–	2,221	2,221
Captain C.A. Barnes	7,983	831	1,860	6,875	69,976	208,334	135,692	644	644
Sir Francis Kennedy	5,250	5,250	–	1,860	166,666	166,666	–	1,421	1,333
Hon Charles Price II	*10,000	*10,000	–	–	–	–	–	–	–
Lord White	–	–	–	–	–	–	–	–	–
	171,638	93,280	10,730	14,488	1,571,402	2,609,963	1,104,870	30,364	30,276

* Held in American Depositary Receipts.

** R.J. Ayling was appointed to the Board on 16 December 1991.

The Directors' interests set out above are in each case beneficial. The options under the Executive Share Option and Savings Related Share Option Schemes are at prices varying between 135p and 210p per share. No Director has any beneficial interest in shares in any subsidiaries of the Company other than those shown above in the 9.75 per cent Convertible Capital Bonds 2005 in British Airways Capital Limited. There have been no changes in the interests set out above between the end of the financial year and 18 May 1992.

BA Annual Report 1991–92: principal investments

As at 31 March 1992

	Percentage of equity owned	Principal activities	Country of incorporation and principal operations
Subsidiary undertakings			
Principal subsidiary undertakings are all wholly-owned direct subsidiaries except where indicated			
Air Miles Travel Promotions Ltd (51 per cent of ordinary shares owned)		Airline Marketing	England
Bedford Associates Inc. (A subsidiary undertaking of BritAir Acquisition Corp mc)		Specialist computer reservations software	USA USA
BritAir Acquisition Corp Inc.		Holding company	England
British Airways Associated Companies Ltd		Airline management services	Australia
British Airways Australia (Holdings) Pty Ltd		Holding company	Jersey
British Airways Capital Ltd (89 per cent of founders' shares owned)		Airline finance	
British Airways Finance BV		Airline finance	Netherlands
British Airways Holidays Ltd		Package holidays	England
Caledonian Airways Ltd		Airline operations	England
Chartridge Centre Ltd		Airline training services	England
Speedbird Insurance Co Ltd		Airline insurance	Bermuda
Travel Automation Services Ltd (trading as Galileo UK)		Computer reservations systems	England
Associated undertakings			
Air Russia	31.0	Airline operations	Russia
Concorde International Travel Pty Ltd	50.0	Airline marketing	Australia
Deutsche BA Luftfahrtgesellschaft mbH	49.0	Airline operations	Germany
Euro-Hub (Birmingham) Ltd	21.0	Airport terminal services	England
GB Airways (Holdings) Ltd	49.0	Airline holding company	Jersey
Galileo Company Ltd	24.0	Computer reservations systems	England
World Aviation Systems (Australia) Pty Ltd	50.0	Airline marketing	Australia
Trade investments			
Covia Partnership	11.0	Computer reservations systems	USA
Hogg Robinson plc	12.4	Travel, transport and financial services	England
Ruby Aircraft Leasing and Trading Ltd	19.3	Aircraft leasing	England
Sapphire Aircraft Leasing and Trading Ltd	19.3	Aircraft leasing	England
Plimsoll Line Ltd	49.9	Airline holding company	England

APPENDIX A4.4

British Airways' new Code of Business Conduct

This is the text of BA's Code of Business Conduct:

> The success of British Airways is dependent on the quality of the decisions and the behaviour of individuals at all levels throughout the organisation. The code has been developed to provide guidance and assistance to both managers and staff in their dealings with all those with whom we do business, with our customers and suppliers, and with each other.
>
> Adherence to the principles will help ensure that our reputation and success that has been built up over the years through the dedicated hard work of you and your colleagues will continue to grow.
>
> Judgment and discretion will need to be exercised in applying the principles where, at first sight, they appear to be at variance with local custom and practice or commercial common sense.
>
> It is the intent of the code to anticipate and provide a framework of governing values and advice on how to proceed when making difficult decisions, namely to establish the norms of business behaviour throughout the company.

General standards

Compliance: Comply with all the laws that regulate and apply to the company, its systems and the conduct of its business.

Fairness: Treat all groups and individuals with whom we have a business relationship in a fair, open and respectful manner.

Integrity: Show respect for the individual, treating each in a consistent way and honouring commitments made.

Openness: Share and declare information on personal and corporate conflicts of interest (political, financial, relationship) including the offer or acceptance of gifts or hospitality of significant value. Seek guidance and where appropriate confirmation from a higher authority before acting.

Honesty: This goes beyond simply telling the truth to ensuring that any misrepresentation is quickly corrected. Do not allow people to be misled. Where there are valid reasons for withholding information, be clear about the motives and if possible explain why you are doing so.

Fair competition: Ensure comparisons drawn with competitors and working partners are based on fact and avoid innuendo. Competition should be based on the quality, value and integrity of British Airways' service and products.

Determination: Demonstrate a sense of purpose and commitment to achieving the optimum even in adversity.

Responsiveness: Recognise changes in the business environment and use a creative flexible style to respond to them.

Enablement: Provide sufficient guidance to enable individuals to act upon their own initiative to solve problems and grow in their role.

Conformity: Promote corporate values and competitive edge through the established performance systems of performance and appraisal.

Through employing these practices and behaviours, staff should:

- Use British Airways' stated goals and objectives as guidance, using your values and judgment to interpret against the principles of this code.

- Treat others as you would like to be treated.

- Be prepared to solicit views as to whether something would be appropriate before action, rather than after.

- Discuss difficult decisions with those whose values and judgment you respect. Use company process to earn respect.

- Ask whether you would feel comfortable explaining your decision or behaviour to your boss, your family or the media.

- Be prepared to challenge if you believe others are acting in an unethical way. Create the climate and opportunities for people to voice genuinely held concerns about behaviour or decisions that they perceive to be unprofessional or inappropriate.

- Do not tolerate any form of retribution against those who do speak up. Protect individuals' careers and anonymity if necessary. Encourage an environment of learning from mistakes and mutual trust in each others' motives and judgments.

- Treat the assets and property of British Airways and its customers and its suppliers with the same respect as you would your own. Apart from tangible assets this would include company information as well as the name, image and reputation of British Airways.

CHAPTER 5

The Co-operative Bank's Ethical Policy

After reading this chapter you will:

- Understand the deeply embedded nature of corporate values

- Be able to identify the marketing advantages of ethical codes and behaviour

- Appreciate the impact of ethical policies on the behaviour of managers.

5.1 Introduction

This chapter examines the case of the UK-based Co-operative Bank, which is an organisation that has long traded on its ethical and fair-trade principles. However, we are principally concerned here neither with the Bank's ethical policy (see Appendix A5.1) itself nor with its impact on the bottom-line, though they do help to provide the context for the research reported here.

Policy statements on ethical issues abound. If all organisations that had mission statements, codes of practice or ethical codes were, therefore, ethical in conduct and performance, business ethics would be non-problematic. However, the effectiveness of corporate codes of ethics is dependent, amongst other things, on the day-to-day behaviour of managers.

Interest in the impact of ethical codes and mission statements on managerial behaviour grew markedly during the 1980s and 1990s (Fritzsche and Becker 1984; Stead et al. 1990; Clutterbuck et al. 1992; Delaney and Sockell 1992; Cohen et al. 1993; Premeaux and Mundy 1993). One further way of enriching our understanding of the ethical behaviour of managers is to focus on actual behaviour in real organisations and to develop case studies that test principles and concepts.

This chapter reports the findings of a 1995 research project aimed at discovering the extent to which the Co-operative Bank's ethical policy influenced the behaviour of those managers at the Bank who are responsible for achieving the Bank's objectives in acquiring new business in the corporate market. It seeks to explore the impact of the Bank's ethical policy on the day-to-day behaviour of a significant group of the Bank's managers.

5.2 Successful ethics

The Co-operative Bank is a commercially successful organisation with strong roots in cooperative values and history, and with a high-profile stance on ethical issues. It operates in the competitive financial services market, which has seen many significant financial scandals over the years, and it does so successfully, at the same time promoting itself very clearly as an ethical organisation.

The Bank's marketing strategy has been a classic niche marketing exercise with a strong emphasis on the cooperative values that created the Bank and provide its dynamic in modern times. Its ethical policy provides a tangible outcome of a marketing strategy that has built upon the traditional values of the British cooperative movement and shaped the Bank's current promotional stance.

Davis and Worthington (1993), in writing about the Co-operative Bank within the context of traditional cooperative values, argued that the Bank's commercial strategy and its market positioning have resulted in a confident re-statement of cooperative values within a highly receptive, if relatively small, sector of the financial services market.

The Bank is convinced that its ethical stance has been good for business. Its 1992 Annual Report stated (pp. 6–7) 'There is an increasing awareness of ethical issues in the UK and a broad spectrum of customers and potential customers would prefer to bank with a financial institution which has developed its customer service to this level of awareness.' It goes on to claim that 'The Ethical Stance is consistent with customer perception of The Co-operative Bank and represents a clear point of differentiation from its competitors.'

The success of the Bank's strategy was reflected in the increase in operating profits (up by £11 million to £53 million in 1992) resulting from higher revenues from a depressed financial services market. Lynn (1993) asserts that the improved performance of the Bank 'was the outcome of the bank's new ethical policy' (p. 44). Increased revenue, however, is only one of the causes of higher profitability. The Bank also bore down on costs – particularly in relation to bad debts.

However, the enhanced profitability of the Bank was a more complex phenomenon than simply a product of its ethical stance and reduction of bad debt. The Bank introduced new products, new methods of providing customer service based on considerable investments in new technology, a Total Quality Management programme and a process re-engineering programme which resulted in some down-sizing and de-layering of the Bank's staffing structure.

5.3 Organisational context

The managers operated within an organisation that had an 'official' description reproduced in the organisation charts, job descriptions, remuneration systems and other organisational policies of the Bank.

Figure 5.1 indicates the organisational structure of the Co-operative Bank as in October 1993. It is included here to indicate the place of the Retail Banking (Sales) Division within the corporate structure.

Figure 5.2 indicates the structure of the Retail Banking (Sales) Division as in October 1993.

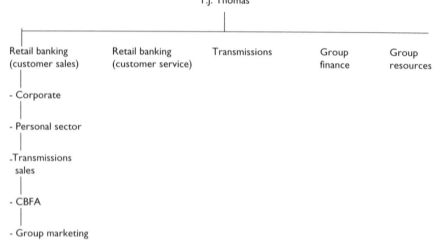

MANAGING DIRECTOR
T.J. Thomas

Retail banking
(customer sales)

Retail banking
(customer service)

Transmissions

Group
finance

Group
resources

- Corporate

- Personal sector

-Transmissions
 sales

- CBFA

- Group marketing

Figure 5.1   Co-operative Bank plc: organisational structure and key functions

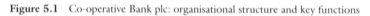

EXECUTIVE DIRECTOR

— FINANCE

CREDIT MANAGEMENT

SUPPORT SERVICES

CBFA

MARKETING

Lending policy
Credit strategy
Advances
Securities
Recoveries
B of E regulations

Resources
Projects
Quality/SLA's
Premises
Training

Sales force-
 management
Business-
 development
Lead conversion
Sabre liaison

Bank group positioning
Product development
Pricing
Public relations
Promotions
Market research

BUSINESS DEVELOPMENT

CORPORATE BUSINESS PERSONAL BUSINESS

Central corporate
 relationships
National relationships
 (key sectors)
Product specifications
 and costings
Telesales
Transmission sales
Task force
Financial director

– North Region
– Midlands Region
– South Region

Corporate network management
Relationship management
Business development
Lead generation

Sales network
 management
Business development
Lead generation
National relationships
 (personal)

Figure 5.2   Retail banking: structure in sales division

Senior commercial managers (SCMs) and commercial managers (CMs) operated within this division. They were located at branches (known as 'commercial units') of the Bank.

The job profiles of SCMs required them to liaise with a wide range of other managers in the Bank in order to ensure the provision of services to clients within a particular geographical area. They involved achieving targets for sales and services, generating new ideas for product and service enhancements, maintaining and developing client relationships, coordinating the work of subordinates, lending within their levels of discretion and preparing proposals for submission to credit assessors within the Bank.

The job profiles also provided details of the knowledge base required by SCMs. The knowledge required was weighted (from 1–3, with 3 being the most important); knowledge about the Bank's ethical stance was weighted as 2.

The CMs' job profile indicated their role in working with the SCMs to ensure that business plans were devised and targets met, the importance of maintaining good client relationships, managing staff, lending within their discretionary limits and preparing proposals for submission to credit assessors. Knowledge of the ethical stance is weighted at 2.

Each commercial unit covered a given geographical area and the number of SCMs and CMs varied in accordance with the amount of the business being carried out in that area.

The remuneration of the managers was based on a structure with three elements: there was a basic pay element that derived from the Bank's Grade and Salary Structure; a Christmas Bonus paid to all staff; and, from 1993, an element derived from the Bank's Performance Management Appraisal (PMA).

PMA was aimed at creating 'a performance oriented culture which will improve the Bank's position in the short, medium and long-term' (PMA User Guide p: 2). It had five performance principles:

- Maintain a competitive base salary (the job rate) for on-target performance

- Pay people up to and at the job rate for on-target performance

- Reward above target performance by means of additional payments

- Recognise the importance of learning and development within a job by encouraging progression towards the job rate

- Continue to employ on-target performers and take action to ensure that everyone meets these standards.

Rewards to staff could be developmental and monetary. 'How this works is that the Corporate Plan sets out the strategic direction of the Bank on a three-year rolling basis. The annual Group budget, Divisional Profit and Operating Plans translate this into targets for the current year. PMA turns targets into actions and actions into results. It pays for results and identifies any training and development that is needed to help people get even better results in future' (ibid. p: 2).

The bank's salary structure indicated the starting salaries for jobs at identified levels and a 'job rate' (achieved through annual increments). To continue to be paid at the job rate required the achievement of agreed performance targets. Performance above agreed targets resulted in payment above the job rate.

The Bank's recruitment policy had changed in this period. The established practice, in common with other commercial banks, had been to 'grow' managers from internal sources. In the mid-1990s, the tendency was to recruit more managers at a younger age from external sources. This is reflected in the findings below.

The job content of the SCM and CM was radically affected by internal organisational change. These changes aimed at developing centralised provision for customer services; incorporating, for example, the armchair banking service (telephone banking), the provision of centralised administrative support for non-personal accounts and the introduction of *Financial Director* (a real-time office finance system used in the commercial units). The overarching aim of these developments was to reduce the impact of day-to-day administrative demands on branches and to release branch-based SCMs and CMs from routine administrative chores to enable them to manage their client relationships more effectively.

5.4   Research findings

A total of 17 managers from 10 different branches were interviewed in their offices using a written schedule (see Appendix A5.2). Responses were recorded during the interviews. The 10 centres were selected to represent the geographical spread of the Bank's operations.

When examining the research findings, it is important to note that, for many questions, managers were not limited in the number of responses they could make; hence, in several instances, the recorded responses exceed the number interviewed

From the total of 17 managers interviewed:

- 10 were CMs, 7 were SCMs

- 13 managers had previously been employed by a different bank (it should be noted that only 2 of these managers came from small banks; most of them had experience of working for the larger clearing banks).

5.4.1   Job content

The purpose of this section is to identify the major components of the managers' jobs so that their responses to the request to identify which parts of their jobs are influenced by the Bank's mission statement and ethical policy can be placed within the organisational context as experienced by the managers.

Managers were asked to identify the major components of their job. It is significant that, from the self-reported job content, the differences between CMs and SCMs were not significant. This appears to reflect the heavy reliance on teamwork and trust at branch or central level, and the deeply shared assumptions about the purposes of the corporate and commercial work of the Bank.

Table 5.1 indicates the managers' self-reported job components and the frequency with which each component was reported.

Table 5.1 Managers' self-reported job components

Component	Frequency
Maintaining a portfolio of commercial accounts	15
New Business Development	14
Managing subordinates	7
Training and development	5
Meeting targets	3
Cross selling	3
Troublesome accounts	1
Team leader/motivator	1
Ensure things work	1

Table 5.2 Job elements managers consider to be influenced by the Bank's ethical policy

Response	Frequency
All aspects	9
New business	11
Existing customers	3
Little impact	2
Partial affect	1

Clearly, the predominance of the first two elements, which are strongly inter-related, indicates a widely held view about the purposes of the job. This reflects the Bank's perception of the nature of the commercial management function as indicated in the job descriptions of CMs and SCMs.

The focus for the managers is fundamentally based on target achievement within the context of competitive commercial banking.

5.4.2 How the ethical policy influences job performance

Managers were asked to indicate which parts of their current jobs were influenced by the Bank's ethical policy. Table 5.2 summarises their responses.

There was a clear view amongst the majority of managers that the ethical policy had proved to be very successful in attracting new business and had played a major role in the commercial and corporate sector of the Bank's work. Three managers reported that existing businesses within their portfolio had been affected by the introduction of the ethical policy – some business had been released by the Bank as a result of a search of existing customers to check their compliance with the policy.

5.4.3 Incidents

The influence of the policy was further investigated by asking managers to identify incidents in which the Bank's ethical policy had helped them in arriving at a decision about a particular client. Incidents that were reported included:

- A chemical waste company applied for loan facilities; the manager was concerned about the processes involved but further investigation reassured him that the processes were sound and environmentally acceptable

- A group of hunt saboteurs were asked to withdraw their business when they failed to give reassurances about being non-violent in their approach

- An incinerator business was investigated in greater detail than would have been the case without the existence of the policy

- The Bank's policy not to speculate against sterling in the foreign exchange market enabled a manager to obtain additional business from charitable organisations

- A manager used the policy to point out to a business that the attempts by that business to evade tax were against the Bank's policy

- A factory-farming business was investigated in great detail and found to be operating within the spirit of the Bank's policy

- A waste disposal company was investigated and, after consultation with the Bank's Head Office, approved

- A political organisation was asked to produce a copy of its aims and rules, and was asked to confirm that it would not be involved in illegal or violent action

- A company wanted finance for a venture involving the processing of chicken manure to produce electricity; the manager was concerned about the links with factory-farms from which the manure would need to be obtained; the business was approved

- A charitable trust wished to deposit large credit balances at the Bank; however, the Chairman of the trust was heavily involved in organising bird shoots and wanted to put the family accounts into the Bank (his wife already had an account at the Bank); the manager felt that the ethical policy raised the issue but did not provide an answer and he referred the matter to Head Office

- During a 'sweep' of existing accounts following the introduction of the ethical policy, a manager became concerned about an account with an abortion clinic; he referred the case to Head Office

- A manager reported a case – currently under investigation – of a company making lipsticks, some of the raw materials for which are tested on animals; the company making the lipsticks does not itself do the testing on animals; the company is not doing very well and the manager is concerned that no other bank would be willing to take on the business if the Bank decides to ask it to withdraw its account

- One manager reported that from a 'sweep' of 5,000 accounts at his branch, 12 or so had been 're-banked' (that is, asked to withdraw their account)

- A manager who targets business in the working men's clubs sector was concerned that there were many smokers in these clubs but, as they were not involved in the manufacture of tobacco products, their business was acceptable

- A manager turned down a substantial new account because it breached the Bank's code on the environmental impact of the business

- A battery hen operation was refused facilities by a manager because it breached the ethical policy; this manager indicated that his decision may have been different if, later in the financial year, he had not been hitting his targets for new business

- A sports organisation approached the Bank for accounting services; this organisation was partly sponsored by a tobacco manufacturer; the manager's view was that, since they were not involved in the manufacture of tobacco and since the cooperative retail organisations also sold tobacco products, the business was acceptable

- A public company put one of its businesses into receivership and wished to buy it back as an attempt to evade tax, the manager declined to grant loan facilities

- A manager was concerned that an approach from a part of the Territorial Army might have been in breach of the code; the business was approved.

From the 19 incidents reported, 6 managers checked with the Corporate Affairs Unit in the Manchester Headquarters of the Bank for advice and guidance; 8 felt compelled to carry out further detailed investigation into a proposition because of the existence of the ethical policy. Seven managers reported no incidents at all.

All of the examples cited above came from the remaining ten managers. Two managers indicated that their decisions were affected by commercial realities – one was concerned that no other bank would take on a business that he felt he wanted to be rid of because it breached the policy, and one admitted that a decision might have been different if he had been below his financial targets.

It is clear from the above that a significant number of managers were influenced in their behaviour by the existence of the ethical policy. It is also interesting to note that, even where a particular case did not directly breach the ethical policy, as it was written, some managers felt that they needed to apply the spirit of the policy as they saw it. This applied in the cases of the hunt saboteurs and the political organisations mentioned above.

5.4.4   Someone to turn to?

Managers were asked whether there was someone at the Bank for them to turn to if they had a problem of an ethical nature. This question did not refer specifically to the ethical policy but to ethical issues generally, whether or not they were incorporated in the policy. Two managers stated that there was no one to whom they felt they could turn for ethical advice or guidance; these were the exception. Twelve indicated that they would turn to the Corporate Affairs Unit at Head

Office and 11 felt that they could discuss ethical problems with colleagues at their own branch.

5.4.5 Ensuring conformity

The methods used by managers to ensure that their investment or client-related decisions conform to the ethical policy produced a variety of answers.

The Bank's procedures required confirmation that the ethical code had been discussed with any new client and managers' discretionary limits were set so that the larger advances were dealt with by Head Office staff. The Bank also required an annual review of each existing account. However, within this general framework, managers appeared to exercise their discretion in different ways.

One manager felt that this was not a real issue. Another stated that he discussed the policy with a new client and relied on the client to disclose relevant information. Other approaches included the view that the ethical policy was quite specific and conformity with it was unproblematic – it was clear when a client did or did not conform.

Nine managers stressed the importance of analysing the work of a company in some detail. Five indicated that they always met with new customers and the ethical policy was always discussed with them. However, two stated that small accounts were usually dealt with solely on documentation. One manager took the view that whether or not a client conformed to the policy was usually obvious from the nature of the client's business or operations.

Nine managers mentioned the significance of the role of the annual review in this context.

Since the exercise of discretion is always likely to lead to different approaches and outcomes, the variety of approaches indicated above is possibly remarkable in the sense that it does not demonstrate widely different approaches being taken. The major difference appears to be the extent to which managers rely on clients to disclose information. However, experienced CMs with successful track records are unlikely to be easily misled.

5.4.6 Managers' personal views

The managers were asked to identify the parts of the ethical policy that were most important to them personally and which were least important. They were not limited in the number of items they could identify in either category. One manager was not able to identify any section as most or least important from his point of view. Table 5.3 summarises the responses.

The very high level of identification of the first section of the ethical policy as personally important is worthy of note. When pressed to identify any regimes or organisations that fell into this category, respondents found some difficulty in doing so. It is also interesting that significant numbers of managers regard the Bank's stance on tobacco manufacture and speculation against the pound as not being significant parts of the policy.

Table 5.3 Elements of ethical policy managers consider personally most/least important

Ethical Policy Section	Most Important	Least Important
1 Oppressing human spirit	9	–
2 Oppressive regimes	3	–
3 Environmental impact	7	1
4 Ethical customers	1	–
5 Speculation against sterling	3	5
6 Money laundering, drug trafficking, tax evasion	2	1
7 Tobacco manufacturers	2	6
8 Customer charter	2	1
9 Animal experimentation	5	2
10 Factory farming	2	–
11 Animal fur	2	–
12 Blood sports	3	1

Managers were clearly more able to identify elements that they personally regarded as very important than they were able to identify elements they considered least important.

The overwhelming response to the question 'Does the Bank's ethical stance accord with your own personal, ethical or moral views?' was positive. Eleven stated 'Yes' without qualification; two indicated 'Yes', but felt that interpretations of aspects of the policy might differ between managers; two indicated 'Yes, generally speaking'; 1 claimed to have an open mind on this question; and another was undecided, but felt that some aspects of the policy went further than he personally might feel disposed to go.

The general support for the policy probably had two major sources. First, the Bank, in developing the policy, consulted widely with customers and staff. Considerable consonance was found between the values of both groups and the cooperative values that formed the basis for the ethical policy. Second, managers were very clear that the policy was an important part of the Bank's market positioning strategy and that it was instrumental in helping them to achieve the targets set (see the responses to the next question).

Sixteen managers responded positively to the question 'Does it help you to gain clients?' The 1 manager not responding positively felt that the policy might have helped him, but not directly.

Managers predominantly felt that the ethical policy made no contribution to their ability to manage their staff. Eleven answered with a clear 'No' to the question 'Does it help you in your management of staff?'; five, however, felt that it did help with the management of staff because it helped in the development of a shared set of values, making leadership and control of staff less demanding for themselves; 1 was not sure.

To the question 'Does it help you in relating to your superiors?', thirteen answered 'No' and four answered 'Yes'. Most managers reported that the ethical policy was less important in this context than organisational goals focused on targets and personal relationships with their superiors.

Claims made about the effectiveness of corporate codes and mission statements (see Campbell and Tawadey, 1992) emphasise their role within the corporation of creating the conditions for effective leadership and direction of staff by managers. It is not clear in this case whether the ethical policy helped significantly in this area of the managers' jobs.

The question 'Are there any aspects of the Code you would like to change?' produced a wide range of responses:

- Six managers did not want to change anything in the code

- One did not wish to change anything, but was personally more relaxed about some of the matters mentioned in the code

- Two felt that the reference to tobacco manufacturing should be taken out.

There were a large number of individualised responses, which produced the following statements:

- Any extension of the ethical policy would require greater specificity or be more widespread in its coverage

- The statement is rather long-winded and could be reduce to 5 paragraphs with a strong emphasis on the customer charter

- The code has to be ever-changing, the detail is less important than the general statement

- The code should be more down-to-earth and include categories such as cleaning up the streets

- The Bank should run diesel cars if it is genuine in its concern about the environment

- Endangered species should be added to the list

- Issues of race, ethnicity and creed should be included

- Alcohol should be included along with pharmaceutical products if tobacco is included

- Issues such as family instability, and law and order issues should be included

- There should be clarification of the tax evasion and tobacco manufacturing parts of the policy.

Most managers (11 out of the 17 interviewed) did wish to propose changes to the ethical policy. This does not imply a general dissatisfaction with the policy; it does, however, show that these managers felt that improvements in the policy could be made. There was a general perception amongst the managers interviewed that they would not be able to influence the content of the policy and that the processes involved in making changes were distant from their own working experience in the Bank.

5.4.7   Hypothetical circumstances

Each manager was asked to indicate what he would do if:

1 One of the companies in which he or she invested went bankrupt;

2 One of his or her clients was convicted of drunk driving;

3 A direct competitor of one of his or her existing clients approached him or her for a loan.

In relation to the first hypothetical circumstance:

- Fifteen managers responded that they would instigate the Bank's receivership procedures

- Two indicated that they would attempt to avoid this situation arising by being alert to developments and intervening to help the company before it got to the stage of receivership

- Four believed that the Co-operative Bank would be more sympathetic to the company than would other banks

- Six, however, stated that they felt that the Co-operative Bank's approach would be the same as any other commercial bank and this meant acting to protect the Bank's interests

- One manager, without prompting, stated that the Bank's ethical policy was not relevant to this situation

- No other manager mentioned the ethical policy in relation to this question.

Responses to the second hypothetical circumstance showed a similar degree of uniformity:

- Twelve managers indicated that their major concern was simply the impact of the drink-driving case on the client's ability to run the business

- Four indicated that they would do nothing

- Two felt that they should not make a moral judgement

- Seven indicated that such an incident might affect their personal relationship with the client involved.

The third hypothetical circumstance produced a wider variety of responses than the previous two. Although, the predominant view was that commercial considerations would be the major factors in a decision, different reasons were given to support this view:

- Managers felt that the new business should be taken because, if they did not, someone else would;

- Two argued that it is a competitive business world in which they operate and that this justified taking the new business on

- One manager, however, asserted that he would definitely not take on the new business because of the danger of having intimate knowledge of two competing clients. He felt that this ran counter to the underlying values of the ethical policy, even if such matters were not explicitly included in the published statement.

- Two felt that, if there were a conflict of interest, they would turn the new business away

- One manager would give the decision to another colleague not person-ally involved with either business, but went on to say that he would try to influence this colleague's decision

- One adopted the approach of turning down the new business but encour-aging the existing one to repay the bank loan as soon as possible to protect the bank from any future decline in the fortunes of this business as a result of new competition

- Three managers introduced the bank's duty of confidentiality into the dis-cussion: one of these stated that he felt that the question posed was not an ethical one because it was covered by the duty of confidentiality, which meant that the new business could be taken on without alerting the existing client because the bank is bound by a duty of confidentiality not to tell clients about other clients' business. The other two simply stated that the duty of confidentiality meant that they should examine the new proposition purely on commercial grounds.

The responses to the hypothetical circumstances indicate that managers approached such cases on the basis of the established procedures of the Bank, based on traditional banking practices as applied within the Co-operative Bank. The ethical policy does not provide clear guidelines to managers about what to do under the various circumstances. It was not intended to. There are rules, regulations and traditions upon which managers draw in such circumstances.

5.5   Conclusions

Did the ethical policy made any difference to the way in which managers performed their duties?

At one level, it is possible to argue that the policy had a significant influence on behaviour within the Bank. Its procedures required managers to confirm that each client, especially potential new ones, was aware of its ethical policy; job profiles indicated the need for managers to have knowledge of the policy. There was also a high degree of awareness of the existence of senior staff at Head Office in Manchester who could be consulted about particular problem cases. The Bank appeared to have been successful in integrating the policy into its processes.

However, within the complex and rapidly changing internal organisation of the Bank, it is difficult to establish the precise influences that the policy had on managerial behaviour. Other factors, such as the process re-engineering, downsizing, vigorous marketing strategy and the new performance management system, are just as likely to have influenced managerial behaviour.

Further, the traditional cooperative values of the Bank, which is an integral part of the cooperative movement, were felt by the managers to be significant in influencing the culture of the organisation and the behaviour of managers towards customers and colleagues. The Bank could argue, with considerable justification, that its ethical policy was simply a market-oriented re-statement of these traditional values.

The managers did feel that the policy had a major impact on their ability to attract new business amongst the target groups (educational establishments, professional bodies, charitable organisations) and it provided an entrée into discussions with these groups. However, they also took the view that the policy was effective in this regard only insofar as it was supported by efficient, helpful and effective services provided by the Bank.

The ethical policy did not appear to have had significant influence on behaviour in areas that the managers regarded as covered by traditional banking practice. This is illustrated in their response to the hypothetical circumstances. In these circumstances, the more traditional banking virtues of confidentiality were seen as predominant in influencing their behaviour.

Chadwick (1993) argues that one danger of professional codes of conduct is that the behaviour of the person affected by the code loses autonomy. The code becomes a replacement for independent moral action. In the case of the Co-operative Bank's ethical policy, this did not appear to have happened. The policy was significant in marketing terms and was seen as helpful for managers in achieving targets. It did not dominate their thinking. Other values, beliefs and attitudes intervened in mediating the code. The more traditional banking values, particularly of confidentiality, were used by managers in justifying their behaviour more frequently than reference to the ethical policy.

Finally, the Co-operative Bank's ethical policy was the product of decisions to include certain features and, necessarily, to exclude others. The Bank was, and is, committed to reviewing and changing its policy in the light of changing circumstances and the changes in the values of its customers. As indicated above, most of the interviewed managers wished to propose some changes to the policy, although each manager's individual proposal would not result in major changes of emphasis. However, most of the managers were not aware of the procedures for review and change. Their sense of ownership of the policy as a marketing tool was considerable. Their use of it in other areas of work and their feeling of influence over its content was limited.

▮▮▮ QUESTIONS AND TASKS ▮▮▮▮▮▮▮

1 Find two other banks from anywhere in the world that claim to have an ethical policy. Compare and contrast these banks' ethical policies with those of the Co-operative Bank.

APPENDIX A5. 1

Ethical policy of the Co-operative Bank

1 **It will not invest** in or supply financial services to any regime or organisation that oppresses the human spirit, takes away the rights of individuals or manufactures any instrument of torture;

2 **It will not finance** or in any way facilitate the manufacture or sale of weapons to any country that has an oppressive regime;

3 **It will encourage** business customers to take a proactive stance of the environmental impact of their own activities;

4 **It will actively** seek out individuals, commercial enterprises and non-commercial organisations that have a complementary ethical stance;

5 **It will not speculate** against the pound using either its own money or that of its customers. It believes it is inappropriate for a British clearing bank to speculate against the British currency and the British economy using deposits provided by their British customers and at the expense of the British taxpayer;

6 **It will try to ensure** its financial services are not exploited for the purpose of money laundering, drug trafficking or tax evasion by the continued application and development of its successful internal monitoring and control procedures;

7 **It will not provide** financial services to tobacco product manufacturers;

8 **It will continue** to extend and strengthen its Customer Charter, which has already established new standards of banking practice through adopting innovative procedures on status enquiries and customer confidentiality, ahead of any other British Bank;

9 **It will not invest** in any business involved in animal experimentation for cosmetic purposes;

10 **It will not support** any person or company using exploitative factory farming methods;

11 **It will not engage** in business with any farm or other organisation engaged in the production of animal fur;

12 **It will not support** any organisation involved in blood sports, which it defines as sports that involve the training of animals or birds to catch and destroy, or to fight and kill, other animals or birds.

Questionnaire for interviews with managers

1 How long have you been in your present role in the Bank?

2 What was your previous role?

3 When did you start your employment with the Bank?

4 What factors led to your being employed by the Bank?

5 Can you tell me your age and qualifications?

6 Please describe the major components of your current job (briefly).

7 Which parts of your current job would you say are influenced by the Bank's:

   (a) Mission statement;

   (b) Ethical code?

8 I would like you to describe up to three incidents in the last 2 or 3 years in which the Bank's ethical code assisted you in arriving at a decision.

9 If you have a problem at work of an ethical nature, is there someone at the Bank you can turn to for help?

10 How do you ensure that your investment or client-related decisions conform to the Bank's ethical code?

11 Which parts of the Bank's ethical code are most important to you personally?

12 Which parts are the least important to you personally?

13 What would you do if:

   (a) One of the companies in which you invest goes bankrupt;

   (b) One of your clients was convicted of drunk driving;

   (c) A direct competitor of one of your existing clients approached you for a loan?

14 In your opinion:

   (a) Does the Bank's ethical stance accord with your own personal, ethical or moral views;

   (b) Does it help you to gain clients;

   (c) Does it help you in your management of staff;

   (d) Does it help you in relating to your superiors?

15 Are there any aspects of the code you would like to change?

16 In relation to day-to-day banking practice, does the Co-operative Bank differ from other banks?

CHAPTER 6

Queens Moat Houses plc

After reading this chapter you will:

■ Be able to identify issues of corporate governance and their relationship to financial information

■ Be aware of some of the issues involved in the leadership of public corporations and the relations between the various stakeholders in the business.

6.1 Introduction

In April 1982, Queens Moat Houses raised £30 million (including a first rights issue) and proceeded to buy 26 hotels from Grand Met, followed by a second rights issue of £10.6 million. This was the start of a ten-year period of expansion culminating in one of the largest corporate losses in history, a complete change of the board of directors, and protracted negotiations with lenders to restructure the finances of the company.

John Bairstow was the founder of the group and remained the driving force until he left the company in August 1993. Jeff Randall of *The Sunday Times* commented that 'the impression of reality created by the Bairstow regime deserves membership of the magic circle'.[1]

During this period, the reported results and financial statements gave little indication of the troubles ahead. Expansion was the mood of the time. In November 1983 the group purchased the Hilton International Hotel and was confirmed as the UK's largest provincial hotel chain.[2] This was followed by a Continental acquisition of the Dutch Belderberg Hotel group for £15.5 million, plus a further 24 hotels on the Continent and, in February 1990, the group gained control of Norfolk Capital for £157 million.

This growth was funded in part by a number of rights issues (see Table 6.1).

Table 6.1 would appear to indicate that the shareholders had faith in the long-term future of the group. This faith was perhaps founded upon the Chairman's statements, which, as late as April 1991, when reporting upon the results for the year to 31 December 1990, gave little indication of impending disaster:

Despite the economic setback in the UK, and more moderately on the Continent, and less favourable trading in the early months of this year in some of

Table 6.1 Funding of growth of Queens Moat Houses (in part) by rights issues

£(*millions*)

1982 12 Apr.	1st rights issue	(Part of £30 raised)
1983 10 May	2nd rights issue	10.60
1985 1 Apr.	3rd rights issue	25.00
1987 20 Aug.	4th rights issue	83.00
1988 13 Oct.	5th rights issue	57.50
1989 16 Aug.	6th rights issue	141.00
1989 4 Oct.	7th rights issue	1.26
1991 29 May	8th rights issue	184.00

the large inner-city hotels, they remain cautiously optimistic. Current trading has been more encouraging and they therefore believe that shareholders can reasonably expect modest progress in 1991 and further improvements in 1992 as the UK economy recovers. A series of re-financing moves have brought the borrowing ratio down to 45 per cent.[3]

A statement on the results for the year to 31.12.91 was, again, upbeat:

On the Continent a strong progress was continued and a good start was made to 1992, with profitability in the first 3 months of this year at new high levels. There is still no sign of a sustained recovery in the UK though some UK hotels also made good headway. The company is strategically well-positioned and the Board anticipates a satisfactory outcome in 1992 and a positive return of growth thereafter. Trading results were close to the record-breaking performances of 1990, and re-financing during the year reduced gearing from 69 per cent to 55 per cent.

Also, the reduction in the net asset value of the group was mainly due to a sensible and prudent reduction by independent valuers of the value of certain UK hotels, which to a large extent was offset by an overall increase in the valuation of Continental assets.[4]

How, therefore could the hoped for profits of £85–90 million for 1992, turn out to be a £1 billion plus loss, the shares suspended at 47½p and effectively worthless, with net liabilities amounting to £338 million, plus debts of £1.1 billion. A new assessment of the property portfolio by Jones Long Wootton put their value at £861 million.[5]

Jeff Randall writing in *The Sunday Times* commented 'the assets and profits seem to have vanished like cards up a sleeve', and proceeded to highlight the following facts:

1 Reported profits of £90 million in 1991, widely expected by analysts to be repeated in 1992;

2 Earlier in the year, when its shares were trading at 59p, its stock-market worth was more than £500 million;

3 In December 1992, Weatherall Green & Smith, the property valuers, said Queens Moat's 200 strong hotels estate was worth £2 billion.

(See Appendixes A6.1 and A6.2.)

6.2 A tale of two valuers

A major issue in the Queens Moat saga was the valuation of the property portfolio of the group, which, in the first instance, was valued in December 1992 by Weatherall Green & Smith at £1.86 billion and then subsequently revised downwards to £1.35 billion. These valuations were followed by a figure of £861 million from Jones Long Wootton, which led to shareholders asking for an explanation for the difference in the figures.

The Royal Institution of Chartered Surveyors, reacting to a call from the former chairman, John Bairstow, agreed to consider the matter, but promptly dropped out of the discussions subsequent to the appointment of the DTI inspectors.

Kirstie Hamilton writing in *The Times*[6] reported that 'on the 26 November 1993, Andrew Coppel, Chief Executive of Queens Moat, said the restructuring proposals will include a full new valuation, but he emphasised that no valuation, however high, could solve the company's problems, which stemmed from an inability to generate enough cash to service its debt'.

6.3 Department of Trade investigation

On 12 November1993, the Secretary of State for Trade and Industry, Michael Heseltine, appointed inspectors to look into various matters drawn to the Department's notice by the new board of Queens Moat. The inspectors were appointed under Section 432 of the Companies Act (1984), which gave them wide powers to obtain documents, and summon past and present directors, officers and agents of the company.

6.4 Corporate governance in action

A major recommendation of the Cadbury Committee, which produced a report on Corporate Governance, was the need to emphasise the role of the non-executive directors in the management of a company.

A comment in *Accountancy Age* (11 November 1993) on the Queens Moat saga questioned the position of the last non-executive directors to resign. 'In the case of Queens Moat, these watchdogs are, however, in the doghouse. David Howell and John Gale were the last of the company's non-executives to resign and, with hindsight, any belief that their credibility with investors would have survived the revelations regarding Queens Moat and its management looks optimistic.[7]

Melvyn Marckus writing in *The Times* on 6 November 1993 quoted David Howell as saying 'I have sought to perform my non-executive duties conscientiously throughout my appointment and I believe the non-executives were clearly misled.'[8] This was in contrast with an earlier statement attributed to Howell by *The Sunday Times*: 'I am definitely staying, Queens Moat is a company with a very good future.'[9]

6.5 Debenture holders and capital reorganisation

At the Annual General Meeting, held on 29 November 1993[10] the chairman stated that 'the group had over £1.2 billion of net borrowing and an annual net interest bill in excess of £100 million to service and that the group's borrowing facilities had been capped at their outstanding level at 31.3.93 and no new money was available to the company from its lenders. The group was not paying some 60 per cent of its interest bill, but was continuing to pay its trade creditors as they fall due to enable the business to continue to trade.'

A further issue of concern to the board was the debenture trust deeds, which required that the value of the secured properties must not be less than 150 per cent of the nominal value of the debenture stocks. Unfortunately, the Jones Long Wootton valuation valued the secured properties at 67 per cent of the principal owed. As a result, default under the trust deed had occurred and consequently the trustee was entitled to take control of the secured properties, which could have resulted in Queens Moat having to cease trading.

It was therefore necessary for a request to be made to the debenture holders, via the trustee, not to enforce the security so that directors had time to prepare proposals as part of the overall restructuring. This was agreed at a meeting held on 30 November 1993.

Reporting on 2 February 1994, the company announced that 'progress has been made towards financial restructuring of the group and that a steering committee of the group's lenders had recommended a continuation of the present arrangements for lender support for a further 2 months'.[11]

6.6 Past dividend payments and shareholders' interests

The investigations undertaken by the new management revealed that the company had paid dividends to both Ordinary and Convertible Preference shareholders – which, under the Companies Acts, it was not legally entitled to do, because the company had insufficient distributable reserves. The total amount involved was approximately £33 million, but the board stated it would attempt to reclaim the dividends paid to the directors.

On the 19 November 1994, the board reported that 'it had been advised that resolutions passed at meetings, amending the borrowing limit in the company's articles, were not valid because recognition was not given to a right to attend and vote at such meetings incorporated in the company's 7 per cent Convertible Accumulative Redeemable Preference shares. The Company had therefore appointed Freshfields and Leading Counsel to assist the directors in resolving these issues.'[12]

Concern was growing amongst the shareholders as to their position after any capital reorganisation, and a Shareholder Action Group was formed to represent their case at the annual meeting on November 29 1993. Denis Woodhams,[13] a shareholder in Queens Moat, issued a petition asking the High Court to declare that the group's affairs were being conducted in a manner unfairly prejudiced to the shareholders.

Mr Beaumont-Dark, supporting the case of the shareholders, was quoted in *The Financial Times*: 'The banks, and one understands it, are protecting their own situation. But people feel other interests ought to be looked at as well. The banks have a certain responsibility. How well did they check before lending money? They're not just innocent victims. The people who are the most innocent are the shareholders.'[14]

6.7 The new management

The new board of directors soon became embroiled in the battle between the various interested parties, and were themselves criticised by the shareholders on the question of their remuneration packages. The annual general meeting held to adopt the company's 1992 accounts (including the £861 million property valuation)[15] was a stormy three-hour debate, and the chairman Stanley Metcalfe was obliged to call for a poll to secure adoption of the 1992 accounts.

The new board – Metcalfe, Coppel and Le Poideven – were criticised by the shareholders, who questioned the validity of the £861 million valuation and attacked their salaries and incentive arrangements. The Chairman, Metcalfe, warned shareholders that the vote to be taken by debenture holders, on whether or not to enforce their security, could threaten Queen Moat's survival. Adoption of the 1992 accounts was defeated by 158 to 80 on a show of hands. In the subsequent poll, 256, 719, 019 votes were cast in favour of adoption and 52, 527, 297 against adoption.

▬▬▬ QUESTIONS AND TASKS ▬▬▬

1 Find out which watchdog bodies exist in Britain for overseeing the financial reporting of large businesses;

2 Make a list of the roles and tasks of each of these bodies;

3 Which of these bodies have legal powers to enforce action by businesses and which operate on a voluntary basis;

4 Find three examples from recent cases, as reported in the financial media, of companies being made to change their practices as a result of action by any of these bodies.

APPENDIX A6.1

News report (Microview Plus Report)

Queens Moat Houses plc [Suspended]

8 March 94: Balance sheet

At meetings held today resolutions amending the borrowing limit of Co and its Subs were passed.

31 March 94: Balance sheet

At meetings held today holders of 10% First Mort Deb Stock 2020 and 12% First Mort Deb Stock 2013, Extraordinary Resolutions to extend, until 30-694, directions to Trustees not to enforce security were duly passed. Steering Committee of Group's lenders has indicated to Co that it has recommended a continuation of present arrangements for lender support for a further 2 months.

8 Apr 94: Dividend

No dividend (1.395p per share) for year to 2.1.94.

8 Apr 94: Results

- Result for year to 2.1.94, figs in £m: Turnover 381.3 (387.4). Operating profit 18.4 (loss 0.7). Exceptional items − net surplus on revaluation of tangible assets 26.0 (Dr 803.9) restructuring costs nil (32.0) loss on disposal or closure of businesses nil (69.2) and amounts written-off investments 0.3 (17.2) foreign currency gains 13.9 (nil) and interest payable nil (16.7). Interest payable 110.1 (112.6). Loss before tax 46.4 (1,040.5). Tax credit 2.0 (Dr 7.0). Net loss 44.4 (1,047.5). Loss per share 6.4 (116.9p) and excluding exceptional items 10.7p (13.6p).

- Analysis of turnover and operating profit in £m: Continuing operations − hotels − UK 134.8 (115.1) and 18.5 (8.0), Germany 91.4 (88.2) and loss 0.9 (loss 10.3), The Netherlands 51.9 (45.5) and 8.0 (8.3), France 24.4(26.1) and loss 0.3 (profit 0.9), Belgium 16.8 (16.8) and 0.7 (1.1), elsewhere 10.3 (9.6) and loss 1.7 (profit 2.2), discontinuing operations − property − UK 24.8 (52.1) and loss 3.8 (profit 4.3), discontinued operations − property − UK 14.2 (21.1) and 1.3 (3.1) and leisure − UK 12.7 (12.9) and 2.4 (1.6), less central costs and provisions nil (nil) and 5.8 (15.5), totals 381.3 (387.4) and 18.4 (loss 0.7).

- Consolidated balance sheet as at 2.1.94, shows in £m: Tangible assets 927.0 (891.1). Add investments 0.6 (1.1) and deduct net current liabilities 1253,2 (1,208.0), creditors due after more than one year 2.0 (4.4) and provisions 49.4 (68.7), giving net liabilities 377.0 (388.9), represented by shareholders deficit.

- Accounts have been prepared on going concern basis which assume that Co and all its Subs will continue in operational existence for foreseeable future, having adequate funds to meet their obligations as they fall due.

- Validity of this assumption depends on: successful completion of financial restructuring; continued provision of adequate facilities by Group's banks and other lenders pending completion of financial restructuring; and holders of Co's First Mortgage Deb Stocks not seeking to enforce their security over assets of certain Subs of Co.

- Board reports that a satisfactory start to current financial year has been made by Group in UK, which has seen increased occupancy rates but lower than projected average room rates. Overheads have benefited significantly from a reduction in wage costs at unit level. In Continental Europe, difficult trading conditions experienced in 1993 have continued into current financial year. However, measures have been taken to reduce Group's cost base in line with current market conditions.

Board has appointed Cazenove & Co as stockbrokers to Co.

Queens Moat House plc: Annual Report 1992

(i) Chairman's statement

I was appointed a director of your company and elected Chairman of your board on 26 August 1993. The results for the year ended 31 December 1992 show that the group incurred losses before taxation of £1,040.5 million (1991 – £56.3 million loss – restated) on turnover of £387.4 million (1991 – £314.7 million – restated). Exceptional losses, which accounted for £939.0 million of the pre-tax losses in 1992, included £803.9 million arising from the reduction below historical cost in the value of the group's properties since 31 December 1991. Losses per ordinary share were 116.4p (1991 – 8.5p loss – restated). No final ordinary dividend in respect of the year has been declared.

As a result of these losses, the group's consolidated balance sheet as at 31 December 1992 showed net liabilities of £388.9 million, compared to net assets of £1,192.6 million as restated as at 31 December 1991. Borrowings as at 31 December 1992 stood at £1,165.9 million (1991 – £860.4 million – restated). These figures include the full liabilities associated with finance leases (1992 – £173.8 million; 1991 – £149.5 million – restated) which, in 1991, were partly treated as operating leases and, therefore, as off-balance sheet liabilities.

In common with the experience of other hotel groups in Europe, the operating performance of the group was disappointing in 1992, reflecting difficult trading conditions. The group made an operating loss of £0.7 million in 1992 (1991 – £22.4 million profit – restated). A discussion of the trading performance of the group's businesses is contained in the Chief Executive's Review which follows this statement.

The group's consolidated profit and loss account and balance sheet for 1991 have been restated as a result of adjustments necessary to reflect the more prudent accounting policies and treatments used for the 1992 accounts. The effects of such restatements are that the 1991 pre-tax profit has been reduced from £90.4 million to a pre-tax loss of £56.3 million and the 1991 net assets have been reduced by £105.3 million to £1,192.6 million.

You will find enclosed within this Annual Report and Accounts the unaudited interim results for the six months ended 4 July 1993, which show that the group made an operating profit of £9.1 million over the period. The group incurred net interest charges of £57.5 million during the period resulting in a net loss before tax of £48.4 million. The interim results for the period ended 12 July 1992 were based on the previous board's application of accounting policies and treatments, which have now been changed. Your board believes that it is not appropriate to compare the 1993 interim results with the 1992 interim results and, for the reasons indicated below, the latter have not been restated.

Background to the 1992 results and reasons for the delay in publications

These results demonstrate a substantially different financial position of your company from that indicated by the Report and Accounts dated 30 April 1992 and the Interim Results dated 12 August 1992. Whilst neither I nor any of the current executive directors were members of your board during the period under review, it is nevertheless necessary for me to explain the background as I understand it. Inevitably, many of the comments made in this statement are based on information available to me and my board colleagues at this time. Accordingly, I have summarised below the principal factors responsible for the changes in the financial position of the group. On pages 19 to 21 is set out a Report by the Finance Director explaining the steps taken to introduce an effective system of financial and management controls, summarising the principal changes in accounting policies which have been made and commenting upon the liabilities of the group.

The delay in the production of the 1992 Report and Accounts has been due to a number of factors. The gravity of the group's financial position was first brought to the attention of the group's banks by the former chairman on 31 March 1993, when it was indicated that the group's 1992 results were likely to fall seriously short of expectations and that the preference dividend due on 1 April 1993 could not be paid. Grant Thornton were appointed to investigate the financial position of the group on behalf of the group's banks and Andrew Coppel and Andrew Le Poideven were appointed as consultants to the group in April 1993. Coopers & Lybrand were appointed as auditors and Morgan Grenfell were appointed as financial advisers in May 1993. It became clear to the board and its advisers at an early stage that a thorough review of the financial position of the group was imperative. As a result, the group's accounting policies were reviewed and appropriate changes made, a rigorous review of the group's contingent liabilities was conducted and Jones Lang Wootton ('JLW') were appointed to value the group's properties.

Given the background to the present situation, the preparation of the 1992 accounts, including the substantial restatement of the 1991 accounts, has taken a considerable period of time. I am confident that the accounting policies on which we have based the 1992 results, and therefore those for 1991 as restated, are entirely appropriate and are the result of considerable deliberation with our auditors and other financial advisers. Certain of those policies were, in fact, accepted by the previous board following recommendations by Andrew Coppel, now the Chief Executive, and Andrew Le Poideven, now the Finance Director, when they were consultants to the company. The new accounting policies are set out on pages 36 to 39 and detailed effects of the changes on the 1991 results and financial position are set out in note 1 to the accounts.

Contingent liabilities have been rigorously reviewed in order to ascertain whether they are in fact actual liabilities, for which provision should be made in the accounts, and your board has endeavoured to provide as appropriate for all known liabilities and potential losses. Whilst the new management team has focused on the stabilisation and recovery of the group, a number of issues have surfaced as the problems of the group have been identified. We have ensured that both the auditors and our legal advisers have, as appropriate, carried out proper investigations into known matters affecting the group. These issues include the payment of unlawful dividends in 1991, 1992 and 1993, other breaches of the Companies Act and the infringement of Stock Exchange regulations and have been referred to, where appropriate, in these accounts. Your board has brought these issues to the attention of the Department of Trade and Industry and the London Stock Exchange.

The Finance Director's Report describes certain serious shortcomings which existed in the group's management and financial controls. In view of these shortcomings, your board regarded it as essential to subject the 1992 accounts to particularly detailed scrutiny. The group's 1991 consolidated profit and loss account and balance sheet have been restated in order to make them comparable with 1992.

Reduction in the value of the group's properties

The principal reason for the exceptional losses in 1992 was the reduction in property values resulting from an independent valuation of the group's portfolio of properties as at 31 December 1992.

At 31 December 1991, the group's properties were valued by Weatherall Green & Smith ('WGS') at £2.0 billion, a valuation which was incorporated in the 1991 audited balance sheet. WGS also presented a draft valuation in respect of 31 December 1992 to the previous board as well as a draft valuation as at 31 March 1993 to the group's bankers in May 1993. Both of these valuations reflected a substantial diminution in value compared to the 31 December 1991 valuation.

In June, the previous board appointed JLW to value the group's hotel portfolio in place of WGS. They have valued the portfolio of properties as at 31 December 1992 at £861 million.

The JLW valuation as at 31 December 1992 differed substantially from WGS's valuation as at 31 December 1991 and also materially from the values presented to the banks on 27 May 1993. The board subjected the JLW valuation to lengthy and detailed examination. Attention was focused on the methodology used, including adjustments made to net operating income, the use of income capitalisation and discounted cash flows in arriving at the actual valuations and deductions relating to capital expenditure.

After careful consideration the board accepted the JLW valuation and the valuation has been incorporated into the group's balance sheet at 31 December 1992. In the UK and Continental Europe there was considerable hotel expansion in the late 1980s fuelled by abundant availability of capital. Circumstances have changed materially over the past few years and the recent market place for hotels in the UK has been dominated by distressed sale values. On the Continent, the declining profitability has lagged the UK but the market place for hotels has shown similar adverse developments. It is this adverse context of declining profitability and limited purchasers' interest in hotels in which the valuation has been prepared. However, the board is optimistic about the long-term recovery potential of the group's asset values.

Further exceptional losses in 1992

The group made further exceptional losses in 1992 of £135.1 million, comprising restructuring costs, the write down of certain investments, provisions for losses on the termination of financial contracts and losses on disposals.

The accounts have been prepared on a going concern basis, which assumes that a financial restructuring will be successfully completed. Accordingly, your board has considered it appropriate to make provisions in these accounts for the costs incurred to date and the estimated further costs which may arise in 1993 and 1994 in connection with the envisaged financial restructuring, totalling £32.0 million.

In addition, the group has provided fully against certain of the group's investments in associated undertakings, some of which are in financial difficulties, and certain other investments. These provisions amounted to £17.2 million.

In the light of the group's financial position, your board has reviewed and continues to review its actual and contingent liabilities very carefully. In particular, full provision has been made for liabilities resulting from exposure on contracts taken out in the past with the intent of limiting the effect of interest and exchange rate movements. These contracts were terminated at a cost of £16.7 million as there was no longer any commercial or financial rationale for retaining them.

Finally, in accordance with best accounting practice, your board believes it appropriate to provide against the diminution in the book value of certain subsidiaries which it has now sold or is in the process of selling. We are also required to write off through the profit and loss account associated goodwill which was previously written off to reserves upon acquisition. This has been treated as an exceptional item although it has no impact on consolidated net assets. The aggregate exceptional loss provided for in the 1992 accounts for book value adjustments and goodwill write-offs was £69.2 million, which has created a reduction in net assets of £40.7 million.

Relationship of the group with its bankers and other creditors

On 31 March 1993, the then chairman of the group met with the group's principal bankers. At the request of Barclays Bank plc, on behalf of the group's banks, Grant Thornton, reporting accountants, commenced an investigation into the group's financial position. A meeting of the group's lenders was held on 7 April 1993 to give them the background to the situation. Subsequently, Andrew Coppel joined the group as a consultant on 8 April 1993 followed by Andrew Le Poideven on 9 April 1993.

At this meeting the banks were asked to agreed to a standstill arrangement whereby the group's bank facilities were capped at the amounts outstanding as at 31 March 1993, payments of certain interest were deferred and strict limits were imposed on capital expenditure by the group. This agreement was to remain in place until Grant Thornton had completed their report. Further, a steering committee was formed, comprising eight banks, led by Barclays Bank plc and National Westminster Bank plc, to represent the interests of all the 65 lenders which provide facilities to the group.

The group and Grant Thornton made a presentation to the banks on 27 May 1993 and Grant Thornton's report was made available to all the banks at that time. At that meeting, the group sought an extension to an amended standstill arrangement until 31 October 1993 to enable management to prepare a strategic plan for the group as a basis for going forward beyond the short term. The basis of the extension provided operational terms more favourable to the group than the previous agreement. All the group's banks either signed the extended standstill agreement or have acted in accordance with its principles.

The group presented its plans and outline restructuring proposals at a meeting of banks on 28 October 1993 and has sought an extension of its interim banking arrangements in order to allow time for the detail of its outline proposals to be put in place.

Some of the group's particularly certain Continental European banks, whose borrowings are well secured, are now receiving interest. We have paid particularly close attention to the banking relationships both in the UK and elsewhere in Europe and we have successfully resolved a series of problems and stabilised a number of difficulties with individual banks.

In addition to liaising closely with the banks, we have also had discussions with the trustee of the company's £215 million First Mortgage Debenture Stocks and, latterly, with a steering committee of the Association of British Insurers. There are two debenture stocks, totalling £215 million, which were issued between 1983 and 1991 and which rank pari passu. The stocks are secured by a fixed charge over 27 UK hotel properties, floating charges over four UK hotel properties and the stockholders also have the benefit of a floating charge over certain UK subsidiary undertakings and assets. Interest on the stocks has continued to be paid. However, following the completion of the JLW valuation as at 31 December 1992, it is clear that there is a material shortfall (relative to the requirements of the Trust Deed) in the value of the property on which the Debenture Stocks are secured and this security no longer covers the nominal value of the Stock outstanding. Interim proposals to seek the support of stockholders are being considered pending the formulation of further proposals to stockholders in connection with the restructuring of the group. A meeting of stockholders is being convened to consider the interim proposals.

At the trading level, the news of the group's financial problems initially had a noticeable impact on suppliers and customers, particularly in the UK, where the publicity was more widespread than in Continental Europe. However, within a relatively short period, the position stabilised.

Financial restructuring

In 1992 the group's consolidated operating loss of £0.7 million compared with the net interest payable, including finance lease charges, of £100.9 million. Your board believes that the level of cash flow generated from the group's operations will be insufficient for the foreseeable future to service the current level of the group's indebtedness on the basis of the financial arrangements which existed as a 31 March 1993. In addition, the group's consolidated balance sheet shows net liabilities of £388.9 million as at 31 December 1992, which should be viewed against net borrowings (including finances leases) of £1,165.9 million. It has become evident to the board that a financial restructuring is essential for the group including, inevitably, a debt for equity swap which will dilute shareholders interests. Once proposals have been formulated, we shall communicate with shareholders.

Following the presentation of the group's plans and outline proposals on 28 October 1993, the Steering Committee of the group's lenders issued the following statement:

> The plan presented to the banks today demonstrates that Queens Moat Houses can be reconstructed to give it a viable future, despite the group's results for the year ended 31 December 1992 and for the six months ended 4 July 1993.

> It was stressed at the meeting that the best way forward for all the banks is to continue to support the group and maintain its stability.

> To this end, the steering committee, led by Barclays and National Westminster, recommended approval of the group's proposal for additional time to allow detailed negotiations to be completed with lenders on the final foRm of the reconstruction.

These circumstances have closely focused the attention of your board on the issue of solvency and the position of the individual directors of the parent company and each subsidiary in the context of possible wrongful trading. We continue to take appropriate advice on this serious issue on a regular basis.

The costs of the enormous amount of work required to get the business back onto a sound footing will be considerable. To date, these principally relate to professional advice to the group and the group's bankers. Your board at all times seeks to minimise these costs but it must be recognised that the severity of the group's financial position demands proper advice and that the complexity of the group's financing arrangements has required a particularly large commitment of resources by the professional advisers concerned. However, as soon as the reconstruction of the group has been completed, the board is confident that professional costs will be reduced significantly.

Board of directors

There have been major changes in the company's board and senior management since the group's problems become apparent. Between 26 May 1993 and 26 August 1993, all the previous board members, with two exceptions, either resigned or did not seek re-election at the annual general meeting held on 26 August 1993. Andrew Coppel joined the board as Chief Executive on 2 July 1993 and he has since been joined by myself, as non-executive Chairman, Andrew Le Poideven as Finance Director and Michael Cairns as Chief Operating Officer – Hotels. Michael Cairns has extensive experience in the international hotel industry, having spent 25 years with Inter-Continental Hotels. Before joining your company he was responsible for the management of Inter-Continental's European, Middle Eastern and African properties. I am confident that the new management team, combining financial, hotel and general management experience, is sufficiently broadly based to attack the group's problems. John Gale and David Howell continue as non-executive directors, and further non-executive directors will be appointed in due course.

In line with the Cadbury Report on Corporate Governance, a remuneration committee has been formed, comprising the non-executive directors, and, on the appointment of additional non-executive directors, an audit committee will be reconstituted, to whom a group internal auditors will report.

Previous directors and advisers

All previous executive directors resigned without prejudice to any contractual rights they may have had. Shareholders should be aware that Mr Bairstow, the former chairman, and Mr Marcus, the former deputy chairman have made claims for wrongful termination of their respective service contracts. Mr Marcus and two other former executive directors, Mr Hersey and Mr Porter are also seeking compensation for unfair dismissal. All these claims are being strongly resisted.

Your board is aware that, in the light of the issues referred to in this statement and otherwise, your company may have rights of action against previous directors or advisers. Such matters are being kept under close review to ensure that the interests of the company are protected.

Listing of the company's securities

The possible relisting of the company's securities is an issue which has been raised by many shareholders and is a matter which is subject to regular review by your board. The board has liaised closely with the London Stock Exchange since the beginning of April 1993. However, it is not appropriate to seek the relisting of the company's securities until such time as shareholders and investors have sufficient information to use as a basis for trading the company's securities. Whilst the availability of this Report and Accounts for 1992 and the unaudited 1993 half-year results is certainly helpful in this context, it is also important for shareholders and investors to be aware of the level of support the group has from its bankers and mortgage debenture stockholders and the form of the anticipated financial reconstruction. As soon as we are in a position to clarity this matter we will review the situation again with the London Stock Exchange and our advisers.

Group pension schemes

Of some concern to our employees and pensioners will be the status of the group's final salary pension schemes. There are two main schemes – the UK Executive Pension Scheme and the UK Staff Pension Scheme. The results of recently received valuations show that the assets of the UK Executive Pension Scheme were valued at £5.8 million, a shortfall to liabilities of some £1.1 million. The principal reason for the shortfall was that the salary growth experience since the previous valuation in 1989 was considerably ahead of the assumed growth rate, but with the departure in 1993 of several high earning executives, the shortfall has been reduced substantially since the valuation date. The latest results of the UK Staff Pension Scheme show that the assets had a value of £4.2 million and there was an actuarial surplus of £1.4 million.

Interim results and current trading

In the six months ended 4 July 1993 the group incurred losses before taxation of £48.4 million on a turnover of £167.2 million. Your board does not have available meaningful consolidated financial information for the 1992 interim period with which these results can be compared. The interim results of the period ended 12 July 1992, which were published in August 1992, were based on the previous board's application of accounting policies which have now been changed. Your board has been unable to find the working papers which were used to construct the 1992 interim results. The absence of these papers, together with the time which would be required to prepare revised comparative figures has caused your board to conclude that it would be inappropriate to delay further the publication of the 1993 unaudited interim results.

At the operating level, the group's UK hotels in the first half of 1993 continued to suffer from the difficult trading conditions present in 1992. However, from the latter part of the second quarter there has been a modest recovery in the performance of this division led by an upturn in occupancy rates. Your board is encouraged by prospects in the UK although no material improvement in room rates is expected in the short term. The trading conditions for the group's Continental hotels have deteriorated throughout 1993 as a result of the general recessionary climate in a number of European economies. We continue to manage our European businesses to limit the impact of this downturn.

Further details of the trading performance of the group's businesses are contained in the Chief Executive's Review.

Serious loss of capital

On 27 September 1993, directors of the company became aware that the net assets of the company had fallen to one half or less of the called up share capital of the company. On 25 October 1993, notice of an extraordinary general meeting, convened in accordance with Section 142 of the Companies Act, was sent to shareholders. The meeting has been convened for Monday, 22 November 1993 to consider whether any, and is so what, steps should be taken in view of the fact that the net assets of the company have fallen beneath the relevant threshold. As it is proposed that the annual general meeting of the company will be reconvened for Monday, 29 November 1993, it will be proposed that the extraordinary general meeting be adjourned until immediately following the reconvened annual general meeting.

Support of banks and employees

The support of our banks has been particularly encouraging during a most difficult period. We have continued to work closely with the joint co-ordinators throughout and we are grateful to them, and the steering committee in particular, for their efforts in a difficult situation. Morgan Grenfell's advice has been particularly valuable.

I would like to conclude by thanking our employees throughout the group for their help in our endeavours to restore stability and to ensure the group's continued viability. The hotel business is very much a people business and the new management team can only be successful if it has their continued commitment, loyalty and determination.

Stanley Metcalfe

Chairman
29 October 1993

(ii) Report of the Auditors

To the members of Queens Moat Houses plc

We have audited the accounts on pages 30 to 72 in accordance with Auditing Standards except that the scope of our work was limited by the matter referred to in paragraph 2 below.

1 As explained in the accounting policies, the accounts have been prepared on a going concern basis and the validity of this depends on the group's bankers and other lenders continuing their support by providing adequate facilities pending the successful completion of a financial restructuring, on the successful completion of such a restructuring, and on the company's First Mortgage Debenture Stockholders not seeking to enforce their security. The outcome of these matters is currently uncertain. Should continuing support from the group's bankers and other lenders not be available, a successful restructuring not be completed, or if the company's First Mortgage Debenture Stockholders were to seek to enforce their security, the group might be unable to continue trading. In this event the going concern basis would be invalid and adjustments would have to be made to reduce the value of assets to their recoverable amount, to provide for further liabilities which might arise and to reclassify fixed assets and long term liabilities as current assets and current liabilities.

2 The Chairman and executive members of the current board were not directors of the company at the time that the 31 December 1991 property valuation was obtained in May 1992. The current directors consider that they do not have a suffi-cient understanding of the 1991 property valuable to enable them to provide a full

explanation for the decline in the property values from 31 December 1991 to 31 December 1992 of £1,341.5 million, of which £537.6 million has been charged to revaluation reserve and £803.9 million charged as an exceptional item in the profit and loss account. For this reason and in this respect alone, not all of the information and explanations we considered necessary for the purpose of our audit have been available.

3 Comparative figures for the cash flow statement have not been presented for the reasons set out in note (b) of the accounting policies.

Subject to continuing support of the group's bankers and other lenders, to the successful completion of a financial restructuring and to the company's First Mortgage Debenture Stockholders not seeking to enforce their security, in our opinion the accounts give a true and fair view of the state of affairs of the company and of the group at 31 December 1992 and, subject to any adjustments that might have been necessary in respect of the decline in property values referred to in paragraph 2 above, of the loss of the group for the year then ended and have been properly prepared in accordance with the Companies Act 1985. In our opinion the cash flow statement gives a true and fair view of the cash flows of the group for the year ended 31 December 1992.

Without further qualifying our opinion above, we draw attention to note 10 which explains that during the year and prior year certain dividend payments were made by the company which were in breach of the Companies Act 1985 as the company did not have sufficient distributable reserves at the time of payment.

Coopers & Lybrand

Chartered Accountants and Registered Auditors
London
29 October 1993

(iii) Finance Director's Report

This report discusses the problems of financial management controls faced by the group and the changes in accounting policies and treatments which have been adopted in preparing the 1992 accounts. The report also comments upon the indebtedness of the group and certain other off-balance sheet liabilities.

Financial control procedures

Shareholders will be aware of the group's rapid expansion in recent years, much of which was financed by the issue of shares and debt. The structure of the group had become extremely complicated, with nearly 200 subsidiaries, which, together with minimal group financial and management reporting systems, contributed to a scarcity of management information at group level capable of being used as a forecasting or management tool. There were no monthly consolidated management accounts to enable the board to monitor the progress of the group. In particular there were minimal group cash forecasts and no clearly defined treasury function.

Since early April 1993, a system of financial and management controls across the group has been introduced. A number of critical group financial functions have been established, including group financial control and group treasury. The first set of monthly consolidated group management accounts was produced in July of this year, and their quality and reliability continue to improve. The monitoring of cash flow has been of the utmost importance in recent months. Indebtedness reporting and cash flow forecasting have been put in place so as to ensure strict control. The increase in resources in this important area has been vital to ensure that the head office finance team is capable of exercising proper and effective financial controls in view of the tight financial constraints now imposed on the group. We have also reviewed the complicated corporate structure and web of complex cross-guarantees governing the banking arrangements.

Prior year adjustments

The 1991 accounts have been extensively restated to reflect changes in accounting policies and treatments which have been adopted in preparing the 1992 accounts. Without such changes, the board believes the 1991 and 1992 accounts would not give a true and fair view of the financial position and performance of the group. The principal changes can be summarised as follows, although shareholders are referred to more detailed explanations in note 1 to the accounts:

Licence fees The group had previously recognised the full fees to be earned in respect of so-called 'incentive fee' or licence arrangements with its hoteliers, regardless of the fact that the fee had only been partially paid and the contract covered a period beyond the end of the accounting period. These accounts are prepared on the basis that incentive fees are time apportioned and only that part of the fee relating to the accounting year in question is recognised as income. Your board believes this change is prudent and appropriate to the business. It has resulted, among other things, in a reduction in net assets in 1991 by £48.6 million and pre-tax profits by £13.5 million.

Sale and leaseback transactions The group had entered into a number of 'sale and leaseback' transactions in 1991 relating to two office developments and eight UK hotels under which the group retains the right to repurchase the assets during the lease and pays rents equivalent to the interest on and amortisation of a loan. Your board considers that such transactions should be treated as finance leases. The effect of this change is to recognise the value of these properties as assets, as well as the full liability of the outstanding lease obligations. Moreover, these transactions, in some cases, were structured to provide initial low rentals. The revised policy leads to the underlying interest expense being recognised in the profit and loss account, rather than the initial rent. The impact of these changes has been to reduce the 1991 net assets by £41.2 million and pre-tax profits by £18.3 million.

Depreciation and repairs and maintenance The group had previously not depreciated its fixtures, fittings, plant and equipment. Your board consider this to have been inappropriate. Moreover, certain repairs and maintenance expenditures were also being capitalised. Provision has now been made in the profit and loss account for depreciation of fixtures, fittings, plant and equipment and relevant repairs and maintenance expenditure is being expensed. This policy change has reduced net assets in 1991 by £2.5 million and reduced 1991 pre-tax profits by £50.9 million.

Acquisition of Globana In the 1991 accounts a fee of £10.3 million credited to the group as part of the acquisition of the balance of QMH France from Globana was included in turnover whereas your board considers that it was in fact a reduction in the cost of the acquisition. Restatement of the 1991 accounts leads to a reduction in pre-tax profits of £10.3 million.

Capitalised expenses The group had previously capitalised certain expenses in connection with certain hotels including interest, pre-opening marketing expenses, professional fees and maintenance wages. Your board considers that such expenditure should not be capitalised. Accordingly, the assets have been written off, with the result that pre-tax profits have been reduced in 1991 by £21.9 million.

Profit on disposals of fixed assets Previously, profits and losses arising on the disposal of fixed assets carried at valuation were included in the profit and loss account based on the difference between the sale proceeds and depreciated historical cost. In accordance with the requirements of FRS 3, this policy has been changed and such profits and losses are now included based on the difference between the sales proceeds and net carrying amount, whether at valuation or at depreciated historical cost. This restatement reduces pre-tax profits in 1991 by £24.2 million.

These accounts also reflect the reclassification of certain profit and loss account and balance sheet items.

In aggregate, the prior year adjustments reduced the group's net assets in 1991 by £105.3 million to £1,192.6 million and reduced the group's pre-tax profits in 1991 by £146.7 million to a pre-tax loss of £56.3 million.

Borrowings, finance leases and operating leases

As at 31 December 1992, the group had net borrowings of £992.1 million (1991 – £710.9 million – restated). In addition, finance lease obligations amounted to £173.8 million (1991 – £149.5 million – restated), bringing the total net indebtedness to £1,165.9 million as at 31 December 1992 (1991 – £860.4 million – restated). The 1991 figures are restated to include finance lease obligations of £30.5 million which were previously classified as 'other creditors', as well as to include obligations arising out of certain sale and leaseback transactions which the board considers should be treated as finance leases. The group had net interest expense before exceptional items of £100.9 million in 1992 (1991 – £79.0 million – restated).

In addition, the group entered into sale and leaseback transactions in respect of seven hotels in Germany in 1991 and 1992 as referred to in note 25 to the accounts. Under these complex arrangements, the group has entered into 20-year operating leases. The group is in preliminary discussion with the owners of the hotels to consider ways in which these sale and leaseback arrangements may be amended in a manner which may lead to these leases being treated as on-balance sheet obligations. At this time the group is not able to quantify any losses which may arise as a result.

The group had rental expense of £12.1 million in 1992 (1991 – £6.3 million – restated). This rental expense increases significantly in 1993 owing to sale and leaseback transactions in late 1992. We are concerned at the onerous terms of certain leases, particularly in France, Germany and Austria, and are examining ways to reduce this burden on ongoing profitability.

Andrew D Le Poideven
Finance Director
29 October 1993

Part III

Ethics and Professional Life

Introduction

Having looked at the general context and five very full case studies, it is appropriate to move on to the ways in which ethical issues can confront individual professionals in their day-to-day jobs. This part of the book is designed to provide insights into major problems and dilemmas that can confront people with a specific job to do in their role as a member of an organisation. It will provide analyses of those problems in ways that will be of help to anyone who works within an organisation of any kind.

A context grounded in business practice is essential to develop an understanding and appreciation of the severely practical but philosophically challenging field of business ethics. Business ethics deals with everyday problems, in the literal sense that ethical problems are problems that can occur any day, in any organisation and will confront almost everyone with decision-making responsibilities. A person's ability to deal with these problems rests partly on his or her ability to recognise them as problematic but also on how well he or she can relate them to a wider context and to general principles. In the chapters that follow, a range of issues will be explored within each of several different functions or roles, and the discussion will be grounded within that context.

We begin with an investigation into the relationship between ethical behaviour and codes of ethics. It might be thought that a profession or an organisation only needs a code of ethics when it is attempting to check the behaviour of individuals who cannot be trusted to regulate themselves. And in such a case, of course, it would be pointless, because individuals such as this are not going to take any notice of a code of ethics in any case. We argue, to the contrary, that codes of ethics are needed not to shore up the resolve of weak and amoral managers, but to provide protection for ordinary decent professionals against pressures that they might otherwise find it hard to resist, and to provide explanations and defences for them in cases where something beyond their control has gone wrong.

Next we consider, in Chapter 8, the very current notion that organisations have responsibilities just as people do. How far is it the business of business, for example, to acknowledge that it has duties to people other than its shareholders?

To its employees, perhaps, or to the community within which it is based? It is clearly in a business's interest to treat its customers well: what about its treatment of its suppliers? And how, as Chapter 9 considers, is the socially responsible culture or otherwise of an organisation attributable to the values and leadership of those at its head?

It is often said that the rate of technological change is accelerating. It is certainly true that information and communication technologies – and especially the Internet – have transformed the context within which organisations operate and the ways in which they can conduct their business. It is, however, worth considering, as does Chapter 10, whether this has simply changed the guise in which fundamental ethical dilemmas arise, or whether it has changed the nature of those dilemmas. Whichever turns out to be the case, no one can close their eyes and hope that the world of e-mails, mobile phones and Internet shopping will just go away. The judge who said 'I don't really understand what a website is' is not an example to follow. (According to the *Sunday Times News Review* of 20 May 2007: 14, 'Judge Peter Openshaw, sitting at Woolwich Crown Court, continues the long tradition of judges who should get out more'.)

Every organisation, not merely business-orientated ones, is expected to have a mission statement, and a clear strategy for implementing and realising its mission. The problem is that many mission statements are bland and unhelpful ('We are committed to the provision of first class service') or else are imposed from the top down. How hard should an organisation strive to define its unique style and purpose, and how far should this be the expression of the whole organisation and not only that of its leadership (or of the consultants they hired)? How far a properly thought through and genuinely 'owned' strategy can affect the ethical behaviour of an organisation is the question examined by Chapter 11.

If the purchasing function is clearly a potential ethical minefield (Chapter 12), it is surprising that it has received comparatively so little attention in the literature. Studies of human resource management (HRM) also show very little preoccupation with ethical issues and yet, as Chapter 14 shows, nearly all HRM decisions show an ethical dimension. On the other hand, both marketing and accounting have received substantial academic attention; Chapters 13 and 15 attempt to do justice to this. Chapter 16 presents an account of the issues that arise from production management and sketches an analytic framework that would help to engage with and manage them adequately.

Chapter 17 returns to the issues raised at the beginning of this section in Chapter 7, and examines the tensions between corporate practice and individual responsibility – between, as it might be said, being a good employee and being a good person. What are the problems raised by the interplay between power, authority and trust, or between confidentiality, loyalty and the public interest? Do you, or should you, work to different principles and values as a member of an organisation from those to which you might adhere as a private individual? This is not merely the main topic of Chapters 7 and 17, however; in a sense, it is what the whole of *The Ethical Organisation* is about.

CHAPTER 7

The Ethical Organisation and Codes of Ethics

LEARNING OUTCOMES

After reading this chapter you will:

- Understand the different roles that codes of ethics play in organisations

- Be able to identify different types of codes

- Understand the relationship between codes and managerial behaviour

- Be able to identify the important stages in the development of an effective corporate code of ethics.

7.1 Introduction

What is a code of corporate conduct? One of the problems is that there is a very wide variety in terminology and it is sometimes difficult to distinguish a code of conduct from a mission statement, a statement of corporate governance or even a statement about the way an organisation proposes to source its raw materials or relate to public officials in countries where corruption is rife. For the purposes of this chapter, we are defining codes of conduct as commitments voluntarily entered into by organisations of any description that state the standards, values and principles to be applied to the conduct of the organisation's business and activities.

According to Nigel Harris (1989) professional codes have increased in number nearly tenfold in the latter half of the twentieth century. At the same time, but especially in the 1990s, there was a similar increase in the numbers of codes designed for the use of employees of a single company. Webley (1988; 1992) surveyed 300 companies in the UK in 1988: from 100 usable responses, 55 had a company code. In 1992, he surveyed 400 of the largest companies in Britain: from 159 usable responses, he noted that 113 had codes. Langlois and Schlegelmilch (1990) surveyed 1481 UK companies and, on a response rate of 25 per cent, reported that 50.5 per cent had codes of ethics, 22.8 per cent had a policy statement on ethics and 42.6 per cent had guidelines for the proper conduct of business.

Webley and Le Jeune (2002) repeated earlier surveys carried out by the Institute of Business Ethics and found that more companies were providing codes of ethics for their employees, using these codes for giving staff guidance rather than for enhancing the corporate reputation. More companies were including compliance with the company code in their employment contracts and were making more use of their codes in disciplinary procedures. However, they also found that fewer companies were training staff in business ethics, reporting on business ethics issues in their annual reports or had a process for revising their code. Clearly, companies see advantages in developing and implementing their codes and enforcing them through contractual and disciplinary means, but seem increasingly reluctant to commit resources to training their staff in the use of the code or in updating their codes. Also, it would be apparent from these findings that companies are becoming less concerned about the impact of ethical issues on their corporate reputation, as fewer are reporting on ethical issues in their annual reports. So, although more companies are developing and implementing codes of conduct, there are concerns about the extent to which the focus moves beyond mere compliance and protection of the company against unethical actions by its employees.

In the USA, the numbers and percentage of companies with codes of ethics is higher than in the UK. Weaver (1993) reported two surveys that took place in 1992. In the first, 83 per cent of the surveyed US companies had codes compared with 50 per cent of the surveyed European companies. The second survey, focused on Fortune 1000 companies, reported that 93 per cent had codes. In a comparative survey of European and US companies, Nash (1991) reported that in the USA, in comparison to five years previously, corporate ethics activity more was widespread, more sophisticated and moving deeper into the organisation. Many European firms, on the other hand, were still not attracted to formalised ethics statements and codes. In Europe, codes and ethics programmes appeared to be less frequent, newer, more dominated by large companies and more widely disseminated than in the USA. Of the US respondents, 83 per cent had some kind of ethics document compared with 50 per cent of the European respondents.

The impact of this burgeoning development of corporate codes of conduct on business and managerial behaviour is difficult to measure with any degree of precision. However, there is no doubt that the language of business has changed and that, even if it is only lip service, an increasing number of businesses feel it necessary to demonstrate their compliance with, if not active support for, ethical standards of business behaviour. A new consensus is beginning to emerge around the issue of ethical conduct. Gordon and Miyake (2001) note, in their analysis of 246 codes of conduct, 'evidence of an emerging consensus on managerial approaches to combating bribery'.

One reason for adopting a code of conduct may be a wish to be seen as self-regulatory, in order to avoid regulation by government. This is a strategy adopted by the press, the stock market and the tobacco industry with regard to advertising. A second reason, connected to this, is a wish by a profession or a company to improve its image either with the general public or its peers in the industry. Such reasons are clearly *prudential* in the sense that they are aimed at benefiting (or avoiding harm to) the company or profession in question. Some would argue (for example, see Chadwick 1993) that acting out of prudential motives is not to act morally.[1] However, some reasons for drawing up codes of behaviour are clearly moral in character. Professional bodies or companies may feel that there are special problems or particular temptations involved in the field in which they operate with which ordinary moral judgement cannot cope. Special advice and guidance may be needed in order to protect their members or employees from moral risk. And, ultimately, they might feel the need for disciplinary sanctions against a minority for the sake of both the general public and their own members or employees. A code can also play a training role in inculcating and promoting the particular values and standards that characterise a profession or a company and which members or employees need to internalise in order to play a full role.[2]

So far, what we have said applies indifferently to both professions and companies. There are, however, obvious differences between professional and company codes, in at least some respects. The first is that a company might employ members of many different professions as well as members of no professions at all. There is therefore a problem about *applicability* – that is, to whom does the code apply? Does it, on one level, apply to the chartered accountant who is currently a financial manager and director, but who is also subject to the professional code of the Institute of Chartered Accountants? And, if it does, which is to take precedence should their requirements come into conflict with each other? On another level, does a company code, given that it is a code for corporate action, apply only to those empowered to act for and on behalf of the company or does it apply to all those employed by the company in whatever capacity? Does it apply to consultants retained on a long-term basis, to sub-contractors or to satellite suppliers with no other outlets? Does it regulate only behaviour expected of its employees by the company, or does it also cover the behaviour of the company towards its employees? Company codes must recognise these problems and allow for some method of resolving them to avoid them being unworkable.

Company codes may be called codes of practice, codes of conduct, codes of ethics, mission statements or value statements. What difference there is between these may be characterised by increasing generality, in that codes of practice tend to be the most specific, whereas value statements are the most general. Codes of practice and codes of conduct also tend to be the most prescriptive in tone (see Harris 1989). But, for the most part, the differences between them are less significant that the fact that they exist at all. What are they for and why are they felt to be necessary? Is it not true, as some might argue, that good people will not need the guidance of such a code whereas the malicious, selfish or stupid will ignore it? In neither case, of course, will the existence of a code make any difference.

Such a position depends on the assumption that good people always know what to do and, also, that those who do the wrong thing always do so for reprehensible reasons. (Also, though this is more obviously false, it depends on the assumption that we can divide people neatly into the good and the bad.) It is not always obvious what the right thing to do is, for ethics is more than a simple set of injunctions that any fool could grasp, and well-meaning people can often go astray for lack of experience or a momentary weakness which in other circumstances might have done no harm at all. We all need to know, or to work out, how general principles are to be made to apply to concrete particular cases. Different people may, in good faith and quite justifiably, come to different conclusions about the rightness of a particular act in particular circumstances – in private life this may not matter at all. But in the public domain there is also a requirement of consistency, which may force us to replace the workings of the individual conscience with a written code or an impersonal process. This may be needed not only to ensure (as far as can be) consistency of outcome, but also to protect those who must make judgements. In employment, for example, a judgement to promote a particular person may be completely reasonable, but it has to be seen in the light of a company's record on promoting, say, women, or members of ethnic minorities. Those promoted, or not, have a right to be treated not only reasonably but also equitably (that is, in a similar way as others). And those who operate the procedures must not, so long as they operate them properly, be seen as personally responsible for the outcome.

One way, therefore, of seeing codes is by analogy with the law. Just as case law and rules of process are needed in order to make it possible for statute and common law to be implemented, so a code of practice mediates between general principles and particular cases. This is, at any rate, how they should operate. It is not, of course, how they always do. Sorell and Hendry (1994: 14–15) point out some of the problems that can be caused by codes or mission statements so vague, general and uncontentious that no one could possibly disagree with them – neither could they hope to get any real guidance from them as to what to do in a particular case. Chadwick (1993: 3) quotes the Johnson & Johnson organisation's: 'We must provide competent management and their actions must be just and ethical' as an example of this. As inspirational rhetoric it may have a function, but as a basis for a code of ethics it is virtually useless without a detailed commentary.

7.2 The development of codes of ethics

Many of those political and economic thinkers and practitioners who claim an intellectual lineage back to Adam Smith may be surprised to learn that Smith himself was concerned to demonstrate the need for ethical values as an essential part of a market economy. He saw the role of moral values as one of exercising reasonable constraint on the single-minded pursuit of profit. It is interesting to note the widespread use of *The Wealth of Nations* as a traditional justification of rampant free market policies and the almost total disregard for Smith's equally important, but much less influential, *A Theory of Moral Sentiments*.

In recent years, the concerns expressed by Smith have been echoed in the literature on company codes, which has expanded considerably (see, for example, Webley 1988; Donaldson 1989; Campbell and Tawadey 1992; Manley 1992).

Three major traditions can be detected in the literature:

- A concern for how businesses may make effective use of company codes with practical guidance on how to draw one up (see, for example, Clutterbuck et al. 1992)

- A concern for the impact of company codes on business practice from a variety of perspectives (for example, Drucker, 1981; Peters and Waterman 1982; Hoffman 1986; Adams et al. 1991)

- A concern to analyse company codes using theories of ethics (for example, Shaw and Barry 1989).

All of these traditions have something to offer.

The philosophical basis for company codes appears to be eclectic in nature. Individual codes draw upon a variety of philosophical traditions, combining utilitarian and deontological statements with those drawing on the Golden Rule and prudential approaches. The content of the codes often lacks philosophical consistency. This lack of consistency can, at least in part, be explained as a product of the circumstances in which the code is drafted and the positions of those responsible for drafting it.

Many codes develop from a defensive posture by senior managers in a company; they tend to have a prudential tone with some basis in utilitarian theory. The example of Fiat is a case in point. Considerable damage resulted to the international reputation of the company following revelations concerning connections between the Mafia, big business and government in Italy. Fiat produced a code for its employees that lays down clear and enforceable rules concerning relations with government officials at all levels. The code ignores many other aspects of employee behaviour that have ethical implications. It was fashioned in particular circumstances for particular reasons.

Unilever provides a clear statement of a prudential approach in its company code, developed in circumstances very different from those of Fiat:

> The success or failure of a company – and Unilever is no exception – largely depends on its people, particularly its managers. Its reputation depends on the way its managers behave. (Unilever 1981: 6)

Unilever's code reflects the company's position as a major multinational corporation. It contains statements about its support for the guidelines for international businesses produced by the OECD and ILO as well as those of the United Nations Commission on Transnational Corporations.

The Royal Dutch Shell Group of Companies provides a similar 'Statement of general business principles' (see Clutterbuck et al. 1992: 304–6). It recognises responsibilities to shareholders, employees, customers and society, asserts the importance of profitability and the benefits of a market economy, supports the OECD and ILO codes, requires honesty and integrity from its employees (any form of bribery is unacceptable), declares itself as an abstainer from party politics. Running through the statement is a concern to be seen as a responsible citizen in all of the countries in which it operates. This is a prime example of a code drawing upon a variety of different philosophical bases – Kantian duties for the workforce, prudential considerations for different Group companies in different parts of the world and a utilitarian approach to the market economy.

The Body Shop's code is in part based upon the Golden Rule.

We declare that:

1 The Body Shop's goals and values are as important as our products and our profits;

2 Our policies and our products are geared to meet the needs of real people both inside and outside the company;

3 Honesty, integrity and caring form the foundations of the company and should flow through everything we do;

4 We care about each other as individuals: we will continue to endeavour to bring meaning and pleasure to the workplace;

5 We care about our customers, and will continue to bring humanity into the market place;

6 We care about humanising the business community: we will continue to show that success and profits can go hand-in-hand with ideals and values. (Ibid.: 303)

The Charter fits neatly with Body Shop's position as a leading supplier of 'ethical cosmetics' and clearly plays a significant role in its business strategy. It originates in the aims and views of the company's founder.

On the other hand, the code of British Gas plc reflects an overwhelming concern with vulnerability to allegations of impropriety (ibid.: 306–8). It covers conflicts of interest, dealing in British Gas shares and those of other companies, purchasing and supplies, declarations of interest, gifts and confidentiality of information. It warns employees that breaches of the code may result in disciplinary action and that they should seek the advice of their superiors if in doubt about any matter concerning conduct.

7.3 Company codes and managerial control

Hosmer (1987: 153) distinguishes between codes of ethics and rules of ethics. He sees ethical codes as 'statements of the norms and beliefs of an organisation' and as 'the ways in which the senior people in the organisation want others to think. This is not censorship. Instead the intention is to encourage ways of thinking and patterns of attitudes that will lead towards the wanted behaviour'. He sees ethical rules as consisting of requirements to act in particular ways – as more than mere expectations or suggestions.

For many employees, this distinction may appear to be a fine one – company codes, in practice, tend to slip easily from being codes of ethics into becoming rules for behaviour. As defined by Hosmer, senior managers produce codes of ethics as a deliberate attempt to influence the ways in which others think. They are products of the managerial urge to control the behaviour of their subordinates. This applies with greater force to ethical rules.

Business codes, then, tend to have a strong imperatival nature in the sense that they expound the duties of the company and, especially, its employees. There is a clearly identifiable strand within the literature on business ethics that sees the use of a code of conduct as an important contributor to managerial control of employee behaviour. Shaw and Barry (1989: 196) state the case for a corporate code of ethics very clearly: 'If those inside the corporation are to behave ethically, they need clearly stated and communicated ethical standards that are equitable and enforced.'

Snoeyenbos and Jewell (1983) suggest that there are three elements in a successful strategy to institutionalise ethical behaviour. These are: first, the adoption of a corporate ethical code; second, the establishment of an ethics committee; and, third, a management training programme that includes ethics training. All three elements are essential if the behaviour of company employees is to reflect well on the company itself.

Campbell and Tawadey (1992: 6) perceive the benefits of a company having a sense of mission as follows:

> People are more motivated and work more intelligently if they believe in what they are doing and trust the organisation they are working with ... If an organisation can provide meaning for an employee on top of pay and conditions, it will inspire the greater commitment and loyalty that we have labelled a sense of mission.

Other significant benefits include clarity of strategy, better decision-making, clearer communication, greater ease in delegation with lower costs of supervision.

Manley's comprehensive analysis of company codes identifies 18 benefits of written codes. They are:

1. Providing guidance to and inculcating the company's values and cultural substance and style in managers and employees
2. Sharpening and defining the company's policies and unifying the workforce
3. Providing overall strategic direction
4. Helping managers to deal with outside pressure groups
5. Signalling expectations of proper conduct to suppliers and customers
6. Delineating the rights and duties of the company, managers and employees
7. Effectively responding to government pressures and rules
8. Enhancing the company's public image and confidence
9. Pre-empting legal proceedings
10. Improving bottom-line results
11. Enhancing the self-images of employees and improving the quality of new recruits
12. Promoting excellence
13. Realising company objectives

- Responding to stockholders' concerns
- Strengthening the British free enterprise system
- Encouraging open communication
- Integrating the cultures of acquired or merged companies
- Deterring improper requests of employees by supervisors and vice-versa.

The underlying approach here appears to be one in which those who prepare, pronounce and protect the company code are in an active mode, whereas those employees (usually below the level of senior management) who are faced with operational problems are passive recipients of the wisdom of their betters.

Although some of the companies that responded to his questionnaire indicated that employees were consulted and their views taken into account, Webley (1988) confirms the perception that a 'top-down' approach is the one most frequently found in the development of codes of ethics by British companies. Healey and Iles (2001) confirm this perception in their study of 80 UK organisations in the IT industry. They suggest that not only does the use of codes of conduct vary significantly amongst the organisations they surveyed, but also that those who initiate such codes are not those primarily seen as being responsible for implementing them.

It seems likely to be the case that the recipients of the code and all the apparatus that goes with it will themselves have at least some beliefs on ethical issues or, at the very least, some general moral attitudes, which will affect their behaviour as much as the official code. Kitson (1994) reports that the managers within the Co-operative Bank appeared to interpret and apply the Bank's ethical policy in ways that reveal the mediating effect of their own values. Forsyth (1992) identifies four different moral philosophies amongst managers. They are differentiated along two dimensions: relativism and idealism. Forsyth produces the taxonomy as shown in Table 7.1.

Forsyth argues that managers with different moral philosophies will react in complex but different ways from each other to the same objectively defined problem. The company ethical code – indeed, any ethical code – will be more important for some than for others. It will be more important for those whose

Table 7.1   Taxonomy of personal moral values

Idealogy	Dimensions	Approach to moral judgement
Situationists	High relativism High idealism	Reject moral rules; ask whether the action yielded the best possible outcome in the given situation
Subjectivists	High relativism Low idealism	Reject moral rules; base moral judgements on personal feelings about the action and the setting
Absolutists	Low relativism High idealism	Feel actions are moral provided they yield positive consequences through conformity to moral rules
Exceptionists	Low relativism Low idealism	Feel conformity to moral rules is desirable but exceptions to these rules are often permissible

personal moral philosophy has some congruence with the values expressed in the company code.

This problem (of active and passive roles) can be looked at from a different perspective. It is possible to argue that any codification of ethics removes (at least, in part) the personal autonomy that philosophers in the Kantian tradition argue is essential for any moral actor. One practical consequence is the 'loophole seeking' mentality. This is the antithesis of the behaviour normally stated as the expected outcome of company codes.

7.4 Who is being protected by the code?

Many companies state that their codes have been produced to help those employees who may be faced with a difficult ethical problem at work. Customers also frequently appear in company codes as the recipients of the intended ethical action. Sometimes the focus is on shareholders; on other occasions, the target is society or the environment.

However, often unstated, the long-term interests of the company seem to represent the paramount cause for the production of the code and the audience appears to be influential sections of the public – mainly political and media groups and organisations.

Clutterbuck et al. (1992: 269) identify the interests of the company as the prime reason for developing a code of ethics. Damage to the company's reputation is not, however, the only thing at risk. There is also the problem of the motivation of people in the company. Unethical behaviour might focus managers' attention on short-term, pragmatic goals and lead to the exclusion of long-term objectives. Furthermore, companies engaging in unethical conduct towards customers, shareholders, suppliers or employees might encourage unethical behaviour towards itself. The case is stated with some force:

The dilemma for top management is that it is expected to maintain an ethical climate, yet has only limited control over the hearts and minds of the people who work in the organisation ... There are at least two major issues here:

- How do executives keep themselves out of trouble?

- How do they control the activities of perhaps thousands of individual employees, any one of whom may be mis-guided or mis-motivated into behaving in ways that may damage the corporate reputation?

Senior executives are being encouraged to see the development of a code of ethics as a device for controlling their possibly unruly employees, as a way of keeping out of trouble and preserving the long-term future of their business.

Within the context of increasing political and public concern about possibly unethical behaviour (Guinness, Polly Peck, British Airways) and what appears to be a swing of the pendulum of public opinion away from the rampant free-market economic policy of the Thatcher years, not only do executives need to keep themselves out of trouble, they also need to be aware of a changing public mood in relation to unethical behaviour in business. Developing a code of ethics as a defensive measure in such a context seems to be a rational response. Whether such codes will stand the test of time remains to be seen. (See, for instance, Example 7.1.)

EXAMPLE 7.1

World Bank

In May 2007, the World Bank published *The Many Faces of Corruption*. This book examines a wide range of corrupt activities and one chapter in particular, 'Corruption in Public Procurement: A Perennial Challenge', has become, according to some, less a resource for development economists and more a goldmine for satirists.

Paul Wolfowitz, the then President of the Bank, became entangled in a controversy caused by his personal relationship with a Bank employee. The salary of his partner, Shaha Riza, was increased to $194,000 following influence exerted by Mr Wolfowitz. Stephen Colbert, an American satirist said: 'He knows corruption is the enemy; and Mr Wolfowitz fights fire with fire.'

The Bank's rules preclude sexual relationships between a manager and a staff member serving under that manager, even if there is no direct reporting relationship between them. The Bank has an Ethics Committee, which is responsible for overseeing the effective implementation of the Bank's ethical code and dealing with any allegations of transgression or potential conflicts of interest.

Wolfowitz initially proposed to the World Bank's Ethics Committee that he recuse himself from personnel matters regarding Riza, but the committee rejected that proposal and Riza was seconded to the State Department, to work under Liz Cheney, the daughter of the Vice-President, promoting democracy in the Middle East.

The Committee also decided that she should be moved up to a managerial pay grade in compensation for the disruption to her career, resulting in a raise of over $60,000, as well as guarantees of future increases. At this point, the staff association became involved and claimed that the pay rise was more than double the amount allowed under employee guidelines. According to Steven R. Weisman in a report published in *The New York Times*, the then current chair of the Committee emphasised that he was not informed at the time of the details of extent of the present and future raises built into the agreement with Riza.

The Bank President's PR man, Kevin Kellems, resigned saying that 'given the current environment . . . it is very difficult to be effective in helping to advance the mission of the institution'.

Mr Wolfowitz fought off calls for his resignation. First, he declared that an investigation by the Bank's executives would exonerate him. Instead, it found him guilty of 'questionable judgment and a preoccupation with self-interest'. He then said he thought he had been asked to arrange Ms Riza's pay, a claim the report says 'simply turns logic on its head'. His last defence is one of acting in good faith. Yet, he reportedly threatened Bank staff with retaliation if they revealed the pay rises and promotions won for his partner.

Mr Wolfowitz resigned in June 2006 following an investigation by the Bank's managing board.

The World Bank is funded through donor governments and exists to reduce poverty and promote economic growth in the third world. It has a complex organisational structure, part of which is its Ethics Committee. On this occasion, the Committee appears not to have worked as effectively as it might have, and it was the outrage amongst employees and donor governments that led to Mr Wolfowitz's eventual demise.

7.5 Implementing company codes

There is a growing body of experience in the processes of implementing company codes and this practical experience is increasingly reflected in the literature on business ethics.

Ferrell and Fraedrich (1994) suggest that the implementation of strategies to encourage employees to make more ethical decisions is not very different from implementing other types of business strategies. They propose an approach to implementation based on four aspects: organisation, coordination, motivation and communication.

Ferrell and Fraedrich assert that the structure of the organisation is a crucial influence on the implementation of an ethical policy and that authority should be delegated in such a way as to ensure appropriate levels of ethical performance. Depending upon the particular circumstances of the company, this may require greater centralisation or decentralisation.

Coordination involves 'arranging and synchronising the activities of all employees so that the company achieves its objectives efficiently, effectively and ethically' (ibid.: 177). Coordination is needed to ensure that different parts of the organisation are not pursuing different ethical goals.

Motivating people to behave ethically involves applying the same principles of motivation that managers apply to other areas of employee performance. These include recognising that different people are motivated in different ways, that modern employees are motivated by the quality of their work environment, their opportunities for personal growth, and the ethical performance of their companies. Job enrichment programmes are seen as providing motivation for such employees to improve their ethical decision-making.

Finally, communication by senior managers is essential to maintaining the ethical climate of a company and as an underpinning to effective coordination and motivation.

This approach to implementation seeks to incorporate ethical issues into the traditional management functions. It is heavily influenced by classical management theory. Classical management theorists (see, for example, Brech 1953) identified a range of managerial functions and gave detailed guidance and advice on how these functions should be carried out. Ferrell and Fraedrich take the view that it is within these traditionally accepted managerial functions that ethical policies should be implemented.

McDonald and Zepp (1989) adopt a more sophisticated approach to the problem of implementation. They propose an approach based on three persectives: the individual dimension, group/peer influence and organisational strategies. The individual dimension emphasises the need for individuals within the organisation to develop appropriate ethical values and sensitivity. McDonald and Zepp assert that, although individuals will possess different ethical values, it is possible to enhance ethical behaviour through training programmes. They advocate a 'basic awareness programme' and specific ethical training programmes, based mainly on seminars focused on ethical dilemmas and encouraging the examination of the actual dilemmas faced by the managers participating in the programme. McDonald and Zepp refer to the work of Lickona (1987), who has provided specific strategies for corporate training programmes. Lickona advocates:

- The use of socratic questioning in order to isolate views and confront reasoning

- Creating open, integrative discussions

- Eliciting a full range of ethical views

- Utilising an experiential approach drawing upon the participants' own personal cases showing value conflict and ethical dilemmas

- Taking care not to present cases that continually show the most difficult choices and high levels of cognitive strain.

McDonald and Zepp also argue that if a business is concerned about the ethical behaviour of their employees, it is easier to hire individuals with appropriate ethical standards than to try to change those of current employees.

The strong effect of peer influence on individual behaviour coupled with the frequent perception of peers as having lower ethical standards than themselves, might, according to McDonald and Zepp, encourage individuals to behave unethically. They argue that greater understanding of the ethical values of one's peers, rather than unfounded perceptions, could help to make an individual feel more secure in their own value system. They advocate small group discussions on ethical issues but warn against the dangers of 'group-think', which sometimes occurs with strongly cohesive groups. Mentor schemes are also seen as useful. Mentors can provide a private and confidential avenue for discussion and guidance.

Organisational strategies include the development of codes of ethics and ethical policy statements. However, they argue that ethical leadership, rather than ethical policies or statements, is most effective in encouraging ethical behaviour throughout the organisation. The use of an ethical ombudsperson, with an investigative, counselling and advisory role, is still unusual, but increasing, in large organisations. McDonald and Zepp warn that such a person must be seen as independent and to have appropriate experience. More widespread, particularly in the United States, is establishment of ethics committees. These deal with policy formulation and, sometimes, with specific violations of the organisation's ethical code or complaints from employees and others. Reward and payment systems, which are often based on performance and output, might encourage unethical behaviour in the pursuit of a target. Reviewing reward systems might facilitate recognition of the need, on occasion, not to achieve a particular target if doing so would mean having to behave unethically.

Clutterbuck et al. (1992) offer very clear guidance in relation to the maintenance of an ethical climate. They suggest that senior managers should set an example through their behaviour, rather than by sending memos. Ethical issues should be on the board agenda and included in the annual report. Opportunities to demonstrate ethical commitments should be taken, the company should be active in charities and it should deliver the same messages internally and externally.

If a company does produce a code of ethics, it should ensure that its drafting is participatory; all employees should receive a copy and be able to discuss its meaning and implementation. Performance against the code should be monitored. Monitoring takes several forms: requiring all managers to confirm that they have not deviated from the code and following this up with sample audits, asking non-executive directors to monitor compliance, establishing an ethics committee, giving the responsibility for monitoring to a senior manager.

Further proposals from Clutterbuck et al. include using reward and punishment mechanisms to reinforce correct behaviour, recruiting ethical people, training, creating a framework for registering concern, building openness into the workplace.

Manley (1992), based upon a detailed study of 125 British companies, argues that the following factors are crucial to the successful implementation of a code of conduct or similar policy document:

- Management involvement and oversight

- Constant consciousness of those written, codified values and standards in recruiting and hiring

- Stressing code values and standards in educating and training employees

- Recognition and tangible rewards for conduct that exemplifies desired values and standards

- Ombudsmen or other designated persons assigned to field employees' questions and reporting

- Thorough concentration on high risk jobs and areas in terms of violating code values and standards

- Periodic certification and auditing to assure compliance with those code values and standards

- Well-defined and fair enforcement procedures, including sanctions.

There is, then, a significant body of experience and guidance in relation to the implementation of codes of ethics developed by organisations. The process of implementation or ensuring compliance with the code is not the last thing to think about in the process of developing the code. The style and approach taken to implementation are often implicit in the process of development. The implementation of a code that is produced as a quick reaction to a controversy (for example, the British Airways case) will be very different from one that is produced following a lengthy and exhaustive process of consultation both within and outside the organisation (as with the Co-operative Bank). Those responsible for the coordination and leadership of the processes leading to the production of the code need to be aware of the problems of implementation from the very beginning of the process. Producing a code that cannot be effectively implemented is an act of cynicism.

The process of production should replicate the values that are being codified and lay the basis for implementation. Process and product are inextricably intertwined. Indeed, both the product (the code of conduct) and the process of its production should be based upon a clear understanding of the underlying ethical principles of the organisation. As Donaldson (1999) puts it, 'Codes, stakeholder concepts and business practices need, logically, to be grounded in an acceptable philosophy if they are to become more than a collection of techniques and expressions of the perceptions of business magnates, however eminent.'

The crucial issue here is that of ownership. Some managers seem to define teams as 'lots of people doing what I want them to do'. Organisations with codes of ethics might define ethical behaviour as that which is in accordance with their code. If, however, the code has not been developed through prolonged and extensive discussion, it is unlikely to reflect the ethical views of the people affected by it. The process of discussion and debate can help to produce a code that is understood by more people and owned by more of them than is likely to be the case if a code appears overnight as a management bulletin. The process of development of the code is an opportunity for people in the business collectively to come to some sort of agreement (total agreement may be undesirable – as well as unlikely) about the basic values of the business and how to resolve at least some of the ethical issues faced in business.

Of course, such discussion might be seen by senior managers as something of a luxury when, for rational purposes, they need to develop a code very quickly. However, once a code – any code – has been published, there is then an opportunity to initiate widespread and effective discussions, provided there is a genuine willingness to adapt it, which could lead eventually to a more open and rational discussion of ethical problems and a greater degree of ownership of the code (suitably amended). It seems that the choice facing companies with a code is either to allow it to ossify, in which case it will fall into disrepute sooner rather than later, or to see the code as merely a starting point in a long-term development – indeed, as a significant part of strategic planning.

7.6 Conclusion

There is a real risk that codes might exist only on paper, and not in practice. Where this is true, then, there will be justice in the cynics' claim that codes are for impressing outsiders and not meant to affect the behaviour of the company or its employees. For codes must not only be explicit and detailed, they must also be internalised by those to whom, and by whom, they will be applied. In the end, a code that is to be worthy of the name must be embodied in the behaviour and the practices of the relevant group of people. This means that actually producing the written part of the code is only one part. The other part is implementing it, and this is something that cannot be done just once. It must be a continuous process. To succeed, a code must be the result of satisfying (at least) the following three conditions:

1 It must be the result of an extensive period of research, consultation and discussion by, on behalf of and between all affected parties;

2 It must be owned by all who are affected by it and not merely imposed by executive fiat;

3 It must be backed by a programme of staff development and training that is ongoing and that opens the code up to amendment in the light of experience.

QUESTIONS AND TASKS

1 Obtain three corporate codes of conduct from three different organisations and identify:

(a) What are their similarities?

(b) What are their differences?

(c) How could you explain these similarities and differences?

CHAPTER 8

The Ethical Organisation and Corporate Social Responsibility

After reading this chapter, you will:

- Be able to analyse and evaluate the social responsibility and sustainability reports of businesses

- Understand the fundamental concepts underlying the notion of corporate social responsibility

- Be aware of a range of resources for developing your insight and understanding further.

8.1 Introduction

An increasing number of businesses, large and small, have begun to develop policies and activities that are described as examples of corporate social responsibility (CSR). Encouraged and exhorted by governments and a range of non-governmental organisations, businesses that have adopted such practices are often lauded as examples of 'good practice'. The leaders of multinational corporations regard environmental and social credibility as having a major impact on the future reputation of their businesses.[1] In business, reputation is a crucial factor. A reputation as a socially responsible business is seen as a significant contributory factor for business success. For example, Cambridge Business School, (April 2003), reported that the Cooperative Bank (2002) found that more than 90 per cent of its customers approve of its ethical policy and that its market share has increased as a result of the active promotion of this policy. MORI research (1998) among British adults found that 17 per cent had boycotted a company's product on ethical grounds; 19 per cent had chosen a product or service because of a company's ethical reputation; and a further 28 per cent had done both.

A report 'Winning with Integrity' (2000), published by Business in the Community (a UK based non-governmental organisation) produced some startling findings that indicate the importance of an ethical reputation. Of the consumers surveyed, 81 per cent agreed that when price and quality are equal they are more likely to buy products associated with good causes; 73 per cent of employees surveyed agreed that they are likely to be more loyal to an employer who supports the local community.

Reflecting the increased concern about the social conduct of businesses, there has been a growth in the number of non-governmental organisations, pressure groups and business-led groups that aim to provide guidance, advice and support for businesses that are seeking to become more socially responsible and to have a strong reputation for social responsibility.[2]

There are many examples of businesses adopting practices that can be described as socially responsible. Examples 8.1, 8.2 and 8.3 illustrate some aspects of CSR and have been taken from a website[3] maintained by the Department for Trade and Industry of the UK government. In each case, business benefits are claimed to flow from CSR. Indeed, this is a major justification used in government policy circles, for encouraging CSR. The case for CSR is sold as a case for enhancing business opportunities and long-term profitability.

EXAMPLE 8.1

Standard Life

Since 1996, Standard Life has been offering the opportunity of a good career to homeless people caught in a vicious circle of poverty.

As one of the largest insurance companies in Europe, the company has a well-established programme of community investment, including work with schools and lifelong learning schemes for adults. In 1996, it launched its 'Pathfinders' project. Each year, this gives 3–5 people who have experienced homelessness an opportunity to become full-time Standard Life employees. Initially, recruits are given a six-month contract. If this proves successful, permanent employment becomes possible.

Candidates are identified through homelessness organisations in Edinburgh. An assessment day identifies candidates' potential and readiness for work. Of the first 12 people taken onto the scheme: six have left for personal reasons, or to take up other employment, or for further education; four have become permanent employees and two are still on temporary contracts.

The benefits to Standard Life of this project include:

■ Access to recruits who are not reached by traditional recruitment methods

■ An enhanced corporate reputation

■ Valuable and loyal permanent members of staff

■ Staff development opportunities for participating managers.

Homeless people benefit from increasing their employability through training and work experience with a major company.

EXAMPLE 8.2

United Utilities

In 2000, United Utilities was awarded the title of Company of the Year by Business in the Community for its 'Impact on Society' programme.

A major public utility business based in the north-west of England, United Utilities delivers around 2,000 million litres of water every day. It also treats massive amounts of waste water each day before returning it safely to the environment. The company has to protect the natural environment in order to protect its future business. To do this, it needs to win the cooperation of farmers whose working practices have major environmental impact.

United Utilities owns more land than any other UK water company. This includes large areas of the upland Lake District. These areas supply large amounts of water to the company. They also accommodate many tenant farmers who make their livelihood from the land and provide rental income to the company.

Recognising that farmers faced both economic pressures and the additional pressures that stem from working within a protected rural environment, the company began a programme to help the farmers improve their efficiency, and protect and improve the environment.

The programme has several elements:

- Encouraging farmers to use the right amount of fertilisers and pesticides
- Helping farmers to obtain grants under the Lake District Environmentally Sensitive Areas Scheme
- Developing a cost effective scheme for removing dead animals that might contaminate water supplies
- Collecting the black plastic used for silage and converting it into garden furniture.

The business benefits of this programme include:

- Customers have more confidence in the quality of their water, and in United Utilities
- Costs of water treatment are falling as farmers reduce fertiliser use
- The amount of black plastic liner in the area is reduced, thereby reducing maintenance costs
- Prompt removal of carcasses cuts contamination risks and saves the costs of coping with such contamination
- Rental income is protected and the value of land and buildings is maintained.

> ### EXAMPLE 8.3
>
> **Design One**
> A small multimedia design and technology company, Design One, has run a student placement scheme for art and design students in the West Midlands, England for several years. In 1999 it started a new scheme.
>
> A local primary school approached the company about building a website for the school. This was an opportunity for the business to become involved in the local community and for the children at the school to become involved in building a web site.
>
> Two workshops were run at the school for IT teachers from local schools to learn more about the Internet. There were also sessions for the children, both at the school and at the Design One studios, to involve them in developing a children's zone for the website.
>
> Children, teachers and parents all benefited from the learning opportunities created by this project.
>
> The business benefits for Design One include:
>
> ■ New business gained from parents, referrals from the school and from the education sector in general
>
> ■ Its staff developed their skills and professionalism through working with a different type of client
>
> ■ The link attracted local publicity and enhanced the company's reputation.

8.2 Defining corporate social responsibility

There are several different definitions of CSR. The Institute of Business Ethics (IBE) (2001) defines CSR as 'the responsibility of a company for the totality of its impact, with a need to embed society's values into its core operations as well as into its treatment of its social and physical environment. Responsibility is accepted as encompassing a spectrum – from the running of a profitable business to the health and safety of staff and the impact on the societies in which a business operates.' However, according to the IBE, CSR is all too often seen as being no more than community development and, at worst, it is seen as an optional extra or marketing tool to improve profits or a public relations smokescreen. The need to manage and protect the reputation of the business has been a strong motive force in the development of socially responsible businesses.

In Europe, a business-driven membership network called CSR Europe has been developed to 'help companies achieve profitability, sustainable growth and human progress by placing CSR in the mainstream of business practice'.[4] CSR Europe believes that there is a strong business case for enhanced CSR.

The CSR Europe view of CSR consists of 7 elements. These are:

■ Contributing to the economic health and sustainable development of communities

- Healthy and safe working environments, good employee compensation, good communication and equal opportunities

- Quality, safe products and services at competitive process

- Minimising the negative impact of business activity on the environment

- Accountability to key stakeholders

- Good governance and high ethical standards

- Fair returns to shareholders.

These seven elements form the principles on which CSR Europe is based and to which members have to sign up on joining. Membership is by invitation only. In carrying out its activities, CSR Europe has identified six themes or issues to act as foci for its work. These six themes are:

- Business and diversity

- Business and human rights

- Communications and reporting

- Education and lifelong learning

- Mainstreaming CSR

- Socially responsible investment.

There is clearly a good deal of overlap and similarity between the perspectives of IBE and CSR Europe. There is broad agreement between them about the meaning and context of CSR.

However, the development of theories of CSR is not a recent phenomenon, although in the last five years there has been a significant increase in publications and activities related to it. It is an idea that has been resurrected following years of Thatcherite and Reagonite economics in which the power of the unfettered market and the reduction of the role of the state were the dominant themes. In Europe and America, the concepts of social responsibility and corporate citizenship have been given fresh impetus and vigour, driven by large, often multinational, corporations.

Hay et al. (1976), offer a model of the history of the idea of social responsibility. They identify three distinct phases of the development of the idea. Phase 1 is labelled 'Profit maximising management'. This is based on the belief that business managers have only one single objective – to maximise profit. Phase 2 is called 'Trusteeship management', which they say emerged in the 1920s and 1930s in the USA. This perspective was based on the notion that managers of businesses are responsible not simply for maximising the stockholder's wealth, but rather for maintaining a fair balance between the competing claims and demands of employees, customers, suppliers, creditors and the community. So, managers are trustees for the various contributor groups to the firm rather than simply the agent of the owners. (In Chapter 1 this view is identified as the 'stakeholder perspective'). During the 1960s and 1970s, Phase 3 emerged. This is called 'Quality of life management '. This is based on the view that economic abundance within the midst of a declining social and physical environment does not make sense. Business, with all its vast resources and expertise should be making a major contribution to the solution of society's problems.

Hay et al. proceed to develop a typology of managerial values that they believe are reflected by managers who hold Phase 1, 2 and 3 beliefs and values (see Table 8.1).

Hay et al. argue that the movement from Phase 1 to Phase 3 can be historically traced through different decades of the twentieth century. This is an oversimplified view and clearly open to question. For example, many of the ideas of the Phase 3 manager can be traced back to nineteenth-century philosophies such as

Table 8.1 Phase 1, 2 and 3 beliefs and values

Phase 1 Profit maximising management	Phase 2 Trusteeship management	Phase 3 'Quality of life' management
Economic values		
Raw self-interest	Self-interest; contributor's interest	Self-interest; contributor's interest; society's interest
What's good for me is good for my country	What's good for my company is good for our country	What's good for society is good for our company
Profit maximiser	Profit satisfier	Profit is necessary, but ????
Money and wealth are most important	Money is important but so are people	People are more important than money
Let the buyer beware (*caveat emptor*)	Let's not cheat the customer.	Let the seller beware (*caveat venditor*)
Labour is a commodity to be bought and sold	Labour has certain rights that must be recognised	Employee dignity has to be satisfied
Accountability of managers is to the owners	Accountability of managers is to all the stakeholders in the business	Accountability of managers is to all stakeholders including society
Technological values		
Technology is very important	Technology is important but so are people	People are more important than technology
Social values		
Employees personal problems must be left at home	We recognise that employees have needs beyond their economic needs	We are responsible for the health and welfare of our employees
I am a rugged individualist and I will manage the business as I please	Although I am an individualist, I recognise the value of group participation	Group participation is fundamental to our success
Environmental values		
The natural environment controls the destiny of man	Man can control and manipulate his environment	Man must preserve the environment
Political values		
That government is best which governs least	Government is a necessary evil	Business and government must cooperate to solve society's problems

the Utopian Socialists. It is also clear that managers in the twenty-first century are a mixed and cosmopolitan group with a wide variety of personal beliefs. So, it cannot be argued that there is an almost uniform, historical movement from one phase to another or that Phase 1 and 2 beliefs and values disappear as Phase 3 takes centre stage. It is a more intellectually plausible argument that the kinds of views expressed within the Phase 3 approach have found an increasingly fertile ground in which to grow but that there are plenty of examples of twenty-first century managers displaying behaviour based on the beliefs found in Phases 1 and 2.

However, despite the shortcomings of the approach taken by Hay et al., the description of the values and beliefs they describe as Phase 3 does provides a basis for the development of notions of CSR that have come to prominence in the last decade in Europe and the United States. Many of the fundamental concepts upon which theories of CSR have been developed are to be found in the description of the values and beliefs of Phase 3 managers.

8.3   The meaning of responsibility

Central to all theories of CSR is the notion of responsibility. Petrick and Quinn (1997) offer a useful typology as a way of explaining the meaning of 'respon-sibility ' within this context (see Figure 8.1). They differentiate between social responsibility and social responsiveness. They define social responsibility as a 'static state or condition of having assumed (internalised) an obligation ' (p. 107). In other words, a social actor (a manager or business) simply accepts that they have to conform to social expectations of their behaviour. There is no sense of a commitment having grown from wrestling with these expectations and proactively deciding what is the right form of ethical conduct in any particu-lar circumstance. They contrast this passive state of acceptance of social norms with social responsiveness, which is 'a dynamic, action oriented external pro-cess indicating the extent to which internal and external stakeholder needs are being met' (p. 107). Social responsibility, as defined by Petrick and Quinn,

	Unresponsive conduct	Responsive conduct
Responsible conduct	RESPONSIBLE UNRESPONSIVENESS	RESPONSIBLE RESPONSIVENESS
Irresponsible conduct	IRRESPONSIBLE UNRESPONSIVENESS	IRRESPONSIBLE RESPONSIVENESS

Figure 8.1   Social responsibility and social responsiveness
Source: Adapted from Petrick and Quinn (1997): 108.

derives from external obligations created by governments or public opinion, often expressed through non-governmental organisations. Social responsiveness derives from the voluntary assumption of responsibilities. They describe imposed social responsibility as 'irresponsible responsibility'.

Obtain

In Figure 8.1, 'irresponsible responsiveness' comprises compliance with externally imposed standards and expectations. It does not involve the internalising by managers and organisations of any sense of social obligation. 'Irresponsible unresponsiveness' involves both a rejection of externally imposed obligations and an absence of any internalisation by managers and their organisations. 'Responsible unresponsiveness' describes an approach in which managers reject externally imposed obligations but have a strong internal sense of their obligations to stakeholders and society. 'Responsible responsiveness' entails a voluntary commitment to external standards and expectations, and a strong internalised sense of social obligation.

This typology is useful in that it describes the fundamental approach taken by advocates of CSR, which involves both the voluntary acceptance of external standards (which have been assessed by the organisation as acceptable and congruent with its own values) and a strong commitment, carried out right through the organisation, to fulfilling social obligations.

The IBE (2001) argues that CSR will only become fully meaningful when companies accept that 'principle must of necessity precede profit'. In addition, the IBE believes that the rewards for this acceptance will have to be delivered by the market. (See Examples 8.4 and 8.5.)

EXAMPLE 8.4

BP and Business Partners for Development

Together with Ecopetrol, Total and Triton, BP operates four oil exploration and production developments in the Casanare region of Colombia – including the Cusiana and Cupiagua fields. Together, the latter represent the largest private oil discovery in Latin America during the past decade. With high oil production levels, and with a backcloth of a nationwide armed conflict, the appointed operator (BP) is applying innovative ways for these operations to contribute to long-term sustainable development in the Casanare region.

In Casanare, BP is working with the 'World Bank's Business Partners for Development' (BPD) programme. BP was a founder member and sponsor of BPD – a project-based initiative that studies, supports and promotes strategic examples of partnerships involving business, civil society and government working together for the development of communities around the world. It aims to demonstrate that tri-sector partnerships benefit the long-term interests of the business sector, while meeting the social objectives of civil society and the state by helping to create stable social and financial environments.

In Casanare, BP has applied this approach since 1993. With BPD's support, BP is helping the Casanare authorities and communities to manage changing circumstances, as well as assisting in accessing new and additional resources to facilitate the sustainable development of the region. In the long-term, the aim has been to ensure that oil revenues contribute to sustainable, non-oil dependent, economic development across the region of Casanare, beyond the operational life of the project.

Amongst the business benefits claimed for BP's approach are:

- Robust channels of communication that increase the opportunities to prevent local disputes and manage social risk

- A durable 'social licence to operate' (for example, access to site)

- A management tool to help close the gap between the social compliance requirements of regulators, investors and corporate HQ, and the social performance of operations on the ground

- Protection of local supply chains and contribution to the local economy

- Reduced community dependency on the company due to the opportunities for communities to engage with other actors from government and civil society.

EXAMPLE 8.5

B&Q

B&Q plc is the UK's largest home improvement chain. In 1999, its profits reached £188 m – a success built not only on products and pricing, but also responsibility and reputation.

When you learn that your brand-new brass letterbox was made by poorly-paid workers in dangerous conditions, the shine begins to fade; the reputation of the company you bought it from starts to tarnish. Ten years ago, B&Q decided to take full responsibility for the environmental and social impacts of their own and their suppliers' operations, launching a programme for continuous improvements. Perhaps the most important aspect of their work has been in inspiring suppliers to adopt, long term, safer and fairer practices.

Taking a country-by-country approach, B&Q first focused on India. There, they worked with factory owners to make brassware casting safer for the workers, helped set up a health clinic for 800 weaving families, and became the first retailer to stock Rugmark rugs, made without the use of exploited child labour. Uncovering problems in how their coir doormats were produced, B&Q looked further down their supply chain to resolve issues by improving wages, starting a savings scheme for the women who beat and spin the coir, and introducing a water treatment process to reduce lagoon pollution.

'Project India' has developed into a permanent relationship with International Resources for Fairer Trade – and, in 1999, the programme was extended to all 13 suppliers and 15 factories in India. The lessons learned are now helping improve conditions in China and South Africa too.

As a leader in responsible practices, B&Q has published reports on its work in developing countries, offering a practical model for other companies to follow.

In 1999, B&Q published a detailed review of their work in *Being a Better Trading Neighbour.*

Amongst the business benefits claimed for B&Q's approach are that:

- Continuous improvement in conditions has made supply chains more efficient

- Managing environmental and social issues through continuous improvement has supported their reputation when there are high profile concerns in these areas

- The company has won coverage on TV and in the national press as a positive example to others

- Child labour and deforestation are emotive issues – employees are proud to work for a company that tackles these issues head-on

- Acting voluntarily, ahead of any legislation, puts B&Q in a strong position and guards against unforeseen costs.

There are two main problems with the approach taken by, inter alia, Petrick and Quinn, and also the IBE. First, the principles and beliefs developed by an individual business might not be such as to lead it to develop an ethical approach to doing business. Second, the values of the society to which a business is responding responsibly may be such as to generate unethical behaviour. A business might be a socially responsible organisation with a strongly held belief in its own value system which accords with the values and beliefs of the society it serves and, dependant on those beliefs, it could exploit its workforce, pay no heed to health and safety, give little consideration to the environment, or use its power to dominate. So, the question remains – what are the principles or values upon which both a business and the society of which it is a part should base their actions and policies. For example, a business that focuses on out-competing its competitors to the exclusion of all other considerations could be said to hold deep convictions about the nature of business activity. If it operated in a society in which it is widely believed that wealth is created by allowing businesses to be as unfettered as possible in their activities, then its values would be congruent with the society. However, it would not be described by any of the models of CSR as being a socially responsible company. (See, for instance, Example 8.6.)

EXAMPLE 8.6

Multi-national corporations

When claiming to be engaged in acts of corporate social responsibility, large multi-national corporations might well be engaged in ensuring their own interests are taken care of in potential new markets.

According to George Monbiot, writing in *The Guardian* in May 2007, death and injury on the roads is the world's most neglected public health issue. Almost as many people die in road accidents – 1.2 million a year – as are killed by malaria or tuberculosis. Around 50 million are injured. Some 85 per cent of these accidents take place in developing countries. The poor get hurt much more often than the rich, as they walk, cycle or travel in overloaded buses. The highest death rate is among children walking on the roads. The annual economic cost to developing countries, in lost productivity alone, is $65–100 bn, roughly the same as the amount they receive in foreign aid.

By 2020, according to the World Bank, deaths from road accidents are expected to fall by 28 per cent in rich nations but to rise by 83 per cent in poorer ones. By 2030, they will overtake the deaths caused by malaria. But while $1.9 bn of foreign aid will be spent on tackling malaria over the next five years, the annual global aid budget for road safety is less than $10 m.

In 1999, the World Bank invited the motor and oil companies to join the Global Road Safety Partnership. It was supposed to bring together 'governments and governmental agencies, the private sector and civil society organisations'. But its executive committee is dominated by giant motor and oil corporations – BP, Total, DaimlerChrysler, General Motors, Michelin and Volvo – are all represented. There are no representatives from civil society organisations and only two from governments.

The Global Road Safety Partnership report emphasised better training for drivers and better safety education for children. These measures do not interfere with the commercial interests of the transport industry: neither, according to Professor Ian Roberts of the London School of Hygiene and Tropical Medicine, do they work. The World Health Organization argues that the solution is to reclaim the roads for pedestrians and cyclists. The Global Safety Partnership Report hardly mentions pedestrians or cyclists.

Similarly, the Independent Commission for Global Road Safety was created to make roads safe. There are, however, questions about its independence.

It was established by the Federation Internationale de l'Automobile Foundation, which is run by motoring and motor sports associations. Of the eight commissioners, one is an executive of General Motors, one runs the Bridgestone Tyre Corporation, one is a trustee of the FIA Foundation, one is Chairman of the FIA Foundation and a president of the Automobile Club of Italy, and one is Michael Schumacher. The Commission's secretary is the Director General of the FIA Foundation.

Its report calls for the developing nations to follow the path taken by richer countries in reducing deaths and injuries. At no point does it mention that much of this reduction was the result of cyclists and pedestrians being driven off the roads. This is a much bigger issue for poor nations – where the great majority of people who use roads do not own cars – than for rich ones.

8.4 Sustainability

Another central notion in theories of CSR is the concept of 'sustainability'. The environmental and social consequences of business activities have increasingly taken centre stage and become matters of concern for governments, societies and businesses. Carmen and Lubelski (1997: 28) write: 'Within both governmental and non-governmental organisations, the idea of 'sustainable' development has appeared of late as a lodestar for orienting policy and strategy alike. Whether North or South, the environmental and social consequences of our actions are coming to light – demographic explosions combined with increasing global social inequality and conflict, exacerbated by massive natural resource depletion and compounded by the effects of industrial waste and pollution.' This provides a potent cocktail of challenges to our ecological and social systems.

Throughout the 1980s, there was a growing concern amongst none governmental agencies that not enough was being done to ensure that business operated in a way that would help to sustain the environment. This growing concern culminated in the 1992 Rio Earth Summit and the United Nations Conference on the Environment and Development. Agenda 21 was the outcome of Rio. This committed over 170 nations to a global agenda designed to ensure environmental and social accountability.

How has business responded to this agenda? There have been several international initiatives such as the International Chambers of Commerce Commission on the Environment in 1989 and the World Business Council for Sustainable Development (WBCSD). This is a coalition of 165 international companies united by a shared commitment to sustainable development via the three pillars: economic growth, ecological balance and social progress. It has members from more than 30 countries and 20 major industrial sectors. It sees itself as a catalyst for change toward sustainable development, and to promote the role of eco-efficiency, innovation and CSR. Its aims are:

- To be the leading business advocate on issues connected with sustainable development

- To participate in policy development in order to create a framework that allows business to contribute effectively to sustainable development

- To demonstrate business progress in environmental and resource management and CSR, and to share leading-edge practices among its members

- To contribute to a sustainable future for developing nations and nations in transition.

There are many examples of businesses seeking to improve their performance and reputation in relation to sustainability. Examples 8.4 and 8.5 are typical of some of the approaches being taken.

In addition to the growth of business-led organisations aimed at enhancing the sustainability of business activities, there has been the development of sustainability reporting[5] (sometimes as part of wider social reporting by businesses), the production of international standards,[6] and the assessment of business performance in relation to those standards and special awards for companies with strong sustainability records.

There are two main strands of criticism of the business-led approaches to sustainability. First, there is the fundamentalist perspective, which argues that there needs to be a change to basic attitudes towards competition as the central driver of business. Second, there is the approach that argues that, although progress is being made, it is neither fast enough nor sufficient in scale.

The first strand is represented by authors such as Hawken (1993) and Carmen and Lubelski (1997). The major stances in this critique are, first, that globalisation and dominance of the world economy by the USA, Europe and Japan is based upon the dogma of the efficacy and inevitability of competition:

> This dogma of competition, having pervaded all spheres of life and not just the world of business alone, makes no economic, ecological, social nor, ultimately, ethical sense and is ill equipped to act as a universal principle to rule the planet. (Carmen and Lubelski, ibid: 29)

Petrella et al. (2001) claim that the traditional business model is based on 'well-having' rather than on 'well-being'. They argue that the world has, collectively, to decide that there are limits to growth and limits to competition.

Second, the assumption that the world's ecological problems can be solved through business-led action alone is false. The approach taken by these business-led organisations is rooted in a culturally specific business paradigm based on the primary need of the business to survive, rather than the primary needs of the rest of the world. Hawken (1993: viii) points out that, even if the best environmental practices in the world were adopted by each and every business, 'the world would still be moving towards sure degradation and collapse'.

Third, even the progressive, business-led approaches to sustainability are still based on a model of massive exploitation of the world's resources to provide for a plethora of consumer goods to a minority of the world's population and results in the exclusion of massive sections of the globe. Middleton et al. (2003) argue that the Rio Summit had less to do with a genuine concern for the environment than with protecting the interests of the North against those of the South.

The second strand of critique arises from a concern to create improvements in sustainability in business through a rigorous application of standards and the continuous pressure to improve. For example, Daniel Litvin (*Financial Times*, 12 May 2003) argues that:

> The flood of worthy reports cannot obscure an awkward fact in this respect: that companies that have taken up the CSR agenda have often continued to face severe public criticism. Many of the companies judged to be the world's 'top sustainability reporters' in a survey last year by the United Nations and SustainAbility, the consultancy, for example, have continued to come under fire in the media on environmental or social issues. Among them are Shell and BP, which run some of the corporate world's most elaborate CSR programmes, both of which companies' annual general meetings last month were disrupted by protesters. In March, Shell was forced to shut down some of its oil production in Nigeria due to community unrest. This was in spite of its increased expenditure on social welfare programmes aimed at fostering local stability.

He argues that even if businesses achieve all they set out to do in their grand statements about CSR, they will still come in for criticism. This is because the businesses have an impossible task: to balance the interests of fundamentally conflicting stakeholder interests. He concludes that:

> All this is not an argument against CSR. Individual companies clearly need to be sensitive to ethical issues: securing broad public approval is crucial for their long-term financial success. But a more rigorous approach to CSR is needed, one that does not pretend that dilemmas can be avoided or promise more than it can deliver in terms of reputation protection. Otherwise there is a risk that the CSR movement, like some other recent growth industries, may prove to be a bubble.

Similar exhortations to improvement can be found amongst those passing judgement on business performance in the sustainability field. For example, the judges for the European Sustainability Reporting Awards in 2002, organised by the Dutch accountancy association NIVRA, called for more quantifiable performance indicators to improve credibility; improved stakeholder involvement throughout the reporting process; and a better balance between the elements of sustainability, with a stronger emphasis on human rights and economic issues.

The Institute of Social and Ethical Accountability (2003) reported that, despite an increase in sustainability reporting by businesses in response to increased stakeholder pressure, reports seem rarely to be used either by stakeholders (including investors) or by management to inform judgements and actions. This report states that, in order for reporting to be more effective, it needs to increase its credibility and, in order to do that, credible external assurance mechanisms are needed. As a contribution towards this improved external scrutiny and assurance, the Institute proposes the use of a new set of standards for assessing sustainability – AA1000.

What all of these criticisms have in common is a desire to see enhanced sustainability in business operations based upon the assumption that the current, competitive, business model will continue in place.

8.5   Socially responsible investment

In July 2001, the FTSE announced a new FTSE4Good index. This index, similar to the FTSE 100 index, is one of a growing list of indices responding to the rising interest in socially responsible investment (SRI). The index selects companies for inclusion that are able to demonstrate a strong and clear commitment to environmental sustainability, universal human rights and strong stakeholder relationships. It excludes companies such as tobacco firms, weapons manufacturers and nuclear power companies. Nestlé, for example, has been excluded from the index because of its marketing strategy with regard to breast milk substitutes.

The index covers four markets: the UK, Europe, the USA and global. Four tradable and four benchmark indices make up the FTSE4Good index series. A committee of independent practitioners in SRI and CSR review the indices to ensure that they are an accurate reflection of current CSR best practice. Companies are regularly added to the indices – which cover UK, European, US and global markets and ranked companies in accordance with their market values: they are reviewed every six months by an independent committee.

While many have welcomed the index, as it is the first of its kind, there have been some criticisms. Friends of the Earth, for example, have questioned the inclusion of some companies, which it says have poor environmental records. In April 2003, the FTSE Group announced a new, more stringent set of human rights criteria for the FTSE4Good index as part of its ongoing strategy to raise the standards for entry into the index series. The enhanced criteria means that companies will have to raise their human rights standards, beginning in September 2003, to qualify for the index series.

The FTSE Group undertook a broad public human rights consultation during 2002, the first of its kind, with almost 200 responses from corporations, fund managers, non-government organisations and private investors. These responses formed the basis of the new criteria.

Companies operating in the Global Resource Sector must meet the higher human rights criteria by September 2003. Companies with significant involvement in high-risk countries, as defined by the Ethical Investment Research Service (EIRIS), had to meet higher human rights standards starting March 2004. In addition to this, the FTSE4Good Advisory Committee announced in March 2004 an implementation timetable for all companies, regardless of sector or geography, to have a basic human rights policy in place.

The US-based Dow Jones Index developed a European series of sustainability indices during 2001. Following the same selection methodology as the Dow Jones Sustainability World Index, it identifies the top performing companies in different sectors. Table 8.2 gives the European rankings in October 2001.

FTSE and Dow Jones are responding to the growing demand for SRI opportunities, and for the information and guidance services that socially responsible investors require. In the USA, in 2001, there was an estimated $2.03 trillion in socially screened investment portfolios under professional management. This is an increase of 36 per cent since 1999. There are now over 250 investment

Table 8.2 European rankings of the top performing companies, October 2001

Market sector	Leading company
Automobiles	Volkswagen
Banks	UBS
Basic resources	Rio Tinto
Chemicals	BASF
Construction	Skanska
Energy	Royal Dutch Petroleum
Financial services	ING
Food and beverages	Unilever
Media	Granada Media
Retail	Boots
Telecommunications	BT
Utilities	Severn Trent

funds in Europe focused on sustainable and ethical investments. Between 1999 and 2002, the value of these funds increased by 41 per cent, representing 15.6 billion Euros being managed by these funds.[7] The growth of SRI in the UK is no less spectacular. Sparkes (2002) estimates that, in 1997, there was a total of £22.7 billion invested in socially responsible funds. This had grown to £224.5 billion by 2001. Businesses are increasingly competing for the investment funds of ethical investors; the type of list such as Dow Jones is producing is being used as promotional opportunities by companies.

SRI is an investment process that combines traditional financial objectives with a commitment to social and environmental responsibility. It involves avoiding socially undesirable investments; such as investments in tobacco, gambling and armaments, and using social and environmental criteria as the basis for investment. According to the UK Social Investment Forum, the SRI industry is split into three main markets, catering to different types of socially responsible investors:

- Institutional SRI, which includes 'mainstream SRI', refers to institutional investment undertaken within an SRI framework that uses screening and/or engagement. Institutions that fall into this category include pension funds, insurance companies, churches and charities.

- Consumer SRI, also known as 'retail SRI' or 'ethical investment' refers to consumer investments made according to social, environmental and/or ethical concerns and personal values. Investments that fall into this category include ethical unit & investment trusts, personal pensions and ISAs.

- Social and green small and medium-sized enterprises, also known as 'social investment ' and 'cause-based investing', is a broad area which covers social banking, community development finance, alternative profit offerings and SEE (social, environmental and ethical) venture capital.

There are two main approaches that can be used by socially responsible investors, either separately or in combination: screening and engagement. 'Screening' refers to the inclusion or exclusion of stocks and shares in investment portfolios on SEE grounds. Screening is usually divided into 'negative screening' (to exclude unacceptable shares from the portfolio) and 'positive screening' (to select companies with superior SEE performance). Screening is typically the methodology used by retail funds, and churches and charities that have strict criteria about certain SEE issues. Engagement, also known as 'shareholder activism', refers to the process by which investors seek to improve a company's performance by means of dialogue and/or voting at annual general meetings. Engagement is typically the methodology used by institutional investors, such as pension funds and insurance companies, but is also used by selected consumer SRI funds, churches and charities.

Ethical or SRI funds and organisations committed to increasing the impact of SRI deal with a wide range of issues, and different funds and organisations tend to focus on different issues. UKSIF identifies the following lists of issues:

Social issues

Access to medicines	Corporate governance
Equal opportunities	Bribery and corruption
Child labour	Health and safety
Community giving	Human rights
Labour standards	Supply chain management
Community initiatives	Conflict

Environmental issues

Air and water pollution	Ozone-depleting chemicals
Biodiversity	Pesticides
Climate change	Resource productivity
Energy	Transport
Environmental management	Tropical hardwood
Mining and quarrying	Nuclear power
Water management	Waste and toxic chemical management

Ethical issues

Gambling	Pornography and adult entertainment
Genetic engineering	Repressive regimes
Human rights	Tobacco
Alcohol	Military
Animal testing and fur	Nuclear power

QUESTIONS AND TASKS

1 Social and environmental reports are increasingly being published by businesses. By searching the web, using some of the useful websites given below, pick out three such reports that have been published in the last two years. Compare the reports and draw up a summary of their main features using the following questions:

(a) Do the reports tell you enough to help you to decide whether, as an ethical investor, you would invest in the business?

(b) How full are the reports; is anything of significance left out?

(c) If you had a substantial amount to invest, would you invest in any of these companies?

2 Examine the annual reports and social responsibility reports of a tobacco company, such as British American Tobacco (BAT). Given that there are ethical issues around the production and retail of tobacco products, how would you advise BAT to develop into a socially responsible company?

CHAPTER 9

Ethical Organisation and Leadership

After reading this chapter you will:

- Understand the relationship between leadership and corporate ethics
- Appreciate the significance of ethical leadership
- Be aware of different approaches to leadership.

9.1 Introduction

In 2002, the Enron Corporation reported massive financial losses. In August 2002, Michael Kopper, a former senior finance official at Enron, pleaded guilty to using Enron's off-balance sheet partnerships to enrich himself and former Chief Financial Officer Andrew Fastow. The Chief Executive of Enron, Kenneth Lay, sold shares for $70million whilst the company was collapsing: some of these sales took place after Mr Lay had been warned by an Enron accountant, Sherron Watkins, that the company may implode in a wave of accounting scandals. Press comment at the time of the collapse spoke in terms of the Enron affair being 'mind-boggling'. Heather Tomlinson, writing in *The Independent on Sunday*, London, stated that 'The effects of its collapse have been wide ranging. Andersen (*Enron's auditors*) have gone. Its shareholders and staff were left out of pocket. Enron seems to have been tainted by a deadly curse, any association with the company leading to dire problems.' Clifford Baxter, a former Enron vice president, had left the company in May 2002 after speaking out in the company about his concerns regarding accounting practices at Enron. He committed suicide rather than face a Congressional enquiry into the affair.

Fusaro and Miller (2002) detail the complicated frauds carried out by Enron executives. More importantly, they deal with the question as to why Enron staff did not blow the whistle. They give two reasons: first, Enron gave lavish bonuses and stock options to their staff; second, Enron management practised a 'rank and yank' policy. This meant that every year managers ranked Enron staff on the basis of their sense of urgency and innovativeness. The lowest ranked 15 per cent were fired. The next two groups of 15 per cent were warned that they were in danger next year. This meant that 45 per cent of Enron staff was constantly under the threat of being dismissed. Such an approach does not encourage outspoken criticism. In the meantime, Enron was regularly praised in the business media as a dynamic and innovative business. Fusaro and Miller do not offer a clear answer as to why the auditors, Andersen, did not report on the malpractices. They suggest it might have something to do with the fact that Andersen were earning $54 million a year from Enron at the time.

The Enron affair left a massive wake in its trail. In this case, and others such as Worldcom and Wessex Water, there was a clear failure by senior managers to comply with good accounting practice. Resignations and ignominy followed for those business leaders, and a great deal of disquiet was voiced in the media and political circles. Comments were made about the responsibility that all business leaders carried towards the business community as a whole. Lack of trust in business leadership and the consequent effects on business activity and long-term profitability were seen to go hand-in-hand. The US Congress took steps to tighten up on financial regulation of business in order to try to restore faith in the capitalist system.

These are stark examples of business failure of a catastrophic nature following on from a leadership failure. The root of the leadership failure in these cases was willingness by the leaders of great corporations to connive in, or even to lead, unethical business practices (see Example 9.1). These were not just failures to comply with technical accounting requirements: they were deliberate and conscious attempts, in the pursuit of great wealth, to mislead stakeholders – investors, employees and customers. There can be few stronger examples of the importance of ethical leadership for the health of organisations and their future prospects.

EXAMPLE 9.1

Shareholders' interests

Business leaders set the moral and ethical tone for their organisations, and their leadership styles have far reaching repercussions. The leaders of public companies have a legal responsibility to act in the interest of shareholders.

In the trial of Lord Conrad Black, the jury was told that he and his senior colleagues received fraudulent payments of $5.5 m (£2.8 m) as a reward for not competing with themselves in an imaginary transaction involving a tiny Californian newspaper. David Radler, the former business partner of Lord Black, described the money as an unofficial tax-free bonus scheme.

Radler admitted to the court that a string of dubious 'non-compete' payments related to the sale of newspapers were neither reported to independent directors nor disclosed to the Wall Street regulator. 'I knew the process for creating the non-compete payments was wrong', said Radler, who gave evidence at Lord Black's racketeering trial in return for a lighter sentence after pleading guilty to fraud.

Lord Conrad Black faced 17 charges alleging embezzlement of $60 m from Hollinger through a pattern of phoney payments and inappropriate expense claims.

According to the US government, these payments began in 1999, attached to genuine deals, but became increasingly daring as they went unnoticed. Eventually, in 2001, Lord Black and Radler paid themselves $2.6 m each for not competing with Hollinger's American division, APC – on which they were both directors. It was justified in an internal memo as tied to 'the final APC sale transactions' in spite of the fact that there was no such transaction.

Lord Black was in the dock alongside three former colleagues: Jack Boultbee, Peter Atkinson and Mark Kipnis.

The prosecution showed the jury a memo circulated by Lord Black in the summer of 2002. In the document, the Conservative peer said Hollinger directors had a 'certain style' of which investors were aware when they bought shares in the company, insisting that he would not countenance a 'Damascene conversion to poverty'. This revealed the mindset of the leaders of the business.

Lord Black argued that it was perfectly reasonable for Hollinger to pay half the salary of a chef at his London home and 28 per cent of the cost of a butler and a waiter, since he often used the house for entertaining. The former press baron added in the memo that he needed the company to fund personal security because of editorial positions adopted by *The Daily Telegraph* and *The Spectator*, particularly their 'opposition to Arab and Irish terrorists'.

Lord Black only owned a minority of Hollinger's shares, with the rest listed on the New York Stock Exchange. But Radler testified that the peer saw it as his own private domain: 'He was saying we would run these companies in the tradition of running private businesses, as opposed to public companies.'

Lord Black and his three co-defendants refused to give evidence under oath at the trial.

The jury had to decide whether Lord Black and his colleagues had defrauded shareholders by receiving these illegal payments. In a complex case, the jury took over eight days to arrive at its verdict.

Lord Black was found guilty of four out of the 13 charges against him in the verdict, which was delivered on Friday 13 July 2007.

Schroeder (2002) argues that there are three types of ethical businesses:

- Businesses that seek to maximise their profits but give generously to charities from those profits; the example she gives here is that of Microsoft.

- Businesses that seek to integrate social values into their everyday business operations; the example here is Ben and Jerry's.

- Businesses that produce ethical products and services; the example given here is Trevor Bayliss's wind-up radio and wind-up torch.

She goes on to argue that, in all these cases, it is decisions taken by top management that have created the ethical business: it is Bill Gates who decided to donate large sums of Microsoft's profits to charity; it was Ben and Jerry, the founders of the business, who insisted on their social values being reflected throughout the organisation; it is the inventor of the ethical product who lays the foundation for the third type of business. Hence, she argues, 'the impetus for ethical business ... has to come from the top, either from managing directors or from owner-managers' (ibid.: 261). Kanungo and Mendonca (1996) state, 'The beliefs and values, the vision, and above all, the actions of the leader set the ethical tone and standards for the organisation.'

The remainder of this chapter will explore recently emergent models of leadership and the extent to which each approach offers the potential for ethical leadership.

9.2   The changing meaning of leadership

Warren Bennis, writing in 1959, asserted that:

> Of all the hazy and confounding areas in social psychology, leadership theory undoubtedly contends for top nomination. And, ironically, probably more has been written and less known about leadership than any other topic in the behavioural sciences. (p. 259)

Dainty and Anderson were saying something very similar in 1996. They refer to a study by Bass (1990), which noted that at that time there were over 7,500 published sources on leadership. They argue that there is no universal agreement on how leadership is defined, that there is no full agreement on what leadership involves, that there is confusion about the qualities required for effective leadership, that there is doubt about which of these qualities can be developed, and that there is a very limited understanding about what leadership at the top of organisations really means.

Distinguishing fact from fiction, myth from reality, views about what leadership ought to be like from views about what it really is like, is, therefore, a task fraught with difficulties. However, it is possible to identify distinct models of leadership or different theoretical perspectives on leadership that have emerged, and to identify the potential for ethical leadership within each of these different intellectual traditions.

However, before proceeding to review the different perspectives on leadership, it is necessary to indicate the areas on which most leadership studies within the social and organisational psychology disciplines are agreed. There is a general consensus (see Kanunga and Mendonca 1996) that:

- Leadership is an organisational or group phenomenon and is a set of role behaviours performed by an individual when there is a need to influence and coordinate the activities of group or organisational members towards a common goal. Before this consensus emerged from empirical leadership studies, the dominant leadership theory was the 'great man' or 'trait' theory. This proposed that successful leaders were always special people with rare characteristics of personality or physical traits and ignored the context within which the leadership function was carried out.

- Empirical studies of leadership provide very little evidence to support the great man or trait theory. Cartwight and Zander (1968: 304) sum up the general view of leadership analysts when they say 'Leadership consists of such actions by group members as those which aid in setting group goals, moving the group towards its goals, improving the quality of interaction among the members, building cohesiveness of the group and making resources available to the group'.

- However, leadership is not just explicable as a phenomenon solely in terms of situational – group or organisational – factors. Leadership arises when followers perceive the leader's behaviour in such a way as to accept the leader's influence attempts and then attribute leadership status to that person. Without followers there would be no leaders and followers perceive certain behaviours as leadership behaviours. They accept the person exhibiting these behaviours as leaders and then attribute leadership status to that person. This is why, for example, some people who have acquired a formally designated leadership role are ineffective as leaders – their behaviour is not recognised as leadership behaviour, they are not accepted as leaders and they are not attributed that role by those who they desire to lead.

- Leadership behaviour is intended to influence followers' attitudes and behaviour within a particular context. This gives rise to three measurements of leadership effectiveness: first, the extent to which a leader is successful in promoting the instrumental attitudes and behaviour needed for the achievement of group or organisational goals; second, the sense of satisfaction obtained by followers with both their tasks and the context within which they operate; and third, the extent to which followers accept the leaders influence. These are broader forms of measurement than the traditional and widely accepted view that the effectiveness of leadership is measured through the achievement of goals or measurement of productivity.

- Management and leadership are not synonymous. Kanunga and Mendoca state that 'most leadership studies in organisational contexts have, in fact, been studies of supervision of day to day routine maintenance rather than the true phenomenon of leadership as observed in society' (p. 21). Supervision or management is essentially concerned with maintaining systems and ensuring efficient and effective operations. It is focused on maintaining the status quo. Several writers – Zaleznik 1977, Jago 1982 and Mintzberg 1982 – have argued that leadership is focused on change – improvements and transformations in existing systems. This distinction is at the heart of the emergent leadership models that we will now go on to examine.

9.3 Altruism and leadership

Kanungo and Mendonca (1996) argue that it is essential for leaders to be altruistic. They argue that leadership is essentially concerned with change and transformation, and that there are three stages in the transformational process. First, the leader identifies deficiencies in the status quo; the opportunities that exist and the organisation's capacity to exploit those opportunities; and the abilities, needs and aspirations of the organisation's members. Second, the leader formulates and articulates a vision that differs substantially from the status quo but embodies a perspective shared by organisational members. Third, the leader takes steps to achieve the vision. These steps are strategies and interventions that are designed to empower the followers to achieve the vision. For the followers to follow the leader, they have to feel that they can trust the leader, and that the leader has the capacity and perseverance to deliver the vision. In order for this to happen, the leader has to behave, in all three stages, in an altruistic – as opposed to an egotistic – fashion.

The typology of altruistic behaviour as perceived by Kanungo and Mendonca is presented in Figure 9.1. The two dimensions in this typology are behaviour concerned with benefiting or harming the self, and behaviour concerned with benefiting or harming others. Genuinely altruistic behaviour is that which has costs for oneself and benefits for others. Utilitarian or mutual altruism can be likened to enlightened self-interest. Kanunga and Mendonca argue that genuine, moral altruism is based on the internalisation of social responsibility.

In the first stage of transformational leadership – that of identifying deficiencies in the status quo and opportunities that exist, and the capacities and aspirations of the organisation's members – leaders with a self-centred (as opposed to other-centred) perspective would be likely to be unsuccessful. They could identify deficiencies in the status quo and develop radical proposals for

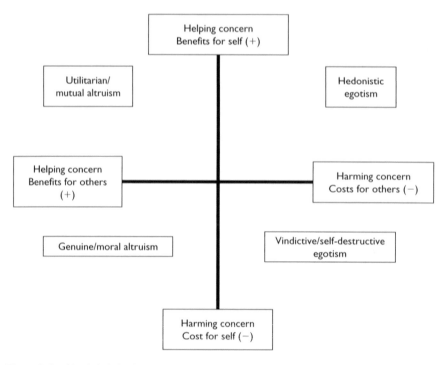

Figure 9.1 Altruistic behaviour
Source: Kanungo and Mendonca (1996)

change; however, it is unlikely that followers would perceive the proposals as based on their needs and aspirations. They would perceive them to be based on the leader's personal needs and aspirations.

Similarly, in stage 2 – that of formulating and articulating a vision – the leader's role is to develop a vision that is shared and to articulate this vision in a way that the followers find inspirational. Clearly, the leader has a pivotal role in the formulation and articulation of the vision, but the realisation of the vision depends on the commitment of the followers and they will need to feel that it is a shared vision. In formulating and articulating the vision, the leader is taking a personal risk. The willingness of the leader to take this personal risk is a product of an altruistic perspective. For the future good of the organisation, the leader has to be willing to step, and lead others, into the unknown. Articulation of the vision requires the leader to demonstrate trust and confidence in their own capabilities and those of their followers. If followers perceive that the leader does not trust them or show confidence in their capabilities and is more interested in protecting his or her own personal interests, then the articulation of the vision will not be shared and the leader will be less effective. Trusting their followers to be able to rise to the challenges of change demonstrates that the leader is willing to place his or her personal and organisational interests in the hands of others.

In the third stage, that of implementation, the focus on others is more evident. In this stage, the leader's task is to motivate others to implement the vision. Typically, the leader will engage in modelling or exemplary acts, innovative and unconventional behaviour that often involves personal risk and sacrifices. For example, Lee Iacocca (see Iacocca and Novak 1984) reduced his own salary to one dollar per year when he took over Chrysler. This was an inspirational, unconventional act that embodied personal risk and sacrifice, and was instrumental in demonstrating to his followers his total personal commitment to the vision he had articulated for the organisation and his determination to see it through.

Kanungo and Mendonca sum up their paradigm by stating that 'the behavioural characteristics that are absolute imperatives for effective leadership can only be demonstrated by a leader who is motivated by a high degree of moral altruism' (ibid.: 44).

They go on to argue that this does not mean that other sources of motivation have no part to play in leaders' behaviour. The needs for affiliation, power and achievement (see McClelland and Burnham 1995) are clearly significant factors in the motivation of leaders. However, Kanungo and Mendonca argue that such motivational needs of leaders are more effective if they are derived from a focus on others rather than self. For example, Boyatzis (1973) argues that the need for affiliation can be divided into two types. There is 'avoidance affiliation' – here, the leader seeks to develop relationships with others that are protective of their own personal interests; and 'approach affiliation' – here, the leader is motivated by a genuine interest in others. Leaders with high approach affiliation needs 'relate to others with the full recognition that they are individual persons with ideas and resources and that they are partners in the problem solving and related activities necessary for attaining task objectives' (ibid.: 46).

Kanungo and Mendonca make similar comments related to the need for power and the need for achievement, arguing that when leaders seek to satisfy these

Table 9.1   Two contrasting leadership motive patterns

	Underlying motive	
	Altruistic	*Egoistic*
Leader's motivational needs	Interested in others in their own right	Interested in others as a way of protecting self
	Motivated by increasing the power of the organisation they are leading	Motivated by increasing personal power
	Motivated by the achievements of their organisation	Motivated by personal achievement
	Willing to control personal needs in the interest of the organisation	Interested in self-aggrandisement
Leader's influence strategy	Empowerment of followers	Control of followers
	Power based on expertise and capability	Power based on rules, coercion and rewards
Leadership effectiveness	High	Low

Source: Kanungo and Mendonca (1996: table 3.1).

needs, they can do so either in a self-centred fashion or in such a way as to demonstrate commitment to the needs of others and the organisations they are leading. Their analysis is summarised in Table 9.1.

The broad argument here is that highly effective leadership, as opposed to effective management, is more likely to occur if the leaders are altruistic in their motivation and adopt influence strategies that are based on respect for their followers as rational human beings who can be trusted. They also tend towards favouring a power base that is founded on expertise and capability rather than rules or coercion. It follows that, if ethical behaviour towards others can be characterised as being based on an acceptance of the equal status of others as human beings, on trust and on rational decision-making based on knowledge and expertise, then only ethical leaders can be effective.

There is a widely held view in business circles – particularly in the USA and often reflected in Hollywood movies such as *Wall Street* – that good leaders are ruthless and dominant, aggressive and focused on results. Warren Bennis (1993) disagrees with this view. He believes that, in modern organisations, such an approach may work for a short period but, in the long run, the organisation will lose its best people. They will not follow such a leader for any longer than they have to and they will leave the organisation. Such an approach might work for the leader and respond to their motivational needs, but is unlikely to respond effectively to the motivational needs of those whose high-level skills and knowledge are essential for success in the modern knowledge-based economy.

Similarly there is a view that, to be effective, leaders must be charismatic personalities. Collins and Porras (1994) investigated 18 US corporations that had the characteristic that they had operated successfully over very long periods. They concluded that the main reason such companies were successful over a long period was not because of the outstanding personal qualities of the different leaders they had had over that period, it was because the companies had in-built corporate capabilities, which are essential for long-term success. There was a shared vision and shared set of values. Collins and Porras call this a 'purpose beyond profits'. These businesses were profitable over a long period, but they were driven by their vision and values not by the urge to make money.

Charles Handy (1992) argues that the role of the leader is to exemplify the vision of the organisation. Without a vision there can be no leadership. The vision needs to be different from current reality; it must make sense to members of the organisation and be challenging – above all, it must be shared. The leader's role is to articulate, clarify and pursue the vision. If followers do not share the vision, leadership will fail. Handy argues that leadership is a process of gaining commitment to a vision. For this to happen, the vision needs to be clear. The leader has to gain the followers' trust and be concerned for their needs and potential. The leader should actively solicit ideas from the followers and inspire, motivate and generate enthusiasm through the setting of example. This does not require the person holding the leadership role to be a charismatic personality; it does, however, require sensitivity to the needs and values of the followers.

9.4 Leadership in learning organisations

Peter Senge's (1990) seminal work on the 'learning organisation' offers a different perspective on leadership. Senge starts from the proposition that organisations destroy people. They shape behaviour in a way that, outside the organisation, people would find unacceptable. He argues that there is a strong link between learning and performance. Learning can be of two types: 'generative learning' is learning that facilitates the development of new ideas, processes or products; 'adaptive learning' facilitates the assimilation of new circumstances into organisational planning and behaviour. Organisations do not encourage either of these types of learning, which would, if allowed to happen, ensure the continuing success of the organisation. The reason why learning organisations are very rare, according to Senge, is that there is a dearth of appropriate leadership.

He argues that organisations can continue to be successful only if they have a clear vision about where they want to be – that this should be different from current reality, otherwise there is no motive for change. If there is no creative tension between where an organisation is and where it wants to be, it will ossify and settle into the status quo. It is the gap between the current reality and the vision that creates the need for learning and leadership. To remove the tension that the gap creates is an inherent organisational dynamic. The tension is uncomfortable for members of the organisation. They can decide either to change the current reality to a new reality to fit with the vision, or they can dilute the vision to make it less distant from the current reality. The role of leadership is to create this tension. To do this, there must be a clear understanding of the current reality. This requires details and factual analysis. However, the analysis of current reality does not produce the vision. This comes from the fundamental values of the organisation's members.

In this context, new roles emerge for leaders. They need the skills of designers to be able to picture the vision. They need to be teachers to ensure that others understand the vision. They need to act as stewards of the vision, protecting it, following it and passing it on to others. In terms of organisational design, leaders have to develop the governing ideas, policies, strategies and structures that will lead to the fulfilment of the vision. They also need to create effective learning processes. Within their teaching role, they have to ensure that there is a shared understanding of current reality. They also need to ensure that the various mental models at work beneath the service of organisational life are brought to the surface; otherwise, there will never be a shared understanding.

It is in the stewardship role of leadership that the ethical dimension comes to the fore. Stewardship is characterised by Peter Block (1987) as 'willing[ness] to be deeply accountable without choosing to control the world around us'. It involves listening, reflecting, trying to understand and to convince others rather than coerce them. The learning leader needs to come to terms with his or her own lack of expertise and wisdom.

Senge argues that, within the learning organisation, new leadership roles are required: building a shared vision, surfacing and challenging mental models, and applying systems thinking to problems.

This concept of leadership reflects a set of ethical values. Leaders do not see themselves as 'in charge'. They encourage and respect others. They are not leading to aggrandise themselves but to ensure that the organisation continues to be effective after they have left it.

9.5   Servant leadership

The idea of leader as servant is summed up in a famous Chinese poem written by Lao Tzu:

> A leader is best when people barely know he exists.
> Not so good when people obey and acclaim him.
> Worse when they despise him.
> If you fail to honour people
> They will fail to honour you.
> But of a good leader
> Who talks little
> When his work is done
> His aim fulfilled
> They will say 'We did this ourselves.'

The view that a good leader is self-effacing, almost retiring in manner and very pleased to let others take the credit for the organisation's achievements is one that jars with the western approaches to leadership. How can you be an effective leader and be almost invisible to your followers?

However, the idea of servant leadership need not be quite as described by Lao Tzu. The essential concept lies in the lines 'If you fail to honour people they will fail to honour you'. In other words, leaders will only be honoured as leaders if they demonstrate by the actions that they value and honour their followers, recognise their contributions and their worth to the organisation.

9.6   Existentialist theories of leadership

A common characteristic of all of the theories of leadership examined earlier in this chapter is that they are essentially based on a 'humanist' perception of leadership. Stone (1997: 34) argues that 'The humanistic model, emphasising as it does the self-concept, the uniqueness of the individual, the importance of values and meaning and our potential for self-direction and personal growth, has had a major and increasing influence upon contemporary thought and management theory'.

Humanists advocate giving employees (followers) the freedom to make autonomous choices as a means of motivating them to develop their personal potential to the full and to contribute positively to the transformational changes being brought about by their organisation's leadership. The basic assumption is that freedom to act (empowerment) is a basic human right that all people need and that, if organisations give this freedom to their people, they will take it, particularly when the leaders have created a safe, no-blame environment in which followers can operate.

The existentialist view is radically different. For existentialists, the exercise of freedom of action or choice creates anguish and uncertainty. According to Stone, the existentialist view is that 'Life is inherently unjust, and although the support of others can be very helpful we are ultimately alone, must make our own decisions, act and deal with the consequences' (ibid.: 41). For existentialists, freedom is a moral challenge. They argue that the human condition is by nature full of uncertainty and anxiety. In modern society, when traditional values and belief systems have eroded, each of us is individually responsible for shaping our own identity and making our existence meaningful. We do this by taking risks, doing what feels right and learning and developing from each experience.

For traditional moral belief systems such as Christianity, human essence precedes human existence. This means that there is something essential about being human that is in all humans. For existentialists, it is the other way round. Existence precedes essence. What we know is that we exist and it is up to each of us to determine our essence through our choices and decisions. What we do with our existence is a matter for us. However, most of us feel constrained in our choices because we need to be recognised by others, and this leads us to live our lives according to certain values – organisational, family, church or social. Now, the choice of this higher authority is a choice that we make as individuals and the decision to act on the guidance of this higher authority is our decision. In a sense, therefore, we 'make our own advice' (ibid.: 43).

Existentialists, such as Sartre, see human freedom as a kind of curse. In his lecture 'Existentialism and Humanism' (1948), he asserts that man is condemned to be free. Man's freedom to create his own essence is both his agony and his glory. This view has been summarised by Morris (1966: 135) as follows:

I am a choosing agent unable to avoid choosing my way through life;

I am a free agent, absolutely free to set the goals of my own life;

I am a responsible agent, personally accountable for my free choices as they are revealed in how I live my life.

Existentialists argue that there is no escape from uncertainty and the need to make choices. Not making a choice is in reality a choice not to change. Consequently, organisations are faced with this dilemma. There is no such thing as a permanently safe and secure environment. Change is endemic within the organisation's environment. Choices have to be made. If we decide not to change ourselves, then the environment will force change upon us. Choosing not to change might be a choice to go out of business, maybe slowly and painfully, but inevitably.

However, most change programmes are built upon humanist values and beliefs, and many managers do not share these values: fundamental values such as these are not challenged by the usual culture change programme and so these programmes have a high proportion of failures. The model used has four elements.

- The current or actual culture

- The desired or ideal culture towards which the organisation wishes to move

- The need to create a safe and supportive environment to encourage organisational members to make the changes needed

- Underlying assumptions about the nature of human beings and how they learn.

As Stone (1997: 61) puts it, 'in some cases we are asking managers to create a liberal environment based on a philosophy of human nature, learning and development that many wouldn't even create for their children in their own home'. She argues that, often, liberal values are foisted on managers who disagree with them fundamentally but choose not to say so. She believes that in most organisations, one third of managers will reject such values as impractical, another third will be willing to try them out, and the remaining third will accept them and work with them. Many managers see themselves as responsible people whose freedom to choose will result in positive organisational benefits, but they see their subordinates as irresponsible people whose choices will be irrational, based on instinct or rewards and punishments.

Effective organisational leadership must, according to the existentialist approach, be based on a willingness to confront the different fundamental values that exist within organisational members, a willingness to make choices clearly and in a committed sense, and a determination to see through the consequences of having made those choices and to do that every day. Effective leaders recognise the importance of clarifying their own and others' personal values and fundamental attitudes. They understand that making choices is difficult and creates anxiety and uncertainty. They do not make any false claims about seeking to create a risk-free environment, and their behaviour constantly reinforces and supports the choices once they have been made.

When Julius Caesar crossed the Rubicon with his army on his return to Rome after his battles in Gaul, he sent a clear message – he was coming to Rome to take control and he was prepared to deal with the consequences of having made that choice. In the words of Stone (ibid.: 171), leaders have to be prepared to cross their Rubicons every day and to live with the consequences of their choices and actions. Followers need to know that leaders are prepared to do this. This is not a comfortable view of leadership. There is no warm glow of humanism here to take the edge off harsh consequences of making a choice. But, if leaders are not prepared to manage the consequences of their choices as leaders, they will be much less effective. Managing the consequences means being willing to take the personal responsibility of confronting the underlying values of others and behaviour that sabotages the change programme for which the leader is responsible. This is very demanding – morally, psychologically and physically. Leaders cannot abdicate their responsibility on the grounds that they are leaving others to make decisions because they believe in empowerment.

Leaders with an existentialist philosophy would believe that they were being ethical if they were authentic in behaviour. That is, if they were prepared to be open about their fundamental values, willing to act consistently on those values and prepared to make difficult choices and live with the consequences. Such leaders would ensure that organisations were not allowed to rest on their laurels and avoid making choices and, once a choice has been made, they would ensure that the decisions made were followed through. They recognise that others make different choices based on their own values but, in leading the organisation, they are determined that all subsequent choices and decisions made by others in the organisation should be consistent with the strategic choices that they, as leaders, are responsible for getting the organisation to make.

9.7 Conclusion

Leadership is a complex social phenomenon. It defies easy, simplistic definition. However, there is, in all the theories examined in this chapter, an underlying presumption that to be effective, leadership needs to be ethical. When leadership is unethical, it fails. This is a bald statement. There have been many examples of business leaders who were regarded as effective but not ethical. Perhaps a more realistic view would be that to be effective in the long term, to build a lasting organisational legacy, leadership must be ethical. Short-term success is possible through unethical behaviour. Enron is a good example – Enron no longer exists.

████████ QUESTIONS AND TASKS ████████

1 Take the list of criteria that you prepared when carrying out the tasks for Chapter 1.

   (a) To what extent does your list reflect the significance of leadership in determining the ethical characteristics of an organisation?

   (b) Do you want to amend your list in any way?

2 Identify a business organisation that has been successful over the last five years. To what extent would you say its success has depended on ethical leadership behaviour? What other factors have been involved in its success? Do you think this business will exist in 10 years' time?

CHAPTER 10

Ethics and Information and Communication Technologies

After reading this chapter you will:

- Understand the major ethical issues raised by the widespread use of computer networks and the Internet

- Be able to identify the major challenges facing computing professionals

- Be able to identify the major issues faced by organisations making use of computer systems in their work

- Be aware of the major ethical issues surrounding the growth of use of the Internet.

10.1 Introduction

The rapid and widespread growth of the use of computer networks and the Internet presents ethical challenges. The fundamental issue is whether these ethical challenges are the same ethical challenges faced by organisations, people and societies in other areas, or is there something special about the particular capacity of the application of information and communication technology that creates entirely new challenges requiring new forms of ethical responses.

10.2 Professional ethics and ICT

Professional bodies have traditionally sought to identify, value and reinforce ethical conduct on the part of their members. Membership of a professional body carries responsibilities and duties that are usually indicated in a code of professional conduct. Breaking the code of conduct can have serious repercussions for erring members.

An example of such a code of conduct in the information and communication technologies (ICT) field is that of the Computer Ethics Institute's 'Ten Commandments' for computer ethics:

1 Thou shalt not use a computer to harm other people;

2 Thou shalt not interfere with other people's computer work;

3 Thou shalt not snoop around in other people's files;

4 Thou shalt not use a computer to steal;

5 Thou shalt not use a computer to bear false witness;

6 Thou shalt not use or copy software for which you have not paid;

7 Thou shalt not use other people's computer resources without authorisation;

8 Thou shalt not appropriate other people's intellectual output;

9 Thou shalt think about the social consequences of the program you write;

10 Thou shalt use a computer in ways that show consideration and respect.

Apart from the obvious attempt to mimic the biblical Ten Commandments and the rather quaint use of language, this statement identifies a wide range of potential ethical dilemmas facing computer professionals. Computer networks are powerful tools used to store and transfer masses of data, including financial data and personal information. Those with the skills to create and maintain such complex systems also have the skills to pervert their use for personal gain.

The 'Ten Commandments' forbid doing damage to others, theft, lying, invasion of privacy, and unauthorised use of another person's property. They also require consideration and respect for others and a consequentialist or utilitarian consideration – the social consequences of one's actions. This is a broad range of ethical issues. It might be seen as too broad a statement, in that individual professionals have to interpret and apply the 'commandments' to their own particular circumstances or in the light of the particular issues they are facing.

The Association for Computer Machinery (ACM) has produced a fuller statement. This code contains the following eight 'general moral imperatives':

Contribute to society and human well-being. This principle affirms an obligation to protect fundamental human rights and to respect the diversity of all cultures, to minimize negative consequences of computing systems (including threats to health and safety), to ensure that products will be used in socially responsible ways, to meet social needs, to avoid harmful effects to health and welfare, and to seek to avoid any potential damage to the local or global environment.

Avoid harm to others. 'Harm' means injury or negative consequences, such as undesirable loss of information, loss of property, property damage, or unwanted environmental impacts. This principle prohibits use of computing technology in ways that result in harm to any of the following: users, the general public, employees, and employers. Harmful actions include intentional destruction or modification of files and programs leading to serious loss of resources or unnecessary expenditure of human resources, such as the time and effort required to purge systems of computer viruses.

Be honest and trustworthy. Honesty is an essential component of trust. Without trust, an organization cannot function effectively. The honest computing professional will not make deliberately false or deceptive claims about a system or system design, but will instead provide full disclosure of all pertinent system limitations and problems.

A computer professional has a duty to be honest about his or her own qualifications, and about any circumstances that might lead to conflicts of interest.

Membership in volunteer organizations such as ACM might, at times, place individuals in situations where their statements or actions could be interpreted as carrying the weight of a larger group of professionals. An ACM member will exercise care to not misrepresent ACM, or positions and policies of ACM, or any ACM units.

Be fair and take action not to discriminate. The values of equality, tolerance, respect for others, and the principles of equal justice govern this imperative. Discrimination on the basis of race, sex, religion, age, disability, national origin, or other such factors is an explicit violation of ACM policy and will not be tolerated.

Inequities between different groups of people may result from the use or misuse of information and technology. In a fair society, all individuals would have equal opportunity to participate in, or benefit from, the use of computer resources regardless of race, sex, religion, age, disability, national origin or other such similar factors. However, these ideals do not justify unauthorized use of computer resources nor do they provide an adequate basis for violation of any other ethical imperatives of this code.

Honour property rights including copyrights and patent. Violation of copyrights, patents, trade secrets and the terms of licence agreements is prohibited by law in most circumstances. Even when software is not so protected, such violations are contrary to professional behaviour. Copies of software should be made only with proper authorization. Unauthorized duplication of materials must not be condoned.

Give proper credit for intellectual property. Computing professionals are obligated to protect the integrity of intellectual property. Specifically, one must not take credit for others' ideas or work, even in cases where the work has not been explicitly protected by copyright, patent, and so on.

Respect the privacy of others. Computing and communication technology enables the collection and exchange of personal information on a scale unprecedented in the history of civilization. Thus, there is increased potential for violating the privacy of individuals and groups. It is the responsibility of professionals to maintain the privacy and integrity of data describing individuals. This includes taking precautions to ensure the accuracy of data, as well as protecting it from unauthorized access or accidental disclosure to inappropriate individuals. Furthermore, procedures must be established to allow individuals to review their records and correct inaccuracies.

This imperative implies that only the necessary amount of personal information be collected in a system, that retention and disposal periods for that information be clearly defined and enforced, and that personal information gathered for a specific purpose not be used for other purposes without consent of the individual(s). These principles apply to electronic communications (including electronic mail) and prohibit procedures that capture or monitor electronic user data (including messages) without the permission of users or bona fide authorization related to system operation and maintenance. User data observed during the normal duties of system operation and maintenance must be treated with strictest confidentiality, except in cases where it is evidence for the violation of law, organizational regulations, or this Code. In these cases, the nature or contents of that information must be disclosed only to proper authorities.

Honour confidentiality.   The principle of honesty extends to issues of confidentiality of information whenever one has made an explicit promise to honour confidentiality or, implicitly, when private information not directly related to the performance of one's duties becomes available. The ethical concern is to respect all obligations of confidentiality to employers, clients and users unless discharged from such obligations by requirements of the law or other principles of this Code.

This code is more detailed than the 'Ten Commandments' and gives clearer guidance to members of the ACM. However, it covers the same broad ethical terrain. The fundamental question, however, still remains. Are the ethical issues presented by the endemic use of computer systems in modern society any different in essence from those faced in earlier periods?

10.3   Organisations and ICT

Rogerson (1998) argues that the increased use of computer systems and networks presents major new, ethical challenges to individuals, organisations and society. He argues that usually new systems are not simply a matter of giving staff a better tool to do the same work, but involve changes to the nature of the work itself. This, in turn, changes the very fabric of the society in which we live. Careful planning and consultation are needed to implement new systems successfully. All those affected by the change must be involved in good time in an appropriate way. They may include customers, suppliers, regulators, business partners and members of the public, as well as employees.

Rogerson believes that, given the central and essential role of ICT in organisations, it is paramount that this ethical sensitivity percolates decisions and activities related to ICT. In particular, organisations need to consider:

- How to set up a strategic framework for ICT that recognises personal and corporate ethical issues

- How the methods for systems development balance ethical, economic and technological considerations

- The intellectual property issues surrounding software and data

- The way information has become a key resource for organisations and how to safeguard the integrity of this information

- The increasing organisational responsibility to ensure that privacy rights are not violated as more information about individuals is held electronically

- The growing opportunity to misuse ICT, given the increasing dependence of organisations on it and the organisational duty to minimise this opportunity whilst accepting that individuals have a responsibility to resist it

- The way advances in ICT can cause organisations to change their form (the full impact of such change needs to be considered and, if possible, in advance) and the way the advent of the global information society raises new issues for organisations in how they operate, compete, cooperate and obey legislation

- How to cope with the enormous and rapid change in ICT, and how to recognise and address the ethical issues that each advance brings.

Thus, there is an ethical agenda specifically associated with the use of ICT in organisations. Rogerson (ibid.) suggests that an organisation seeking to come to terms with this ethical agenda can do so by adopting the following methodology:

1 Decide the organisation's policy, in broad terms, in relation to ICT. This should:

- Take account of the overall objectives of the organisation, drawing from such existing sources as the organisational plan or mission statement

- Use the organisation's established values, possibly set out in its code of practice, for guidance in determining how to resolve ethical issues

- Set the scope of policy in terms of matters to be covered;

2 Form a statement of principles related to ICT that would probably include:

- Respect for privacy and confidentiality

- Avoid ICT misuse

- Avoid ambiguity regarding ICT status, use and capability

- Be committed to transparency of actions and decisions related to ICT

- Adhere to relevant laws and observe the spirit of such laws

- Support and promote the definition of standards in, for example, development, documentation and training

- Abide by relevant professional codes;

3 Identify the key areas where ethical issues may arise for the organisation, such as:

- Ownership of software and data
- Integrity of data
- Preservation of privacy
- Prevention of fraud and computer misuse
- The creation and retention of documentation
- The effect of change on people both employees and others
- Global ICT;

4 Consider the application of policy and determine in detail the approach to each area of sensitivity that has been identified;

5 Communicate practical guidance to all employees, covering:

- Clear definition and assignment of responsibilities
- Awareness training on ethical sensitivities
- The legal position regarding intellectual property, data protection and privacy
- Explicit consideration of the social cost and benefit of ICT application
- Testing of systems (including risk assessment where public health, safety and welfare, or environmental concerns arise)
- Documentation standards
- Security and data protection;

6 Whilst organisations have a responsibility to act ethically in the use of ICT, so to do individual employees. Those involved in providing ICT facilities should support the ethical agenda of the organisation and in the course of their work should:

- Consider broadly who is affected by their work
- Examine whether others are being treated with respect
- Consider how the public would view their decisions and actions
- Analyse how the least empowered will be affected by their decisions and actions
- Consider whether their decisions and acts are worthy of the model ICT professional.

This is clearly a massive agenda. For organisations, a major issue is who is best equipped to carry forward this agenda and ensure that the organisation's information and communication systems, their management and the application are made to correspond with ethical standards. Clearly, a major responsibility rests with the leaders of the organisation. However, it may be that the leadership lacks the technical expertise to ask the right questions and understand the significance of decisions made regarding particular systems and their implementation – until it is too late. For organisations to be able to respond effectively to the ethical agenda created by the massive increase in the use of ICT, those making the strategic decisions need to have sufficient expertise and understanding of the technical issues and possibilities to enable them to make informed and rational choices, and to defend the organisation's long-term interests and fundamental values.

10.4 Hacking

The computing professionals and those organisations making extensive use of computer systems have a legitimate concern with ensuring the accuracy, currency and security of the data held in their computer systems. The phenomenon known as 'hacking' presents them with serious challenges in the maintenance and protection of their information systems. (See Scenario 10.1.)

SCENARIO 10.1

Phishing

The increasing use of the Internet and communications technologies has created opportunities for criminal activity on a vast scale. According to Apacs, the UK trade payments provider, phishing attacks by web hackers seeking sensitive personal banking details soared by a factor of 80 times between January and September 2007. Their numbers, released in December, also suggested that the number of phishing attacks has surged since the summer.

High-profile cases, such as that involving the TJX Companies in the US, have also brought home the risks. The company, operator of TK Maxx discount retail stores in the UK, admitted in March 2007 that a security breach into its computer systems was more extensive than previously reported.

The growing problem of identity theft and fraud is estimated to cost the UK economy more than £1.7bn a year. As a result, security consultancies have seen demand for their services from a range of companies rise dramatically. Four of the top five retail banks now have an online identity verification service made by GB Group, from Chester, either under evaluation or installed in one or more of their divisions. The system works by crosschecking personal information provided by an individual at the point of acquisition against a comprehensive range of data sources, such as the electoral roll and information held by utility companies, and the server information complies with the Financial Services Authority. However, it also carries out checks for 32Red's website, which makes its money out of customers playing casino, poker and sports betting.

The financial services industry remains one of the largest corporate spenders on IT in the world. While retail banks look to combat methods of fraud, other institutions such as investment banks, hedge funds and pension funds increasingly rely on robust, reliable and sophisticated technology to conduct business and give them a competitive edge.

Long term business success relies on trust between buyer and seller. The impact of computer and internet based fraud on this trust is a major concern of businesses.

Caelli et al. (1989) provide two definitions of hacking:

1 *In programming, a computing enthusiast.* The term is normally applied to people who take a delight in experimenting with system hardware (the electronics), software (computer programs) and communication systems (telephone lines, in most cases).

2 *In data (information) security,* an unauthorised user who tries to gain entry into a computer, or computer network, by defeating the computer's access (and/or security) controls.

The second definition is the most widely used.

Hackers have regularly appeared in news stories during the last two decades. They have traditionally been presented as teenaged whizz-kids or insidious threats. In reality, it can be argued that there are different degrees of the problem. Some hackers are malicious, whilst others are merely naive and, hence, do not appreciate that their activities may be doing any real harm. Furthermore, when viewed as a general population, hackers may be seen to have numerous motivations for their actions (including financial gain, revenge, ideology or just plain mischief-making). However, in many cases it can be argued that this is immaterial as, no matter what the reason, the end result is some form of adverse impact upon another party.

Surveys conducted by the UK Audit Commission (Audit Commission 1990, 1994, 1998) consider the general problem of computer abuse (encompassing various types of incident including hacking, viruses, fraud, sabotage and theft) across a number of industries/sectors (including government, healthcare, banking, retail and education). The consequences of the incidents in terms of financial losses that may have occurred directly or indirectly as a result of the incidents are significant. It is, however, likely that other, less measurable consequences might also have occurred as a result (for example, disruption to operations, breaches of personal privacy or commercial confidentiality, and so on).

The Audit Commission's reports show a total of 56 reported hacking incidents in the UK in 1998, which constituted 11 per cent of all disruptive incidents. The resulting financial loss was £360,000. According to Warren and Furnell (1999), it is frequently speculated that the true figures might be much higher than this, but organisations are choosing to remain silent in order to avoid adverse publicity.

Warren and Furnell (ibid.) provide a list indicating the variety of the activities in which hackers have been known to engage. In many cases, there have been reported incidents of hackers not only gaining unauthorised access (that is, potentially breaching confidentiality), but also altering data or service provision (that is, affecting integrity and/or availability):

- Modification of medical records

- Breach of military systems

- Monitoring and alteration of telecommunications services.

Such breaches offer significant opportunities to inflict damage (both to organisations and individuals) and illustrate the nature of the hacker threat. Many systems are vulnerable and existing security can often be breached, even military sites.

The major ethical objections to hacking arise from breaches of confidential information and the alteration to information held on databases that might result in incorrect information being used for decision-making, thereby rendering some information unusable. The consequences for some organizations and individuals affected by changes made by hackers could be severe. The general effect of successful hacking attempts is to reduce the public level of confidence in computer systems, and this may have a long-term effect on business activity.

10.5   Ethics and the Internet

The creation and rapid expansion of the World Wide Web (Internet) raise ethical issues that go beyond those faced by professionals and leaders within organisations. The possibility of moral corruption of children through their access to pornographic material, chat rooms and discussion groups is one such concern. The restrictions placed on access to the Internet by governments anxious to protect their citizens from undesirable influence from alien cultures is another. The potential for fraudulent behaviour seems to be enhanced through the Internet, as does the ability of those in positions of authority to invade the privacy of employees or citizens. Control over the Internet can bring great power to those exercising that control. These are the main ethical issues surrounding the growth and use of the Internet.

10.5.1   Access to the Internet

An article posted by electricnews.net on *The Register* (an electronic newsletter, www.theregister.co.uk) on 26 September 2002 argued that a UK survey of parents whose children use the Internet showed that only a minority employ a filter to restrict access to certain websites.

The survey (conducted in late 2001 by the BBC, the Broadcasting Standards Commission (BSC) and the Independent Television Commission (ITC)) found that, while nearly 70 per cent of parents said they monitored their children's use of the Internet, only 32 per cent said they used a technical filter that limited access to certain kinds of websites. The survey concluded that the Internet as a medium raises more concerns and uncertainties than television for parents monitoring their children's media consumption.

Media publicity has made parents cautious about sites featuring pornography and paedophilia, and about chat rooms. Even when they were confident in their children's ability to regulate their own use of the Internet, they still worried about accidental exposure. However, when it came to actually controlling their children's usage, parents did very little, according to the survey findings. Most control, as with television, tended to be informal – such as placing the computer where it was visible or only the parent to being allowed switch on the computer. Parents in the survey felt this was the most effective way of balancing their anxieties with the educational potential of the Internet. Out of the 32 per cent of parents whose children were Internet users who said they used a technical filter of some kind (either software or ISP-based), around 62 per cent of this group thought they were effective, while 11 per cent thought it blocked too little.

Most parents felt that the current technical tools available for controlling their children's use of the Internet were too complex to install and lacked simple age categorisation. They wanted simple labelling and easy to use filtering systems. However, the propensity for accidental exposure meant that there was a greater urgency among many of the parents surveyed that more needed to be done to deal with the unregulated nature of the Internet.

'The whole issue of censorship and control has been left way behind by technology because, as soon as people got the Internet into the house, there was something so new and so different and potentially so dangerous for children in people's houses, and I don't think either the law or protection has really caught up with that', said one parent in the survey.

Some parents were aware of informal actions (such as using the history button, registering site warnings and using top-level domain names) but few knew about more effective parental or server-based control mechanisms (such as password protection or the Internet Content Ratings Association (ICRA). The study included interviews with 36 parents, carers and children from London, Solihull, Newcastle, Cardiff and Glasgow from homes with and without access to multi-channel television and the Internet. In addition, over 500 parents of children aged 5–16 years took part in the survey.

In most societies, a child is normally perceived as requiring protection from harm, especially in those areas where the child sees little, if any, danger. Parents and others have a responsibility to protect children. However, the question is how far this protection extends before it becomes unethical? When should people be able to make their own choices about how they use the Internet? Is there a danger that access to information and different perspectives can be prevented in the name of protection? Different societies define childhood in different ways. Rules regarding the age of responsibility, legal restrictions regarding the use of alcohol, the right to marry, the right to carry arms, the acceptance of responsibility for others and so on vary enormously between societies. So, different societies treat people of the same age in different ways. Childhood is not universally defined.

Should students in further or higher education (that is, after they have left the normal school system) be allowed unfettered access to the Internet or should their colleges or universities seek to restrict access. If so, on what grounds should this be done? Many colleges and universities, along with many employers, seek to restrict access to material considered to be undesirable or immoral: much of this is labelled pornography. Protecting adults against pornography raises a significant ethical issue. Adults are people who have achieved the right to decide for themselves: however, most societies seek to regulate the social and personal conduct of adults as well as children. This is done through legal, judicial and value systems. Acceptable conduct is socially defined and more or less rigorously enforced.

China has attempted to control access to the Internet by blocking access to certain search engines and by seeking to develop its own China Wide Web, which is used to prevent access to a large number of websites.

So, regulation of access to the Internet presents the same ethical issues that are involved in decisions taken by a society about acceptable conduct and how such conduct will be reinforced. The reality is that is impossible to police every point of access to the Internet, just as it is impossible to police every act of social interaction in complex societies.

10.5.2   Crime and the Internet

Fraud and identity theft through the use of the Internet are frequently reported, as Examples 10.1 and 10.2 demonstrate.

EXAMPLE 10.1

Information highway robbery

It became clear that I needed a new(er) PowerBook. Even with cable access, Amazon.com took 2.5 minutes to load. The computer matching my needs was hard to find. So I went to eBay. It was even slower than Amazon, but I persisted. In only an evening, I located an auction for the machine I wanted. I checked the seller's User Feedback, and it was pretty good, so I posted a bid.

Next day, eBay cancelled that auction: the seller was a fraud. Whoa, I thought, it's good to see eBay has sharp security procedures in place.

Those words would come back to taunt me.

I found another PowerBook being auctioned by someone screen-named 'Mypaltoo,' and made damn sure this one was praised by all eight previous customers. I entered that auction – and won!

The seller then identified herself by e-mail as Aleksandra Rubleva of Auburn, Wash., and insisted in very broken English that I make payment through a service called MoneyGram, which only takes cash. I didn't want to wait for a cheque to clear, most private individuals aren't equipped to take Visa, and for all I knew Russian emigrés don't believe in money orders. I sent Aleksandra Rubleva more than a thousand dollars. Never heard from her again.

After increasingly urgent e-mails went unanswered, I went to eBay. In mere hours, I was able to obtain Confidential Member Information on Mypaltoo – who, in reality, is a nice woman in Ohio named Gail. I phoned, and she was shocked and sympathetic: She hasn't visited eBay in more than two years. Someone hacked into eBay's password records and pirated her identity – and God knows how many others.

You'd think that – receiving input from a member inactive for two years, from a different state, using a different e-mail and IP address on a different computer containing none of the 'cookie' files eBay insists on placing on computers as a condition of membership – eBay might smell a rat. You'd be wrong. If it's taken any steps to detect identity theft, I can't imagine what they might be.

I managed to notify eBay of the fraud despite the procedures it provides for that purpose, which make voicemail look like fun. Finally, eBay said (a) it would launch an internal investigation, the results of which would not be shared with me, (b) reporting the matter to the authorities was my problem, and (c) I could ask for a token partial refund of $175 maximum – much less than I lost – but my claim must be filed no less than 30 days and no more than 60 after the fraudulent sale. And might not succeed.

Guess what law-enforcement authority has jurisdiction? The two-man RCMP detachment out here on my remote island (pop. 3,000), I swear to God. Corporal Greg Lui, an outstanding officer but no Internet maven, took my complaint, and has been diligent in updating me on progress. But we both know there won't be any.

On my own initiative, I posted feedback about Mypaltoo. For days, I received urgent e-mails from members confused because I said she was bogus, and eBay still listed her as legit. I was able to save them thousands. Apparently, it took eBay almost a week to deregister Mypaltoo.

When the statutory 30 days had passed, I'd already bought – without eBay – a new PowerBook. That 2.5-minute homepage now loads in six seconds. So I've only spent 12 hours of the past four days trying to file my Fraud 'Protection' Claim.

To apply, you must use the proper Fraud Protection Claim Form. It took me three attempts to secure one. The first two requests – hours each – produced autoresponse e-mails telling me I needed the form I'd just requested, and directing me to a place I'd already been where it didn't exist. It may be coincidental that I mentioned this newspaper on my third, successful attempt.

Then I submitted my claim – and, since I faxed it, was promised a decision in only three weeks. Two days later, eBay e-mailed me: my claim might be denied unless I supply the original auction page. Well, eBay knows that's impossible: It took that page down after the auction – 30 days ago. I faxed them that news.

Then I left home for two days. I returned to find the last straw, a two-day-old e-mail from eBay: it would cancel my claim within 72 hours unless I reconfirmed that it hadn't been resolved. Barely making the deadline, I assured them 'Aleksandra' had not spontaneously made restitution. And I started writing this column.

Apparently, eBay uses utterly ineffective security measures to protect its customers – and a brilliantly effective system for covering its own ass after the inevitable thefts occur, making even its inadequate token refund exquisitely difficult to obtain.

If, by some miracle, my $175 claim is granted, I'll have spent only $900 for an amusing e-mail – and wasted enough writing time to have earned five times that much money. If I were an investor thinking of putting money into online commerce, I'd be too stupid to have any money. Cyberspace is chock full of crooks – InfoHighwaymen – and the cyberauthorities clearly can't or won't stop them.

P.S.
After submitting this column, I sent eBay a copy for comment. Within two hours, someone named Duke (no last name) e-mailed to tell me my claim's been approved, and a cheque is you-know-where.
(Robinson 2002)

EXAMPLE 10.2

Fake bank website cons victims

West African criminals have used a fake version of a British bank's online service to milk victims of cash, say police.

The fake site was used to squeeze more money out of people they had already hooked.

The site has been shut down. But UK National Criminal Intelligence Service, (NCIS), said at least two Canadians had lost more than $100,000 after being taken in by the fake website.

The scam behind the fake web domain was the familiar one that offers people a share of the huge sums of money they need moved out of various African nations.

NCIS said the use of the web was helping the conmen hook victims that would otherwise spot the scam.

Convincing site

News of this latest scam was revealed by BBC Radio5Live. It found that an unclaimed web domain of a UK bank had been used by conmen to get more cash out their victims.

An NCIS spokesman said the domain looked legitimate because it had 'the' in front of the bank's name.

'I have seen the microsite myself and it's very sophisticated', said the NCIS spokesman. 'It's very convincing especially to people not very experienced online.'

Once the con was discovered, it was quickly shut down. However, the people behind it have not been caught.

NCIS does know that at least two people have lost more than $100,000.

The bank involved has bought up the domain used in the con, as well as many other permutations of its name, to limit the chance of it happening again.

'Web spoofing is going to be a big problem', said the NCIS spokesman.

Domain games

Usually people are first hooked in to what has become known as Advanced Fee or 419 fraud by replying to an unsolicited fax or e-mail offering a share of any cash successfully moved out of Africa.

The '419' refers to the part of the Nigerian penal code dealing with such crimes.

Like any con, there is no money to be moved at all and instead anyone taking the bait is asked to pay increasingly large sums to supposedly bribe uncooperative officials and to smooth the passage of the cash.

Although this con has been practiced for years, people still fall victim to it.

NCIS estimates that up to five Americans are sitting in hotel lobbies in London everyday waiting to meet people connected with this con.

Cutting edge fraud

Often, the conmen provide fake banking certificates to give the con an air of legitimacy.

But a spokesman for NCIS said fake or spoof websites are now being used in place of the certificates.

'To many people nowadays, the cutting edge of banking technology is web technology', said the spokesman.

One of the first groups of conmen to use this method set up a fake website that supposedly gave victims access to accounts held at the South African Reserve Bank, the country's national bank.

Typically, victims are given a login name and password, and are encouraged to visit the site so they can see that the cash they are getting a share of has been deposited in their name.

But before they can get their hands on the cash, the victims are typically asked to hand over more of their own money to help the transfer to go ahead.

Once the South African police discovered the ruse, they declared it a national priority crime and soon arrested the 18 people behind it.

Modern gloss

A briefing paper prepared by NCIS in August on organised crime noted that criminals were increasingly turning to the web to lure new victims and give old cons a modern gloss.

The NCIS spokesman urged people who have fallen victim to 419 fraud to come forward and help it track down the perpetrators. He said in the last two months it had arrested 24 people overseas involved with this type of fraud.

He said any e-mail, fax or letter making an offer that looks too good too be true, undoubtedly is.

One of the first companies to fall victim to website spoofing was net payment service Paypal.

Conmen set up a fake site and asked people to visit and re-enter their account and credit card details because Paypal had lost the information.

The website link included in the e-mail looked legitimate but, in fact, directed people to a fake domain that gathered details for the conmen's personal use.

(Report, www.bbc.co.uk, 8 October 2002)

Example 10.1 covers fraudulent dealing over the Internet (which caught out an intelligent and street-wise individual and is an example of the problems involved in policing the Internet. Example 10.2 involves the setting up of fraudulent websites that appear, at first sight, to be legitimate.

There is widespread concern about the way in which the Internet affects behaviour and encourages criminal activity. 'It's a place where crime is rampant and every twisted urge can be satisfied. Thousands of virtual streets are lined with casinos, porn shops, and drug dealers. Scam artists and terrorists skulk behind seemingly lawful Web sites. And cops wander through once in a while, mostly looking lost. It's the Strip in Las Vegas, the Red Light district in Amsterdam, and New York's Times Square at its worst, all rolled into one – and all easily accessible from your living room couch' (*Business Week Online*, 2 September 2002).

Illegal online gambling has mushroomed on the Internet. Despite online gambling being illegal in the United States, it is now estimated to be the eighth largest activity on the Internet in the USA (*Business Week Online*, ibid.). Illegal drugs are widely available over the Internet. Child pornography is easily available. Money scams and identity theft (as in Example 10.1) are common.

How does the Internet encourage criminal behaviour? First, it reduces transaction costs involved in fraud. It is possible to purchase email lists and to send out messages to all those on the list very simply. The fraudster needs just a few of those on the list to respond. Second, the Internet makes anonymity easier. It is possible to communicate on the web from anywhere in the world and to hide an identity beneath layers of addresses. Third, purchasing illegal goods and services on the Internet is a private act. No one can see you doing it (unless they are looking over your shoulder). Fourth, as the example above indicates, policing illegal activity on the Internet is very difficult.

It is difficult to know whether the Internet simply facilitates criminal behaviour by those who intend to behave in a criminal fashion or whether it encourages others, who would not normally behave in a criminal fashion, to do so. Is the Internet simply a technical tool that can be used for good or ill, or does it, by its very nature, encourage criminal activity? Clearly, the decision to behave criminally is taken by people. The opportunities to behave criminally may be increased by the Internet and the likelihood of discovery may be reduced (thus increasing temptation), but the decision to behave in a particular way is an individual one.

10.5.3 Email and privacy

The burgeoning growth of the use of email by organisations for both internal and external communication raises several ethical issues. The use of email to abuse another colleague (referred to as 'flame-mail') is one such issue. If abuse of another person would generally be regarded as unethical, in that it demonstrates an absence of respect for the other person, the use of 'flame-mail' is an example of such abuse. The difference is that email can make the abuse easier to deliver because it is not done face-to-face. The difference between an abusive email and an abusive letter ('snail-mail') derives from the spontaneity and instantaneous nature of email. Drafting a letter requires time, and time may cool tempers. Email has no such constraints.

However, the major ethical issue in relation to email is privacy. All systems managers have access to user files on their systems. Email is basically just a file that is stored in the user's system. The systems managers are able to examine all emails sent within and from the organisation. Some employers tell the user that mail might be monitored. Such organisations fear that users could be divulging confidential commercial information to competitors via email. Also, systems managers for the computer networks that receive emails from external sources are able to examine all incoming emails. This would take considerable effort on the part of the systems managers, but could be done. Public authorities can also perform the same filtering process.

So, email, as a communications system, has the potential to be very open and to lack complete privacy. Do employers have the right to invade the privacy of the communications of their employees? What rights do employees have to privacy at work? If it is commonly accepted that employees have the right to engage in private conversations during work hours, does this mean that they have the right to use email as a private form of communication? In this regard, email may be seen as analogous to traditional, written forms of communication. Are written memos and reports regarded as private, just a matter for the two persons in communication? Clearly, some are marked as confidential and have a restricted circulation; others are more widely circulated and regarded as public documents. However, no one person is able to monitor the complete range of written forms of communication within an organisation – unless they are able to open the envelopes and read all the contents. Email is different, in that one person – the system manager – is able to read the content of every email, whether marked confidential or not.

Encryption of emails involves using a program to scramble the contents of an email, which is unscrambled by the receiver using a key or password. The US government wishes to outlaw commercial encryption packages and wishes its own package (Clipper) to be used by all organisations and people using the Internet. This is for security reasons – to protect the best interests of the country and secure it from possible terrorist threats or highly illegal activity. The counter argument is that this would be an invasion of the citizen's privacy and be tantamount to introducing a society in which private communications are exposed to the gaze of the government machinery.

10.5.4   Freedom, justice and the Internet

In his essay *On Liberty* (1859), John Stuart Mill explains the nature of freedom. He argues that there are three basic freedoms: the freedom of thought and discussion; the freedom of tastes and pursuit of plans as long as others are not harmed; the freedom of uniting for any purpose except to harm others. Mill's view is often described as a 'negative' view of freedom, in that it rests on the absence of constraints. He argues that there should be no constraints on freedom other than the injunction that others should not be harmed in the exercise of freedoms.

Moor (1999) argues that freedom requires more than merely the absence of constraint. To exercise freedom properly, humans must have abilities, resources and opportunities to share their ideas and activities with others. Moor asserts that the worldwideweb amplifies our abilities, increases our resources and generates numerous opportunities for the exercise of a wide range of freedoms. The web is a freedom amplifier. The web allows not only the members of one society, but also people around the world to express their views, to pursue their interests and to unite with others.

The open and accessible nature of the worldwideweb makes censorship of alternative political and social views very difficult to impose. Traditional news and comment media such as TV, radio and newspapers are easier to manage, but anyone with a modem and Internet connection can post their own views for all to see.

Control over the web can bring with it great riches and great political power. For example, Microsoft's bundling of its Internet Explorer browser in its *Windows '95* software was challenged by rivals Netscape as a monopolistic device intended to drive consumers of software into Microsoft's hands. Governments, such as the Chinese government and several in the Middle East, attempt to censor and control their Internet critics by tracking and closing down critical websites and restricting access to Internet search engines. In the future, the group that controls the net will control what the world thinks and does. If the worldwideweb is to retain its open nature and its potential for critical views to be aired, then dominance by any business or governmental body will need to be avoided.

However, it is sometimes possible for those in the developed world to forget just how few of the world's population actually have access to the web – less than 4 per cent of the world's population, according to Moor. The distribution of current users of the web is not evenly spread. To access the web a user needs access to hardware, software and telecommunications: these are not evenly available throughout the world. In addition, most websites are in English, and non-English speaking parts of the world find the material inaccessible because of the language problem. Non-English website developers usually have to ensure that an English translation of their material is available, otherwise their access to potential markets is much reduced as web usage is concentrated in English speaking countries – particularly the USA.

Freedom of speech on the Internet can be a powerful tool in criticisms of those in power. However, such freedom of speech can sometimes verge on the libellous and abusive. For example, the extracts given in Example 10.3 are taken from a posting on www.salon.com. The article reported a court case going through the New York court system at that time.

EXAMPLE 10.3

Free speech and the Internet: a fish story

The plaintiff in the case of Robert Novak vs APD List Members, filed last May in a federal court in New York, seeks damages of more than $15 million. The FBI has even been notified, although there is no public evidence to date that it is conducting an investigation. But now the defense fund itself has become a legal target – and that raises questions of just what kind of comments are protected speech on the Internet, and how far a company can go in attempting to guard its trademarks. For [some], the lawsuit may be frivolous, aimed at stifling criticism, but for Robert Novak, the founder and owner of PetsWarehouse.com, the reputation of a company is at stake.

The Internet makes it easy to express your opinion; anyone who's ever been caught in the crossfire of an all-out flame war knows that. But does it make it too easy? And when litigation follows flaming words, how far will an online community go to fight back?

The hot water started with a simple post to an Internet mailing list frequented by people whose idea of a good time is growing plants under water.

> The chatter on the Aquatic Plant Digest (APD) mailing list typically runs to tame fare like algae, platyphylla, nematodes, snails and African frogs. But in typical online forum fashion, the aquarists also swap information about their experiences with the companies from which they've bought plants or supplies.
>
> On May 15, 2001, according to court documents, Dan Resler, a computer scientist at Virginia Commonwealth University in Richmond, posted a message that made a blunt recommendation: 'Thinking of buying plants from Pet Warehouse? Don't.' He went on to detail his gripes about the company's customer service, based on what he said was a delayed shipment of plants he'd ordered.
>
> Resler – apparently realizing he'd left out an 's' in his original post – later followed up with this amendment 'to clarify: Pet Warehouse OK, Pets Warehouse NOT.' In classic Net slambook fashion, other members of the list responded to Resler's messages by sharing their own experiences with Pets Warehouse. One post on May 22, 2001, as recorded in court documents, quotes Sean Carney of Weslaco, Texas, sloganeering: 'Remember petSWEARhouse, buy their plants and you'll be swearing.'
>
> (www.salon.com, 4 April 2002)

The posting of a complaint against a provider of goods and services on the Internet has the capacity to create a wave of similar responses from similarly disgruntled customers. The fact that anyone anywhere can read the complaints creates great pressure on businesses. A business might see what appears to be an orchestrated stream of complaints, decide that they constitute an attack on the reputation of the business and subsequently take action to protect that reputation. This is what happened in the case in Example 10.3. Robert Novak felt that he had to protect his business's reputation by taking out a lawsuit against his detractors. The complainers felt they had the right to say what they thought about the company in their discussion group. But their discussion group was on the Internet and therefore open to all to 'listen in'. Usually, in most legal systems, private discussions amongst friends are not seen as providing a basis for legal action. In this case, the discussion could be seen as taking place in a public arena, and consequently subject to legal rules regarding libel or slander.

▌ QUESTIONS AND TASKS ▌

1 Find out, from searching the Internet, how the Chinese government seeks to restrict access to the Internet amongst its own population. Then find out what the policies of the British government are in relation to access to the Internet. How do the two approaches differ? Do they have anything in common?

2 Find out what the policy of the British government is towards the use of encryption software in the use of email. Compare this with the policies of another European country of your choice. What are the similarities and differences?

3 Obtain a copy of your university or college's policy on the use of computers by students. Compare this to the 'Ten Commandments' or the ACM ethical statement. How does your institution's policy match up to either of these approaches? Could you suggest any changes?

CHAPTER 11

The Ethical Organisation and Strategic Management

After you have read this chapter, you will:

- Understand the relationship between strategic management and other functional areas

- Appreciate the ethical issues raised by:

    - Remuneration of senior post holders

    - Organisational structure

    - Globalisation

    - Missions and vision

- Realise the importance of stakeholder theory.

11.1 Introduction

Strategy is the area in which any organisation makes its most far-reaching decisions (in scope and time). Hence, one could argue that it is here that ethics also has its most decisive role to play. Since strategic decisions have a major integrative and directive role for the other functions, ethics at this level will also inform the ethics of other functions. Moreover, it is at the strategic level (articulated in mission statements, and aims and objectives) that the most fundamental questions about the ends and means of a business organisation are tackled:

Ends

What is the real purpose of this organisation?

- What is its scope to be?

- Where is it to be in five or ten years' time?

Means

How are we going to get there?

- What principles and values will guide the process of change?
- What limits will be put on how far the means can justify the ends?

(See, for instance, Example 11.1.)

EXAMPLE 11.1

Strategic management

In 2001, Switzerland's national airline collapsed because creditors would no longer supply fuel for its aircraft. The trial of all 19 members of the Board, which ended in Zurich in March 2007, revealed the self-delusion that destroyed the quality Swissair brand and tarnished the national reputation for reliability and efficiency.

Swissair's 'Hunter' project, adopted in 1997 under Philippe Bruggisser, the newly appointed Chief Executive, was to build a new global alliance led by Swissair and centred at Zurich. Never mind that the population of Zurich is only 350,000 or that, since Switzerland remains outside the European Union, Swissair did not enjoy the benefit of Europe's open skies: bizarrely, the 'Hunter' scheme was presented as an answer to this problem.

However, other airline partnerships had already been created by major airlines and Swissair had to focus on Sabena, Air Liberté and Volare as potential partners. These partners went bankrupt and Swissair's strategy cost it billions of euros.

According to *The Financial Times*, at no time did the strategy ever connect with reality. It appears that critics were slapped down. The Credit Suisse analyst who exposed the scale of the airline's liabilities claims he was forced to recant and was then fired. His boss sat on the Swissair board. In early 2001, Mr Bruggisser was dismissed, and a process of realising assets and containing liabilities began: but it was too slow and too late.

Former directors and executives in the Zurich courtroom tried to blame each other for the debacle. They said the problem lay not with strategy, but with execution. However, effective strategy is not separable from execution and is not based on visions and dreams but, rather, on a match between capabilities and activities.

All 19 defendants were cleared of financial malpractice but the prosecutors, in June 2007, were considering making an appeal to a higher court.

The relevance of the ethical nature of the answers to such questions can be seen in the enduring difference of many companies founded on self-consciously ethical lines, such as Quaker companies in the last century (Bradley, 1987). Other notable examples include the Co-operative Bank and Scott-Bader, and also smaller companies such as Traidcraft. What this points to is the power of those at the top of any business organisation (particularly its founders) to shape its strategy (for good or ill), and also to set the ethical tone of the organisation in terms of acceptable behaviour. Certainly, newspaper headlines of corporate misdemeanours have highlighted the involvement of very senior managers, not just because they make crucial strategic decisions, nor just because their high profile strongly links them with the organisation's reputation, but because the public now expects them to give ethical leadership as well. Strategic management can involve top-down decisions with critical outcomes such as closing certain plants, operating in different countries, management buyouts, mergers and acquisitions, major organisational restructuring, and so on. But strategic management can also depend on those lower down the organisation who have to own these changes and make them work; otherwise, even the most brilliantly conceived strategy will fail. A consideration of strategy and ethics therefore cuts across all levels of an organisation.

11.2 Significant ethical issues in strategic management

Ethical issues of particular concern in strategic management need to be discussed in relation to stakeholders. How stakeholder interests are balanced depends partly on the legal structure of business organisations so, to some extent, ethical issues in strategic management must be worked out within what is 'given'; however, this is not always adequate. MacIntyre (1977) argues that we live in an imperfect (and imperfectly structured) society, but that to live in such a society is something that can of itself be done well, or badly. If you want to ensure you do it badly, then either you say that the problems and injustices are not yours (and take a Friedmanite view of business and society), or you can say they are a legitimate concern but you cannot do anything about them. MacIntyre deems neither approach as morally adequate. From the point of view of far-reaching strategic decisions, business has an obligation both to work within the given structures and to go beyond them. The following therefore emerge as the most significant ethical issues in strategic management.

11.2.1 Setting the vision, aims and objectives

Although the linear approach to strategic management has come increasingly under fire (Stacey 1993; Mintzberg 1994), there seems little doubt about the importance that a strategic vision plays in strategy and ethics (Whittington 1993). This is usually articulated in the form of a mission statement. It seems it does not matter whether you write it down or not, so long as the company has thought long and hard about what the company is to be, and the rules and values it is to live by (Campbell and Yeung 1994). The ethical issue is: to what extent do other stakeholders have a right (or, even, duty) to be involved in developing and articulating the strategic vision that will greatly affect their lives? Success stories can suggest that a charismatic CEO who has this vision can do it all him/herself. 'Failure' stories point out the weakness of this approach; employees and other stakeholders are reluctant to make work a vision they had no part in developing. Employees, in particular, will have to live with the resultant organisational culture. Remembering that there is no such thing as a purely rational decision based on pure data and that all decisions have a significant value element (Andrews 1989), it seems desirable that more people than just the CEO and senior managers should be involved both on ethical grounds and on grounds of good strategic management.

11.2.2 Leadership and senior managers' remuneration

David (1991: 21) suggests that the very high salaries of those at the top of a business organisation are justified on the grounds that those people not only make the long-term success-or-failure strategic decisions, but also carry the 'moral risks' of the firm. Directors can be said to have a number of 'contracts' with other stakeholders (Canon 1994:88). For example, the 'knowledge contract' obliges them to use their competence and skill for the benefit of the enterprise as a whole; their 'efficiency contract' requires them to minimise waste and sustain effort–reward standards. They also have a 'psychological contract' to motivate and give recognition to stakeholders, and offer some security. Obviously these contracts are severely at risk when senior executives award themselves protectionist remuneration packages (golden parachutes and such), especially in the face of major company redundancies. In fact, the shareholder revolt in the case of GlaxoSmithKline (*The Times*, 20 May 2003) suggests that the contract is real and can be broken. We are back to stakeholders and the questions of 'Whose company is it anyway?' and 'For whose benefit is it to be run?'

Moreover, in terms of ethical leadership, 'managerial capitalism' sends certain signals cascading down through the organisation, sanctioning opportunist behaviour. There is no doubt that actions at the top of an organisation carry a heavy, symbolic and concrete element, that both contributes to the culture of an organisation and strongly influences what people understand as ethically acceptable behaviour in that organisation. If David's (1991) argument is right, what if moral leadership is not forthcoming? Remuneration committees are one way in which justice might be seen to be done; however, the continuing existence of a strong 'corporate veil' can easily subvert this (Chryssides and Kaler, 1993: 241–7). When such huge personal financial implications are tied up with strategic decisions, there must be an unreasonable temptation to compromise fiduciary duties, prejudicing the management of the company as a whole, with certain stakeholders unjustly losing out. This raises ethical issues of loyalty and the 'psychological contract'. (See Case Study 11.1.)

CASE STUDY 11.1

Settlement packages

Company X has seen a reduction in its share value of 50 per cent, with the consequent closure of some sites and a large tranche of redundancies. The current CEO has been voted out of office by a shareholders' meeting. However, the package she negotiated on joining the company stipulated that, in the event of her contract being terminated before its specified expiry date, she would receive compensation in the form of a one-off payment of three times her annual salary together with share options and a pension, at sixty, of one half of her retirement salary. The whole package is estimated to be worth £3 million. Since this is due to her by the terms of her contract, the board of directors have argued that it has no choice but to meet it.

(a) Should the shareholders oppose the settlement package?

(b) Should the law be changed to outlaw settlement packages of this kind?

11.2.3 Implementing strategic change

Strategic management often entails large-scale changes in the nature of our work, the people we have to work with, our workspace and lifestyles. The nature of change has altered in several ways in the twentieth century, not least in its speed and scope (Toffler 1970; Lynch and Kordis 1990). But regarding strategic management, there is another aspect of change that requires attention. Before the Industrial Revolution, when 80 per cent of the population worked on the land, people were used to change but in a different manner. The seasons changed regularly and reasonably predictably; there were occasional one-off changes such as earthquakes, floods and unexplained crop failures. The 'imposed' nature of such changes was accepted with resignation because they were 'acts of God'. Nowadays, though, many major changes (particularly in the nature of our working lives) are clearly imposed upon us by the acts of other humans and, as such, people are less ready to accept them as legitimate.

The ethical question in strategic change again draws on the notion of stakeholders who can legitimately ask to what extent the change is really necessary. Could a different strategic solution not be found that had fewer negative impacts? Does the factory have to close? Do I have to move 300 miles to a new location? The way these questions have been resolved in the past is simply by the exercise of raw stakeholder power. The option is that, if one does not like the changes, one is free to leave. Is this really ethically adequate?

11.2.4 Changes in ownership of the organisation

In the 1980s, a favourite strategy was growth through mergers and acquisitions; this, in turn, also generated an increasing number of management buyouts (MBOs) as unwanted parts of acquired businesses were sold off. More such activity took place in the early 1990s as companies re-appraised their strategies in the light of the recession and got back to their core businesses and competencies. The strategic rationale behind such moves has always been either to diversify or to gain a more dominant position within a particular industry. The latter rationale is subject to the Monopolies and Mergers Commission (MMC), but the former has mainly gone ahead without much scrutiny.

What has been left out of the debate is an ethical view of such activities (Cooke and Young 1990: 254–69). Historically, takeovers involved a healthy company rescuing a failing one, but now even the most healthy company may be subject to a takeover bid. Although many acquisitions are friendly and mutually beneficial, hostile takeovers have increased. Does the maxim: 'The strong do what they will, the weak do what they must' always have to apply? Another ethical issue is that of 'corporate raiders', who use the threat of a takeover to force the target company to buy back shares at a premium – a technique known as 'greenmail'. Not surprisingly, such activities have provoked defensive strategies such as 'poison pills', whereby various tactics ensure that the potential buyer will have to put up a disproportionate amount of capital in order to gain a controlling interest. An ethical issue here is: what is the cost in time, energy and money of all this, and would stakeholders not be better served without the attitudes that drive such behaviour? Who really are the stakeholder winners and losers in all this activity? Moreover, will the merger genuinely enhance the company mission? Synergy gains are not automatic, let alone resolution of the problems involved in merging two company cultures and management styles. Above all, how does the concept of company loyalty (to and by employees) fit with all this?

11.2.5   Global strategic operations

The growing size and geographical scope of business organisations has been perhaps the key feature in postwar economic development. A number of Multi-National Companies (MNCs) wield more financial muscle than the GNP of some countries (Goyder 1993: 4). Legally, MNCs can be everywhere and nowhere, as they transcend national legal frameworks and tax authorities. They can invest rapidly having a major effect on the local communities of the host countries; and they can pull out almost as fast as comparative and competitive advantage is sought on a global playing field. Indeed, some developing host countries deliberately lower their employment standards in order to attract companies, and their less-developed consumer regulations invite the dumping of unsafe or inappropriate products.

The key ethical question in global strategic management is simply: when in Rome, should one do like the Romans? (Bowie 1990). The issues go beyond mere cultural sensitivity (for example, should Europeans be obliged to go without alcohol in an Arab country?). They go beyond whether a westerner should offer bribes in order to get a sales contract. They concern the level of employment rights and safety standards when operating a plant in another country; one might easily achieve the host country's standards, but be quite far below the standards of one's own country. Should a chemical banned in one country be sold in another that legally allows it? Which standards should be adopted – or perhaps some standard in between – and why? One answer to such problems may be a form of relativism (see section 4.3). (See Case Study 11.2.)

CASE STUDY 11.2

Fair trade and pricing

Company Y buys components of its cosmetic product from a developing country in South America. It wishes to pay a fair price to the producers of these components. However, if it were to buy at what would be their market price in Europe, the farmers would earn in a month what their peers in the country earn in a year. Not only would this be a serious disincentive to the farmers to produce the quantities that company Y requires, it would also hugely distort the local economy for other goods.

(a) Should the company pay a fair (European) price?

(b) If it decided to, how should it act to avoid ruining the local economy?

(c) If the company decided not to, how might it rescue its fair trade reputation?

11.3 Illustration: Strategic visioning and mission statements

Ordinary employees of Traidcraft developed the company's statement of objectives over a six-month period. The executive directors attended very few meetings, believing that the staff should decide what the business was all about. Their mission states:

> Traidcraft aims to expand and establish more just trading systems, which will express the principles of love and justice fundamental to Christian faith.

> Practical service and a partnership for change will characterise the organisation which puts people before profits.

Its objectives are listed under five main headings:

1 Just Trade – Fairer systems;

2 Just Trade – Developing people's potential;

3 Just Trade – More and better jobs;

4 Just Trade – Fairer relationships within Traidcraft;

5 Just Trade – Efficient and practical structures. (Evans, 1991: 875)

Compare this with IBM's mission statement given by the CEO, Louis Gerstner:

> IBM's mission is to be the world's most successful and important IT company, helping customers apply technology to solve their problems. IBM's success will be based on being the basic resource for much of what is invented in this industry.

IBM's strategic imperatives (objectives) are based on:

Exploiting technology much better

Increasing market share

Re-engineering the way value is delivered to customers

Rapid expansion in key emerging geographic markets

Using size to achieve cost and market advantages.

It is clear that the process of arriving at, and the content of, these two sets of mission statements and objectives will send different ethical messages down through their respective organisations. Although the examples compare a David with a Goliath, the principles remain valid. The IBM example sets a tone of self-aggrandisement, the use of corporate muscle and an implicit assumption of profits before people.

Compare these with the middle road, a medium-sized organisation such as the British Airports Authority (BAA). After wide consultation, they arrived at the following mission statement:

BAA's mission is to be the most successful airport company in the world. This will be achieved by always focusing on customer needs and safety, and by seeking continuous improvements in the quality and costs of service. The company culture will enable BAA employees to give of their best.

BAA's chairman Sir John Egan stated that their mission statement made BAA's intentions absolutely clear. Their mission statement evolves continually.

It is clear that strategic management starts with articulating and communicating a vision of what a business organisation is to be all about. The mission, aims, and objectives, and their interpretation, are all influenced by people's values and ethics (in turn influenced by existing organisational forces). Strategic management is also about real change, which requires changes in beliefs, values and assumptions – a change in ethical orientation. In short, ethics dictate strategy formulation. There appears to be no reason why any stakeholders should be excluded from having some sort of say in what the organisation's mission is to be, or in how the changes are achieved.

11.4   Principles underlying an ethical approach to strategic management

11.4.1   Stakeholder theory, strategy and ethics

Stakeholder theory stems from the suggestion that business should be regarded as an activity made possible by social structures. Hence, business has responsibilities to a much wider range of stakeholders than merely its shareholders, directors and creditors. It therefore raises the question of whether those who are affected by a company's strategic decisions should have a say (at some level) in the process by which those decisions are reached. It therefore challenges (or seeks to qualify quite significantly) the traditional belief that a manager has the sole right to manage, and raises questions about responsibility and accountability. Stakeholder theory is also an attempt to avoid the view that ethics can be simply 'bolted-on'. This stems from the very persistent basic picture of self-understanding that the business community has about itself, which is the organisation doing its best to 'survive' in a 'hostile environment' (Davies 1992:1–40). The danger with a wide acceptance of this approach is that it promotes the habit of seeing strategy merely as a reaction to internal and external threats (which, where they have an ethical dimension, need responding to in the same manner – in ethical terms). Ethical strategy then becomes a kind of veneer forced upon businesses by various stakeholders. Ethical policies are therefore only acceptable when they contribute to good business sense in the prevailing climate; if this requires being ethical, then so be it.

An alternative way of looking at ethics, strategy and stakeholders is to view business as having a pro-active role in creating an ethical society (Goyder 1993).

The argument is that business activity is such a pervasive and powerful force in contemporary life, shaping lifestyles and expectations, that, even if it is an unwanted responsibility acquired merely by historical default, it can no longer legitimately understand itself as essentially a narrow universe of accounting goals separate from society.

11.4.2 Loyalty and the psychological contract

Strategic change often breaches what is known as the 'psychological contract'. This is implicit in the relationship between every employer and employee, and is often couched in terms of loyalty. There are philosophical problems with the notion of loyalty to 'an organisation' (Ladd 1982; Baron 1991), but it is still a key perceived element of the psychological contract. Employees will have built up certain expectations about how they will be treated (based on personal relationships with organisational members). They are then prepared to make sacrifices for 'the organisation' in return. All changes require sacrifice of time and energy; but changes in ownership often additionally shatter the relationships with key people on which someone's psychological contract is based. A new owner buys the assets and liabilities of a company, but what expectations of loyalty to, and from, does it also 'buy' in that same transaction? Overnight, many years' worth of 'loyal' sacrifices for 'the company' may count for nothing: a whole level of management may be removed en masse regardless of the actual contributions and competence of the individuals concerned; a whole factory might be closed by the new owner just because it is now considered strategically to be in the 'wrong' geographical location. Whilst shareholders may gain, a lifetime employee may lose their job. There is a question of justice here. Why should the latter suffer more than the former; if such actions become commonplace, why should an employee have any loyalty for the new employer? But successful strategies require strategic change, and this, in turn, requires the commitment, energy and creativity of the organisational members – in other words, their loyalty, underpinned by perceptions of their psychological contract. The ethical issue therefore lies in persuading people that the changes are legitimate. If their own perceptions of the psychological contract remain unbroken, then a sense of loyalty to the company will continue.

11.4.3 Cultural relativism

One solution to the problem of how to react to differing cultural standards has been to accept what is known as 'cultural relativism', which means that one should adopt the norms of the country where one is. In other words, you cannot take moral beliefs across national borders (Donaldson 1989; Bowie 1990). If bribes are part of normal business practice, then that fact must be accepted. At first, cultural relativism seems plausible enough. But, to be a genuine cultural relativist, one must accept any practices within national cultures, across time, and even hypothetical situations, however extreme. Jailing a thief is no better (or worse) than chopping off their hand; the old Samurai practice of testing a new sword by cutting an innocent traveller in half is acceptable; one would even have to accept the sacrificing of first-born children to 'the gods', were it a national cultural practice. If an unequivocal endorsement cannot be given to all these situations, then one is not a cultural relativist. The moment this admission is made, (that some practices are universally wrong, no matter what the supporting cultural belief system) then we have to look elsewhere for some international framework to guide the strategic actions of MNCs when operating in other countries (Donaldson 1989). Cultural relativism means more than merely having to make difficult choices: it can lead to truly impossible ones. For a cultural relativist, the view, in one country, that bribery is acceptable, must be accepted. However, the relativist must also accept that, in another, it is not. For a relativist, therefore, bribery is both unacceptable and acceptable: nothing (or anything) follows from such a position.

As globalisation becomes a fact of life, being a global player is an increasingly important strategy for continued long-term survival, so the difficult ethical issues surrounding cultural relativism and the regulation of MNCs are likely to increase. But ten or more years' worth of negotiations have so far failed to produce any UN Code of Conduct for Transnational Corporations (Donaldson 1989). Some better way of coping with cultural diversity is still needed. As a possible starting point, during the 1990s MNCs, and most other businesses, began to acknowledge serious acceptance of the arguments of environmental rights; so why not human rights?

11.5   Conclusion

As pointed out in the introduction, first and foremost, strategic management addresses fundamental questions about a business organisation's purposes, its ends and means. But the strategic question: 'What is to be the purpose of this organisation?' is informed by assumptions and beliefs about a deeper question: 'What should the purpose of business organisations be anyway?'

The answer to this question has, for many years, been strongly influenced by the legal status of companies, which has in essence remained unchanged for well over one hundred years (Goyder 1993). The Companies Act of 1862 recognises only shareholders, creditors and directors: this remains the same today. It was made long before the world of MNCs, the welfare state, trades unions, giant privatised monopolies and social expectations of certain democratic rights. Company law does not recognise shop-floor workers, technicians, managers and wider stakeholders: it is now wholly out of line with social reality and expectations.

To this extent, debates about the moral status of corporation (can companies be held criminally negligent?) and corporate governance (the Cadbury Report) are unable to get to the heart of the matter because both company law and beliefs about the general purpose of business organisations have not been radically re-examined and updated. The growth in the stakeholder concept is an attempt at second best, given the above. No legal framework exists to give the ethical position support, force and credibility.

Although, ultimately, ethics drive strategy, business still suffers from a low status, being viewed only as a quasi-profession. With the traditional professions, the driving ethic is easy to identify. For law, it is justice; for medicine, it is health (and the Hippocratic oath); for the priesthood, it is spirituality. What is it for business? No one single ethical concept springs easily to mind. Suggestions such as sustainable development will remain sidetracked until there are legal changes, such as in the annual reporting of results. If wages were on the profit side (contributing to the economy), and businesses' free use of 'the commons' were properly costed in, then the ethics that drive business strategy would be taken more seriously.

QUESTIONS AND TASKS

1 Which would be better: for the senior management to devise and promote strategy, or for it to wait and see what emerge from consultations with the workforce?

2 'When in Rome, do as the Romans do': but what if they do not all do the same thing?

3 What would be the ideal mechanism for determining the remuneration packages of senior executives?

CHAPTER 12

The Ethical Organisation and Purchasing

After you have finished this chapter, you will:

- Appreciate the range of ethical beliefs held by purchasing staff

- Understand the issues raised by the purchasing function

- Be able to apply ethical theory to problems arising within purchasing.

12.1 Introduction

At one time, it was not uncommon for Christmases in certain households to be marked by the influx of quantities of spirits, cigarettes, turkeys and other small gifts: these were offered by suppliers of materials and equipment to the owners or managers of businesses. At the time, it was not thought at all odd that someone in a position to determine highly lucrative purchasing contracts was bombarded with gifts. The bottle of whisky was simply a courtesy gift, thought of as little more than a consumable Christmas card. As Rudelius and Buchholz (1979: 3) put it: 'a bottle of whisky at Christmas may be acceptable, but a case smacks of a bribe'.

The purchasing function of modern organisations has changed from a relatively low status, clerical role to that of a strategic business function. This is due in no small measure to the increasing importance of material costs in the total production function and is allied to developments such as just-in-time (JIT) supply and total quality management (TQM) within production operations. These have led the way in changing the traditional adversarial relationship between supplier and buyer into one of partnership purchasing, which works best when there is open communication and trust. Parallel to this change in the status of purchasing as a business function have been changes in the quality of those employed in purchasing. There has been a rise in the educational base of buyers and a greater willingness to seek professional qualifications as an aid to a more professional approach. Alongside this has gone increased attention to ethics, reflected in the growth in the number of codes of ethics in existence and company policies for ethical purchasing. However, there is evidence that unethical practices persist and continue to cause concern.

Purchasing managers occupy a boundary-spanning role where, inevitably, they have to face situations where they must judge what is right (ethical) and wrong (unethical). Buyers can, by their actions, affect the company's profitability and reputation (Barr 1993). Therefore, maintaining a strict ethical stance can be important in projecting the right image of the company. Other business functions remain sceptical of the honesty and independence of buyers, whilst gift giving and entertainment remain endemic in purchasing. Dubinsky and Gwin (1981) reveal how relatively little attention has been paid to perceptions of buyers, and their ethical standards, by their peers. Many of the issues of ethical concern in business arise within the purchasing function: deception, bribery, price rigging, unsafe products and public safety. In many ways, the purchasing function has been the forgotten function of business – unseen, disregarded and undervalued – and this has been reflected in the status and salaries (and perhaps the ethical standards) of the professionals involved. Furthermore, there is a surprising dearth of published studies of purchasing ethics when compared to the much larger literature available, for instance, on marketing ethics (Murphy and Laczniak 1981).

12.2 Ethical issues in purchasing

Forker and Janson (1990) argued that, though the evidence needed interpreting with care, their research indicated that purchasing personnel adopt high ethical standards. This reinforces the conclusions of Browning and Zabriskie's (1983) study that: (1) buyers are ethical in their dealing with salespeople; (2) buyers' actions are more ethical than their beliefs; and (3) younger, better educated buyers were more ethical than their older, less well educated colleagues. Nonetheless, this study, and that of Forker and Janson, still uncovered evidence that buyers continued to accept gifts and entertainment. Sibley (1979) examined the image held of the purchasing department by themselves in comparison with the image held of it by other departments in one organisation. His study revealed the importance ethics can play in forming images of the professionalism of different groups. He argued that the continued practice of accepting gifts from vendors created an image among their colleagues that purchasing staff were vendor-loyal, though this was not part of the image purchasing personnel held of themselves. Rudelius and Buchholz (1979) reflect the concern of purchasing personnel themselves to adopt more ethical practices when they reported their desire for more top management guidance on ethical concerns. The purchasing managers they surveyed readily distinguished which of the scenarios raised ethical concerns. They also argued, dubiously, that only the acceptance of high value gifts had ethical implications.

Ramsey (1989) and Barry (1992) and Narayanam (1992) all reflect this tendency amongst purchasing personnel to regard some favours as acceptable, whilst others are clearly not.

CASE STUDY 12.1

Favouritism

Gary Brown was a newly appointed purchasing manager at Culcutt Engineering, reporting to Alan Fitzgerald, the General Manager. The company operated a system of first line suppliers who enjoyed stock orders, and a number of second line suppliers to fill in shortages. Gary was given complete discretion on the selection of second line vendors and the volumes that were to be given to them. After a number of months, it became clear that Fitzgerald took an interest in the second line spend and offered Gary favourable comments on the price and service of one particular supplier. Shortly afterwards, a representative of this company called and commented that the figures were a little low and unlikely to qualify for the holiday this year: 'It would be a shame if your General Manager missed it this year.' What should Gary do?

CASE STUDY 12.2

Pressure

Bill Lancaster was the Purchasing Officer of Denver Components Ltd. During an average week, he received calls from up to twelve representatives, though he did not always grant them a hearing. Bill was a member of CIPS and prided himself on the professional standards he set in his work. He was therefore taken aback when one representative he had known for a number of years, Gerald Aspey of Deakin Steel Stockholders, suggested that Bill reveal information he had on the prices of other steel suppliers to enable Deakin to undercut them. In return, they would offer Bill's company information on their competitors. Gerald and Bill had a cordial working relationship that, up to this time, had been strictly professional, with only gifts of minor value having previously been offered and accepted. Deakins was a good competitive supplier who received the bulk of Denver's order for steel. However, Bill had heard that their new owners were aggressively pushing for increased sales. What should Bill do?

The evidence that purchasing is still plagued with unethical buyers is readily available. Rudelius and Buchholz (1979), Dubinsky and Gwin (1981) and Felch (1985) all provide lists of the common unethical practices prevalent in purchasing. Most of the evidence comes from the USA, although there are one or two articles published in the UK and a preliminary study conducted by Wood in 1994. Only Barry (1992), in a UK study, strikes a dissenting note in observing that buyers are increasingly saying 'no' to lavish gifts and entertainment. Certainly, he provides evidence that major companies, such as Whitbread and Allied Dunbar, are tightening their policies on the acceptance of gifts or entertainment by their buyers.

The offering of free gifts, free meals or free entertainment appears still to be widespread both in the USA (see Forker and Janson 1990) and in the UK (see

Ramsey 1989; Wood 1994). It remains the most frequently cited issue of ethical concern in purchasing. Ramsey (1989) and Narayanam (1992) argue that the giving of gifts is endemic in purchasing. Narayanam (1992:25) states boldly: 'There is no denying the fact that bribery is rampant among professionals and that not much is done to combat the evil.'

Forker and Janson (1990) report on the 1987 study commissioned by Ernest & Whinney in the USA in which they compared replies to this survey with one taken in 1975. In 1987, no fewer than 97 per cent of the respondents had accepted one or a small number of favours (gifts or entertainment), whereas only 79 per cent had done so in 1975. The mean value of those favours was also higher (though that might be purely a reflection of inflation). However, the frequency with which offered favours were accepted was lower in 1987 than in 1975. Wood (1994) reported that 82 per cent of the respondents who reported unethical practices mentioned the giving of gifts, free hospitality or free holidays.

Many of these gifts are of such low value that they do not appear to be designed to gain undue influence. Yet, Ramsey (1989) argues for 'no bribes please' (in his article) and he describes gifts or offers of entertainment as *unprofessional characteristics* that the buyer considers in making the purchase decision compared with *professional characteristics* such as delivery, price or quality. He strongly emphasises that the professional buyer does not accept gifts of any value and stays firmly at what he calls the 'righteous' end of his spectrum of purchase characteristics. Supporting evidence on the continuance of the practice of offering sales inducements – or bribes, as Ramsey calls them (1989: 33) – is found in Rudelius and Buchholz (1979), Dubinsky and Gwin (1981), Barry (1992) and Wood (1994). The Chartered Institute of Purchasing and Supply (CIPS 1977) allows its members to accept gifts of very low value – such as pens and calendars, which are primarily promotional materials. However, Ramsey sees gifts of alcohol or chocolates – particularly prevalent at Christmas – as bribes, even if ineffective ones. Gifts such as expensive holidays in exotic locations, or even cars, might be more blatant but should be seen as different in degree rather than kind from other gifts.

Why are buyers so reluctant to employ the word 'bribe'? Ramsey (1989: 33) argues it is because buyers recognise that using the word 'bribe' suggests a willingness to be influenced. They go to elaborate lengths to explain how the 'gifts' do not influence them, and refuse to see the gifts for what they are – which, according to Ramsey, are bribes. The purpose of giving a gift to a buyer is to gain influence, and the value of the gift is irrelevant to that intention. Gifts of low intrinsic value should be seen merely as inefficient means to achieve influence, but that does not alter their purpose. Ramsey calls on purchasing departments to come clean and call a bribe a bribe: 'If a company feels that it is acceptable for their purchasing staff to receive bribes, then that is their business, but at least let them have the guts to be honest about it (ibid.: 33).

We might want to question whether it is entirely their own business, but the meaning of Ramsey's stricture is clear. He continues: 'They should give all their suppliers a break and put up a board in the company's reception area stating "Our purchasing department accepts bribes." This would simplify everything and cut out the need for all of the basic ritualistic behaviour that goes on around Christmas' (Ramsey 1989: 33).

However, many of the studies indicate (Rudelius and Buchholz 1979; Forker and Janson 1992) that the vast majority of purchasing managers are honest and ethical. In Wood's (1994) survey, many managers expressed their resentment at the offering of gifts, even those of low value. Sibley (1979) and Ramsey (1989) would retort that the image of purchasing managers held by their managerial peers is very much coloured by the prevalence of the giving of gifts.

The second major area of concern covers a number of practices that can be placed under the generic heading of 'deception'. Purchasing personnel can, and do, exaggerate the difficulties their company is experiencing to place undue pressure on suppliers, either to cut prices or improve non-price factors. Rudelius and Buchholz (1979) and Dubinsky and Gwin (1981) report that this practice causes considerable concern to purchasing managers themselves. Those purchasing managers who adopt a professional approach to their work regard this practice as unethical, likewise with the allied practice of inventing competition purely as a ruse to pressure suppliers on current price or quality and delivery. One purchasing manager described this as a pressure tactic to 'see what they will give' (Wood 1994). Other deceptive practices include calling for quotations, or even pre-sales services, where there is no intention to offer orders subsequently – or even, in some instances, recompense for the pre-sales services. Suppliers find it difficult to object to such practices because proof is not readily available, and objections at the time might sour relations for the future. The development of a partnership approach to purchasing (Clutterbuck et al. 1992), where a fully open relationship is developed between suppliers and purchasers, helps to eliminate many of these deceptive practices.

A third major group of issues in purchasing ethics relates to discrimination, particularly in the form of showing favouritism toward certain suppliers. The basis of discrimination can vary: for instance, favouring those suppliers who are also good customers; favouring any supplier known to be favoured by senior management; giving orders on the basis of personal preferences; the practice of allowing suppliers to deal directly with other departments that do not adopt a strict professional approach to procurement. All these practices work against the development of a professional ethic by purchasing managers. These practices may prevent a company obtaining supplies on the most favourable terms available. It can make the choice of supplier arbitrary rather than the result of open and free competition. However, for the purchasing professionals themselves, the practice that causes greatest concern is when other departments are allowed to deal directly with suppliers. In the survey by Wood (1994), 20 per cent of respondents registered their resentment to this practice.

The final broad grouping of unethical practices in purchasing relate to the issue of information disclosure. There are various studies reporting a number of practices, all of which breach confidentiality (see Dubinsky and Gwin 1981; and Felch 1985, for instance). Some suppliers seek information on their competitors with the implied promise it will be of benefit to the purchaser. Purchasing managers themselves divulge information to favoured suppliers, not having obtained the relevant permission to release such information in this form. Companies openly reveal the price of the current supplier to create a 'Dutch auction' in which other suppliers compete to offer the lowest price. Finally, some companies operate a tendering system in which the criteria for selection are released to some suppliers but not others.

The growth of the corporate hospitality industry over the last ten to fifteen years is further evidence that the practice of sales inducements is not necessarily dying out, merely changing its form. Corporate hospitality is a highly effective marketing tool, and Robson reports on a survey by Business Marketing Services that indicated corporate hospitality is more effective in attracting business than are advertising, direct mail, brochures or exhibitions in influencing customers (Robson 1992: 28). Robson also quotes the Marketing Manager of Keith Prowse Hospitality as saying that the targeting of corporate hospitality is impeccable. The whole issue of corporate hospitality, whatever its effectiveness, is fraught with ethical problems. The whole tenor of the approach suggests that it is a 'hard sell in a soft package', where half the purpose is to get customers to drop their objectivity in viewing products or services. If the case against the unethical nature of corporate hospitality is not already clear, then Business Marketing Services note that some companies do not use it with new clients because 'they feel it is too direct and perhaps too close to bribery' (Robson 1992: 28). Given the foregoing, it is hardly surprising that Barry is able to report David Sheridan (former purchasing chief at Whitbread) as saying: 'it is almost impossible not to suffer some softening up as a result' of accepting a supplier's goodwill (Barry 1992: 24).

Buyers must remember that there is no such thing as a free gift, for the cost of such gifts or any entertainment is ultimately borne by their employers in the price of the goods they buy. Corporate hospitality is expensive, but it is also a normal marketing expense for the companies who provide it for customers and clients, therefore it will be reflected in the price.

12.3   Codes of ethics and purchasing

Browning and Zabriskie (1980) report that 90 per cent of their respondents stated that their companies had a policy on ethics. Forker and Janson (1990) reported that 72 per cent of companies in the Ernest & Whinney survey had company ethics policies, though this was a reduction on the 78 per cent reported in the 1975 survey. Bradley (1989) reported that 72 per cent of the companies in his survey had formal ethics policies or codes. Barry (1992) gives specific examples of codes in action in leading UK companies.

Further, both professional bodies for purchasing professionals in the UK and USA have had formal codes of ethics or practice for some considerable time; in the case of the Chartered Institute of Purchasing & Supply (CIPS) in the UK, their code dates from 1977. Browning and Zabriskie (1980) recorded that a majority of the respondents to their survey were aware of the code of the National Association of Purchasing Management, the American professional body. Similar evidence concerning the awareness of the CIPS code amongst purchasing personnel is not available for the UK. Nonetheless, evidence is given in Barry (1992) and Clutterbuck et al. (1992) that public and private organisations

are attempting to tackle some of the more common problems of unethical practices in purchasing – for instance, on the acceptance of gifts and entertainment.
Bradley found that only 35 per cent of the companies he surveyed had specific
ethics policies for purchasing, which might suggest the need for a more tailored
policy to deal with the specific problem of ethics in this area. Rudelius and
Buchholz (1979) and Sibley (1979) offered some support for this observation
when they reported their respondents as pleading for much more policy guidance
on ethical issues in purchasing from their organisation's top management.

12.4 Examples

Examples 12.1 and 12.2 (fictitious, but realistic) illustrate situations very common in purchasing. Both explain the ways in which purchasing personnel are
often pressurised to act unprofessionally and unethically.

Gary Brown faces a dilemma that many purchasing managers strongly resent,
whilst that faced by Bill Lancaster tends to be regarded as more of a nuisance
by purchasing managers. Brown would want to be loyal to his general manager
but would not want to take unprofessional characteristics into account in his
decisions on second line suppliers. He could discuss the situation with Alan
Fitzgerald, setting out his objections to the approach from the supplier, but
would probably feel inhibited from so doing. This is a situation where a company
code of ethics, with specific provisions for purchasing, would assist a manager
in resolving his difficulties. In the real case, the supplier was highly competitive
so they obtained many orders as of right, but Brown decided not to artificially
engineer orders just to allow the general manager to win the holiday.

For Bill Lancaster his already cordial relationship with Gerald Aspey should
allow him to explain his objections to giving any information on other suppliers
because it is unethical. Again, a company code would offer good support here
to a manager in this situation. Clearly, Lancaster, as a member of the CIPS, has
recourse to their code, which specifically forbids this sort of trading of information. Deakin Steel and Gerald Aspey must be told that orders are given on the
basis of price, quality, delivery and other relevant factors, but on no other basis.

12.5 Ethical principles in purchasing

A cursory knowledge of the major ethical theories is sufficient to be able to
conclude that most of the practices described in this chapter are unethical, even
if they are legal. Most of the practices involve some form of bribery, corruption or
deception, all unethical. There is, perhaps, one exception to this assertion, in that
managerial egoism generally allows any form of behaviour if it is in the actor's
self-interests. This can be interpreted as the individual's or the organization's
interests, but it should be readily apparent to the reader now that such a view
is not conducive to the conduct of business. It would be impossible to trust
anyone, if managerial egoism were allowed free rein.

Utilitarianism is an ethical theory with which business feels comfortable. The
utilitarian approach of measuring the net benefits of actions intuitively appeals
to managers whose daily lives are preoccupied with similar decision-making

methodologies. Clearly it may be possible to demonstrate that some of the practices we have described (such as exaggerating company difficulties or inventing competition in order to induce suppliers to lower their prices or to improve delivery and quality) might be shown to produce an overall net benefit to society, though there is no clear reason why this should necessarily follow. Utilitarianism is often seen as the philosophical underpinning for free market economics in which the rationale of the maximisation of economic welfare is seen to result from the free interplay of market forces, rather than from any system of planning or control. Many of the unethical practices in purchasing that have been described in this chapter (for example' showing favouritism to particular suppliers, or allowing the offering of gifts or hospitality) are not likely to lead to the maximisation of economic welfare, which results when free competition forces economic efficiency to the highest possible levels. Where, because of the unethical behaviour of the purchasing manager, an organisation does not gain its supplies from the most efficient supplier, having taken all factors into account, then society's economic welfare cannot be maximised. A failure to disclose necessary information to some potential suppliers but not to others would also be seen by utilitarians as being unethical. In the end, most of the unethical practices identified would lead to a retreat from the maximisation of economic welfare which, utilitarianism argues, should be used to test the justness of any action.

Unethical purchasing personnel are likely to find even less support for their actions in any of the duty-based theories than they did in theory of utilitarianism. These duty-based theories, which argue that actions are best judged without regard to consequences, contend that moral laws take the form of categorical imperatives, in Kant's phrase, which should be followed by all as a matter of duty. Kant's categorical imperative (Act in such a way that the action taken could be a universal rule of behaviour for everyone) is unlikely to be acceptable to those who themselves are happy to engage in bribery and corruption. If such an action were to operate against their interests, they are unlikely to want to see it universalised for, if it were, then the advantage they had gained by their unethical actions would disappear. However, discussions with purchasing personnel reveal that the majority of them regard the offering of gifts as widespread – almost part of normal practice. Nonetheless, it is unlikely purchasing personnel would argue that it should become a universal behaviour. Clearly, deception in any form – for instance, the showing of favouritism and the selective use of information – is designed to gain the individual, or their organisation, an advantage which, were it universalized, would disappear. Kant would be astounded if such behaviour were not felt to breach his categorical imperative.

Consideration of the unethical practices that have been detailed in this chapter in terms of Ross's prima facie duties (Ross 1938) leads us to conclude that several of his duties will be breached. The duties of fidelity, gratitude, justice and non-maleficence are breached by the acceptance of gifts; by engaging in deception – for example, by inventing competition; by showing favouritism to those suppliers favoured by senior managers; or by revealing confidential and commercially valuable information. Ross's prima facie duties propose the primacy of honesty in all actions, in equality and fairness, and in acting so that we respect the special obligations we have to other actors, such as employers.

Garrett (1966) supports this approach and adds that we must examine the intentions behind the act, not simply the act itself. Ends, for Garrett, are only properly evaluated if we examine the intrinsic nature of the acts rather than merely their consequences. Many of the actions that are viewed as unethical in purchasing are so viewed because, intrinsically, they are designed to give an unfair advantage to an individual or to an organization.

Rawls' theory of justice (1972), with its two principles – liberty and difference, offers no support to any of the actions detailed in this chapter. Under his liberty principle, Rawls is arguing for maximum liberty, freedom of information and action. Further, under Rawls' principle of difference, actions are acceptable only if they do not increase inequalities and do not operate to worsen the position of the least advantaged. Both of these principles are likely to be breached whenever bribery, corruption, deception and other such practices are present.

Another approach that derives partly from the Aristotelian school might be described as 'virtue ethics' (see McIntyre 1981), where 'virtue' is about the development of good habits, amongst which Aristotle suggested truthfulness, justice and generosity. None of Aristotle's virtues result from the unethical practices found in purchasing.

It would seem that purchasing personnel, at best, only receive minimal support among ethical theorists for the practices that have been explored in this chapter. Many purchasing personnel recognise this and so, in surveys, they always claim that they themselves are not in favour of such practices. The puzzle is, then, why do such practices persist?

QUESTIONS AND TASKS

1 What possible explanations are there for the discrepancy between what purchasing staff claim about their ethical beliefs and the practices discussed in this chapter?

2 'A bottle of whisky at Christmas may be acceptable, but a case smacks of a bribe.' Discuss.

3 How might a workable distinction between promotional material and unacceptable gifts be made?

4 To what extent would ethical behaviour in purchasing also be good business? Can you think of any exceptions?

CHAPTER 13

The Ethical Organisation and Marketing

After you have read this chapter, you will:

- Appreciate the factors that can affect the ethical status of marketing decisions

- Be aware of the ethical issues raised by different areas of marketing

- Understand that some marketing practices may be more ethically suspect than others

- Be able to align ethics in marketing with the ideals of an ethical organisation.

13.1 Marketers and ethics

Ferrell and Gresham (1985) have proposed that a useful standpoint from which to judge ethical behaviour in marketing is through the recognition of those factors that affect ethical or unethical decisions in marketing. Whether the eventual marketing outcomes are thought to be ethical or otherwise is an issue that can be judged from the perspective of the various publics or stakeholders: shareholders, marketers, suppliers, competitors, customers and commentators. They suggest that three sets of elements are likely to affect the ethical status of the marketer's intentions and the marketing output. These elements are:

- Personal factors: the marketer's knowledge, beliefs, values, attitudes and intentions, influenced by the moral standards transmitted by family, education and the cultural context.

- Significant others: the marketer's reference groups within the organisation. The extent of influence from such groups is affected by the social distance the marketer experiences from those groups and by the organisational climate. If top management is visible, its inherent power will ensure it exerts greater influence, whereas peers will be more influential where management is remote.

- Opportunity: increased opportunity for unethical marketing behaviour will make it more likely. Companies and professions that promote and enforce ethical codes raise standards of ethical behaviour and, conversely, fewer penalties and higher rewards associated with unethical behaviour will tend to increase it.

The first and second elements agree with such well-established work as that of Engel et al. (1993) on consumers and Hakansson (1983) on organisational buyers, and most marketers would expect to find these influences having an effect on people's behaviour. Support for the second and third elements comes from Chonko and Hunt (1985), who found that a strong lead from top managers reduced their employees' perception of ethical problems or ambiguity. The Ferrell and Gresham model proposes that in the face of a given ethical dilemma, any particular marketing decision will be mediated by the three areas of influencing factors. Of course, society's judgement may be quite different from that of the marketer. As with many behavioural models, it does not purport to provide a measurement in a general sense. It is a guide to the factors that observers may consider.

SCENARIO 13.1

Marketing

Many doctors in Bangladesh believe that manufacturers of baby formula push their products too aggressively, sometimes breaching the stipulations of an international code, drawn up in 1981, on the marketing of formula milk, ratified by member states of the World Health Organization, and enshrined in law in Bangladesh since 1984. Why? Because, without access to clean drinking water and sterile baby bottles, bottlefeeding is dangerous. Many poor families in Bangladesh do not have access to clean drinking water and sterile baby bottles. The result is that the formula is mixed with dirty water and the babies get diarrhoea. In Bangladesh, diarrhoea can – and does – kill. Virtually no breast-fed babies get diarrhoea. Some doctors in Bangladesh would like to see formula milk and bottles removed from general shops, and available only as a last resort, on prescription; they feel their colleagues are much too quick to suggest bottle-feeding as a solution to feeding problems.

The code on the marketing of formula milk had been prompted by public support of an international boycott of the products of the company that seemed most culpable 30 years ago: Nestlé. The code could have ended the boycott, but campaigners continue to flag it up because, they claim, the company – and many other baby-milk manufacturers – fail to abide by its requirements. Despite the safeguards it affords, they say, mothers in developing countries – the most vulnerable of mothers anywhere, the ones least able to afford formula milk, the ones whose babies most need the breast milk they could and should be getting for free – were being, and continue to be, targeted by corporate giants bent on carving out their share of a valuable market. (Save the Children, which recently published a report on the baby-milk industry, reckons that the total value of baby-milk and baby-food imports is worth almost £16 m a year in Bangladesh alone – but the potential, if more mothers were bottle-feeding, is a lot higher than that).

(Supplied by Joanna Moorhead.)

But, if this has given some indication of where to look for clues as to the marketer's ethical intentions and directions in marketing decisions, what might motivate a company to take an ethical stance in its marketing decisions? There is some evidence that a strong steer from top management on positive ethical policies not only creates a working climate with fewer conflicts for employees, it also gives rise to a higher level of organisational commitment from them. Hunt et al. (1989) found a positive association between corporate values and organisational commitment in a sample of more than 1200 professional marketers comprising marketing managers, marketing researchers and advertising agency managers.

Reinforcing the idea that ethical judgements in marketing are affected by circumstances, they found also that the marketers' notions of corporate ethics were apparently related to their own marketing specialisms. Moreover, just as Ferrell and Gresham (1985) had suggested, they found that age, education, income and some occupational features affected their evaluation of the ethics of particular marketing decisions.

A more persuasive idea to convince top management that adopting an ethical corporate policy is beneficial is the suggestion that it can have a positive effect on the company's success. Donaldson and Davis (1990) argue that such policies will improve 'the bottom line'. Taking the view that management can only operate effectively on a system of shared values in terms of each functional area of the business, they propose the view that some sort of ethical standpoint, good or bad, is integral to those shared values. The argument to adopt ethical values that are 'consistent, justifiable and without need of further improvement' rests on the view that managerial decisions and actions will be seen more favourably, and that the organisational culture and relationships between people will be strengthened. These effects, they say, will lead to higher quality in products, processes and services, and better output and achievements generally in the organisation.

Essentially, these beliefs constitute the rationale for implementing internal marketing and total quality management (TQM). Alternatively, it might be said, they present the profit motive in ethical garb. Donaldson and Davis (1990) acknowledge that some people will respond with scepticism to this approach and, to counter this, cite examples of manufacturing and retailing companies with practices from both sides of the ethical/unethical divide to support their case.

13.2 Empirical evidence

But how far do companies agree with this approach? Some studies of senior executives in companies show them claiming to hold relatively high ethical principles in relation to business. Burke et al. (1993) carried out a study examining attitudes to business ethics amongst a sample of top decision-makers and other professional groups. They obtained responses from 498 senior managers and 165 junior managers to their questionnaire on business ethics. The overwhelming majority of the senior managers had authority in functional, decision-making roles, where ethical judgements enter the considerations; 13.5 per cent of the senior managers were in marketing. The other functional areas represented were company secretaries (10.0 per cent), personnel (16.9 per cent), finance (18.6 per cent), and other directors (2.9 per cent). The Co-operative Bank Ltd, an organisation that has publicly espoused a stringent ethical code and promoted this theme in its advertising campaigns since 1992, supported this research.

There were four areas under investigation: conduct of business, employee relations, social responsibility and environmental concern. Of these, conduct of business focused on aspects that the researchers identified as being 'at the heart of business'. The constituent parts were defined as: marketing, pricing, and direct relations with competitors and customers.

The study concluded that senior managers and professionals had a high level of concern for ethical issues in general, whilst maintaining awareness of the importance of 'a profit oriented competitive position'. Their results indicated that more than three quarters felt that ethical behaviour in business was possible and disagreed with the idea that 'telling lies in business is plain common sense'. The vast majority, claimed they thought 'it was always possible to tell the truth when promoting or selling products and services', 77 per cent disagreed that in business 'there was one rule – make as much as you can', and 88 per cent disagreed that tax evasion was a necessary or legitimate business tactic.

Nonetheless, the sample of respondents did not adopt an anti-competitive stance; free market ideology and practice was supported. Two thirds of those questioned were unconcerned about the destination of invested funds, believing this to be the company's concern only, and nearly a third believed a high interest rate on money lent for high risk ventures was usually defensible. Burke et al. (1993), concluded in their discussion of the survey cited above: 'When it comes to making money, individuals appear less ethically sensitive than they are when dealing with colleagues or considering issues such as the environment.'

The expressed concern for ethical approaches in business by the senior managers in the survey was not related solely to high quality, high value products or services. The fundamental marketing notion of customer focus was cited as the justification for selling low quality goods; that is, the practice is quite acceptable if that is what the customer wants. This approach accords comfortably with the Institute of Marketing definition of marketing: 'Marketing is the management process that identifies, anticipates and supplies customer requirements efficiently and profitably.'

13.3 Marketing strategy

The scope of marketing decisions includes strategic marketing planning as well as operational marketing management. At the strategic level, the company adopts a stance towards competitors. Most strategic marketing theory and terminology derives, as does corporate strategy, from a basis in military strategic thinking. So, the language of such strategy is couched in terms of warfare, rivalry and aggression, with recommendations to attack or defend, to surprise or outflank. The objectives have been to establish an invincible position, either as market dominator (which entails the eventual extinction of some other companies in the same market) or as a specialist in a niche market (the main player in a specific sector). Suppliers and buyers are characterised as part of the competition (Porter 1980). The arguments in favour of this standpoint are persuasive. Successful national and international companies can be seen to be highly competent in these areas.

Such strategies reduce choice for the customer, maximise the cost–price gap initially, might reduce employment in the competitors as they lose market share or fail and, if adopted widely, perhaps adversely affect whole economies. The corollary is that many medium-size companies operating in the same market are adrift strategically. This overlooks the fact that in stable markets there is sufficient competition to stabilise prices, and many firms will operate successfully over many years. It lacks the explanatory power to deal with the advantages of long-term buyer–supplier relationships and with the need for these in the era of online, electronic data exchange between buyers and suppliers as a tool of quick response to the market. Moreover, it does not explain the confidence generated in a market where customers perceive a substantial number of firms operating, so that they believe that they are able to compare market offerings and have real choice in what they buy. Blanchfield et al. (1994) found that whilst customers had considerable dissatisfaction with the UK high street banks, the market concentration meant that they felt helpless to make their complaints heard and there was a lack of trust.

13.4 Market research

Supporting the marketing effort might well be a programme of marketing research. To carry out a rigorously organised survey of customers or internal employees, without sampling or respondent bias or error, and with strictly appropriate statistical treatment and interpretation of results, is, in itself, a demanding exercise. The dangers of unintentional misrepresentation or mistaken analysis of results into market predictions are always there. Unfortunately, there is also the possibility that results may be massaged to produce the predicted or desired outcomes.

The Market Research Society has high ethical standards for members to observe in all aspects of the market research process. There are organisations and individuals who attempt to pass themselves off as carrying out market research, when they are engaged in thinly disguised selling operations. To the public, accosted in shopping centres, over the telephone or on their doorstep with the initial claim that their interviewer is a market researcher, the apparent differences between these activities and genuine market research might be small. These activities contaminate the general image of the market research process as a respectable procedure.

13.5 The marketing mix

The marketing mix elements each offer complex opportunities for marketing decision-making, and thereby contain the potential for ethical and unethical choices by marketing and business personnel. The marketing mix comprises McCarthy's 4 'P's (product, price, promotion and place), applied most often to products available in the market, and the additional 3 'P's of people, process and physical evidence (Booms and Bitner 1981). This marketing mix conveniently elaborates the distinction between the decision areas crucial to product and service offerings in the market, whilst extending the mix concept to explain the key issues in long-term transactions between buying and supplying organisations; that is, the notion of relationship marketing.

13.6 Product

Marketing decisions about products are not confined to quality and relative value. The corporate level decisions of what business and markets to be in – and, therefore, what product to offer – might be seen as ethically loaded. The industries that produce, say, tobacco, infant milk supplement or nuclear fuels, attract interlinked ethical and environmental arguments that are marshalled to both criticise the effects of the products in general and the decisions to offer them in particular markets.

At a less controversial level, the range of products produced, the numbers of product features and their availability can be fine-tuned not just to existing customer demand but to influence and stimulate future demand (see Example 13.1). Offering new features without losing a product's identity is a familiar way of stimulating sales in the consumer market. The updating of many consumer products – such as books, computer software, the re-styling of cars, the seasonal cycle of garment fashions and related but slower movements of style in home furnishings – all meet a latent consumer desire for some aesthetic stimulation and change.

EXAMPLE 13.1

Advertising and peer pressure

It is well known that children and young adults are particularly prone to peer pressure, especially over their appearance. Most fashion manufacturers and retailers have realised this, and almost every major designer label has a diffusion range targeting younger wearers.

Whilst there need not be any concern about the products as such, it is worth remembering that, often, the purchasers are parents who are, themselves, under pressure not to make their children feel odd or unusual. It is not just schools and teachers who favour uniforms for schools; frequently, parents will prefer schools with a strong uniform policy.

Discuss the issues involved in a campaign for marketing expensive designer trainers that targets children between 8 and 12.

Some critics characterise this as manipulation of buyers, especially in consumer markets where discretionary income is more easily spent on impulse. Moreover, the investment required for the introduction of restyled products usually involves the withdrawal of the market offerings that are selling least well or making less profit, perhaps leaving a section of consumers no longer able to obtain the product they want and can afford, or unable to find parts and service for an existing consumer durable.

Nonetheless, the dissatisfactions associated with the need to withdraw a product, or product elimination, are not just a problem for the consumer. Harness and MacKay (1994) recount how the major firms in the financial services industry are legally obliged to keep track of small numbers of customer accounts that the firm would prefer to close, for perhaps 25 years after the issue date. However, when banks and building societies fail to inform existing customers that new financial packages with more attractive terms have been launched, the media are often quick to report this. In these circumstances, the financial companies are often castigated for *not* exercising product elimination. They are seen as leaving their loyal customers in a less advantageous position in respect of either their savings or their liabilities than the newly recruited customers.

Conversely, the rise of environmental awareness on the part of the consumer, resulting in pressure to withdraw products from the market, might not always be to a company's disadvantage. Concern about depletion of the ozone layer has affected the market acceptability of many products. Amongst them has been the gas known as CFC, blamed as damaging to the ozone in the upper atmosphere of the earth and widely used in the manufacture of refrigerators and as the propellant in aerosol sprays. The development and commercial substitution of an alternative product became a priority in the early 1990s, with a few major chemical companies rushing to satisfy the new consumer demand for a non-CFC aerosol propellant. In 1994, however, industry analysts pointed out that the patent on the original product was coming to an end. This allowed a more competitive market to develop in its manufacture and supply. The substitute product is at an early stage in its patent life and, by responding quickly to the changing consumer demand, and thereby supporting the aerosol market, the chemical companies involved have ensured their share of the profit. (See Example 13.2.)

EXAMPLE 13.2

Transparency in advertising

Organic doesn't necessarily mean better, purer or healthier and with processed food, it is always worth reading the label. The organic version of Ambrosia creamed rice has twice the fat (3.7 g compared with 1.9 g per 100 g) and twice the saturated fat (2.2 g compared with 1.1 g per 100 g) of the non-organic version.

This means that a marketing campaign for organic creamed rice which foregrounded the usual perceived virtues of organic produce could easily raise ethical issues about honesty and truthfulness. (*The Guardian*, 15/07/03: G2, 11)

Discuss how you *would* market such a product.

13.7 Price

Setting the price element in the marketing mix is subject to frequent consumer and media speculation but evidence of the ethical direction of the marketing decisions is not always visible. Price is not the chief criterion for all consumers when making purchasing decisions, and even those who do judge some products primarily by price do not apply the same criteria to everything that they buy. The rise in consumer concern with healthy eating, which some UK dairy firms identified as a serious consumer market issue in the 1970s, has raised demand for food products that are low in fat. A report by Peta Cottee (1994) of the Food Commission criticised food manufactures for exploiting the public's anxieties about fat content in food when surveys had revealed that low fat products were priced at around 40 per cent higher than their non-reduced fat equivalents. Marks & Spencer and Ambrosia priced low-fat and regular versions the same.

When launching new products or entering new markets, marketers conventionally distinguish between the pricing strategies of 'market skimming' and 'market penetration'. Market skimming occurs when a product is initially set at a relatively high price affordable by relatively well-off opinion leaders, thereby establishing the product's perceived quality status, the price subsequently being lowered as sales volume builds. Market penetration takes place when a product is set at a relatively low price at the outset in order to build market share more quickly. Both these strategies may be successful in relation to particular market conditions and neither necessarily involves any unethical market behaviour where customers are unlikely to be dependent on new products.

Experienced buyers in both domestic and business markets hold an internal estimate of price bands within which they expect to pay for goods or services of particular quality levels that they purchase with varying degrees of frequency. The idea of a fair price for a given standard of quality is based on prior purchasing practice and is usually shared within the buyer's reference groups. Only the knowledgeable business-to-business purchaser may be in a position to be able to calculate the costs to the producer of bringing a product to market. For the small business buyer, the relevant information is usually obscured by the size of the supplier or the supply chain, and the consumer has little chance of appreciating the gap between costs and price. The consensus about the right price to pay is therefore a key criterion in buying decisions.

Where market competition exists between many organisations of sufficiently equivalent power and size, it would be anticipated that unethical pricing practices (such as operating a cartel to keep the price artificially high to the buyer) are less likely to survive, as any of the firms can bid for increased market share by cutting their margins and prices whilst maintaining their overall profit in an increased volume of sales. However, few markets exist in the economist's paradigm of perfect competition; some are highly fragmented with a lack of shared information, some highly concentrated. Power is frequently unequal between direct industry rivals, and between suppliers and purchasers in the supply chain. Large companies wage price wars on small companies in order to gain market share. The small company might seek rescue from a 'white knight', or friendly larger company; hostile takeovers might occur where no rescuer can be found. The customer may benefit from reduced prices in the short term, as was the case in the newspaper price wars in the UK during 1994. When smaller firms are bought out and the market becomes more concentrated, however, customers may expect firms to attempt to maximise the cost–price gap. The existence of Anti-trust legislation in the US and the requirement for the Department of Trade and Industry to investigate any threat to 'public interest' from proposed takeovers and mergers in already concentrated industries by referral to the Monopolies and Mergers Commission is a formal recognition of this tendency. (See Example 13.3.)

EXAMPLE 13.3

Market-share and fair competition

The sale of the Safeway chain of supermarkets to Morrisons raised many concerns about market-share, fair competition and so on. A less obvious and unpublicised effect might be to cause widespread economic distress in the West Indies.

A potential buyer for Safeway was the US chain Wal-Mart. When Wal-Mart took over Asda recently, it decided to switch procurement of bananas from the West Indies to less expensive (and largely US owned) American suppliers. Many Caribbean agricultural industries are monocultures – they produce sugar cane or bananas and nothing else (virtually). Bananas grown in the Caribbean are also more expensive than those grown in the Americas – because they are grown less intensively and using less modern methods. If a Wal-Mart takeover of Safeway had led to a switch from Caribbean to American suppliers, then a substantial part of the UK market for bananas would have been sourced from the Americas, the price of bananas would have fallen and many West Indian producers would have been bankrupted.

Should this have been a factor in determining the legitimacy of takeover partners for Safeway? How far should law be used to keep competition within a market?

Well before this stage is reached, small and medium-sized firms may find themselves squeezed by the arrival of a large player in their market. During the autumn of 1993, publicity highlighted how the independent town-centre retailers in the toys market were experiencing tough price competition from a chain of toy superstores located on out-of-town sites. Offering very well-priced goods and a wide choice of products but largely accessible only to car-owners, the toy supermarkets could force the small toyshops out of business. If this happens, there will be reduced access and choice to lower-income families without cars whose contribution to market volume is too low to sustain the independent toyshops. The decision to adopt a market penetration strategy might be seem to pose a social dilemma, if not an ethical one.

13.8 Place

By 'place', marketers mean the sum of locations through which the product moves from the supplier to the customer, including the means of distribution, before arriving at the final point of sale to the customer. For retailing, this means the whole supply chain up to and including the location of the retail outlet. With non-store retailing, the communications mode selected and the delivery service become part of the 'place'. For business-to-business marketing, the supply chain is, again, part of the 'place' concept, as is the point at which the customer is able to access the information required concerning the goods or service they wish to buy. In business, repeat purchases occurring on a frequent basis will be made by ordering from the supplier – perhaps electronically or from catalogues. Less regular business purchases requiring specification and negotiation might involve a personal visit from the supplier's sales staff.

Marketing decisions about the extent to which the goods will be available in locations to all who might wish to buy will naturally be tempered by the need to protect against losses if a particular channel of distribution is unprofitable. So, business-to-business marketing properly includes the elimination of sales calls on customers deemed unprofitable and retail location decisions will keep some suppliers out of reach of less well-off consumers. Generally, there are other suppliers who will step into those markets, sometimes with 'cheap and cheerful' operations.

Consumers are, and feel themselves to be, particularly vulnerable when the supply chain is invisible to the public. Individual employees might be reluctant to admit operator error, although monitoring procedures should overcome this. Some domestic consumers are brand loyal to certain, trusted food retailers precisely because they are uncertain whether others have, for example, the integrity, the profit margins or the necessary insurance to jettison products that are marginally damaged in the supply chain. Where consumers fear that unobservable and unspecified contamination of products could occur, some companies adopt stricter codes of practice than regulations demand in order to safeguard their reputation and sales.

13.9 Promotion

Marketing promotions or communications are inevitably subjected to greater public scrutiny than other aspects of marketing. Perceived lapses in ethical standards in selling, public relations and advertising quite rightly attract media attention. The rise of consumerism and the protection of the consumer and small businesses have been stimulated through television and radio and certain crusading sections of the press. Popular TV and radio programmes and press campaigns often highlight pernicious practices that have succeeded in deceiving customers, not because they were exceptionally gullible, but because most firms with which they dealt could be trusted. An unfortunate side-effect of the publicity attached to the dishonesty of a few has been to bring into question the integrity of marketing as such. That selling is an essential part of the supply chain, that public relations and advertising keep the customer informed, and that each part contributes to the viability of the economy, can be overlooked.

The selling practices that attract most adverse attention tend to be those of intrusive, 'hard' sales techniques where the customer feels oppressed by the process. 'Soft' sales techniques using the consumers latent desires and emotions as outlined by Packard (1969) have been heavily satirised and are now familiar to most consumers and, thus, more transparent. The 'hard sell' has attracted such a bad press that it is frequently subject to legal restraint. For example, pressure to sign a sales agreement on the spot may be increased by positive inducements, such as a discount offer available only there and then. This has led to a legal requirement for a short 'cooling off' period, post-sales, during which consumers can reconsider and retract their decision, but it does not apply to all goods. Similar pressures applied to captive holidaymakers to invest in holiday property whilst they are abroad are now well-known, itself a protection for most of the public.

Firms that train their sales staff courteously to advise customers whose needs they cannot supply adequately to go to another supplier, even sometimes providing details of such, might receive gratitude from the individual customer but rarely public recognition. A policy of honesty and politeness in sales might build customer loyalty and company reputation, but it is difficult to quantify such effects. This approach to selling is advocated as part of an overall 'customer care' strategy and attempts to combine an ethical stance with a measure of long-term self-interest.

Potentially damaging for the public image of marketing is the practice previously known for 20 or 30 years as pyramid selling, relaunched in the late 1980s variously as network marketing and multi-level marketing. Consumers are recruited to a selling operation that relies on their each reselling goods in which they have invested, to a minimum number of people who must also resell the goods and so on along an ever-enlarging chain or network. Croft (1994) showed in the results of his careful and detailed research into this area that the practices of these so-called marketing operations are virtually indistinguishable from the original pyramid concept, for which a simple mathematical calculation demonstrates that the population of the UK could not sustain the predicted sales. The selling appeal at recruitment is often to people who have very limited financial resources, who could ill-afford to be left with unsold goods.

In the UK, the honesty, legality and fairness of the content and context of advertising is protected by the Advertising Standards Authority (ASA). This body responds to complaints from the public and, after adjudication, may require advertisers to withdraw material it believes to be offensive, misleading or illegal. There are also published rules with which advertisers must comply and breaking these is sufficient to cause the ASA to intervene without external request. Statements overtly attacking competitors' products fall into the 'forbidden' category. The ASA regularly advertises itself, reminding the public of its existence and how to contact the organisation to make a complaint.

Some of the most controversial advertisements on which the ASA took action in the early 1990s were those for the Italian clothing franchise chain Benetton. Clothes were not portrayed, instead, the advertisements showed arresting and disturbing images from contemporary life. A huge bill-board picture of a new-born infant was shown, but images of international terrorism and the death-bed scene of the family around an Aids sufferer were not allowed on advertising display in the UK.

An advertising campaign launched in May 1992 that was intended to be not only ethical in itself, but also to portray the ethical policies of the company was that of the Co-operative Bank Ltd. The bank had not previously used television advertising extensively, so was not well-known in areas of the country where they lacked a strong branch network. The advertising message expressed with clarity the bank's ethical stance on investment – that is, on the ways that it would and would not use their customers' money. Press advertising was used to complement the Co-operative Bank's television campaign.

By implication, the message contrasts the Co-operative Bank's actions with those of its far larger rivals. At the time of launch, as Blanchfield (1994) says: 'the media interest was noticeable amidst reports of scandal and crises in the dealings of financial institutions'.

Its impact was reflected in the national press immediately: 'After recent fiascos, it is difficult to believe that ethics and moral values can have anything to do with banking. The Co-op Bank has proved otherwise with the launch of its new ethical policy' (*The Guardian*, 1 May 1992).

The Co-operative Bank, however, stated that they had maintained an ethical approach to business since their establishment in 1872. The Bank's mission statement consists of eight principles. Blanchfield (1994) notes that the eight principles not only set out commercial goals, but also address the Bank's social objectives. They refer to factors such as: the quality and excellence of service; education and training; quality of life; and freedom of association in social, political, racial and religious matters, and the bank places great emphasis on integrity. Its ethical stance has been widely recognised and commended, and has received a number of national awards.

The very impact that this campaign has made relies on a contrast effect with the public's more usual perception of banks and their standard of customer care. It is not a message free from risk, since any failure to meet the claimed standards could rebound badly on the bank.

13.10   People, physical evidence and process

Lewis (1991) reports from her empirical findings how customers' expectations of service quality have risen over an extended period, creating greater potential for competition in the financial services. The three service aspects of the marketing mix (people, physical evidence and process) are involved in the five dimensions of service performance identified by Parasuraman et al. (1985). These are:

- Tangibles (physical facilities, equipment, appearance of personnel)

- Reliability (ability to perform the promised service dependably and accurately)

- Responsiveness (willingness to help customers and provide prompt service)

- Assurance (knowledge and courtesy of employees and their ability to inspire trust and confidence)

- Empathy (caring, individualized attention the company provides its customers).

The adoption of the customer care approach inherent in these aspirations for a service has sound business objectives – customer retention through customer satisfaction and loyalty. Keeping existing customers makes sound marketing sense, since the costs are higher in recruiting new customers. Variations of customer charters abound as companies and politicians recognise this. An ethical organisation will make approaches based on the five dimensions of service performance possible by also adopting policies and practices towards its own staff that enable them to meet these objectives. When insufficient account is taken of the needs of the employees in training and resources to meet the exacting new standards set for interaction with their stakeholders, greater customer dissatisfaction is aroused, with potentially dire consequences for public confidence in the service provider. In the specific area of financial services, Gibbs (1993) says, 'lack of confidence and the need for trust may form a vicious circle'.

Earlier, Lewis (1991), found that bank customers in both the USA and the UK had very high expectations of service across most of the dimensions of service investigated. In general, the UK customers were more satisfied than their US counterparts. The areas in which they had most confidence and satisfaction were related mainly to the personal qualities of the staff, possibly reflecting the banks' training exercises with staff. However, on issues of facilities and knowledge of personal needs of customers, they were low in their perceptions and evaluations of service.

13.11 Conclusion

So, how importantly does marketing feature in the health of a company's ethical stance in business? Fearnley (1993) found 'corporate reputation' to be a selling point, but also largely a 'wasted asset'. It mainly comprises the sum of experiences of employees and external groups, hence its existence and nature is intimately associated with the elements of the marketing mix. As with a product brand, the corporate reputation is composed of several elements but is predominantly a matter of stakeholder perception.

However, Fearnley (1993) also asserts that 'the most dominant factor in a good corporate reputation' is the quality of the product and/or service, for, although the customer increasingly buys 'the company along with the offering', it is the offerings themselves that continue to be the main interest, concern and focus of the customer.

Hence, marketing ethics cannot be divorced from the issues that concern business ethics as a whole. As with any less than scrupulous practice in whatever functional area of business, adopting a compromise in ethical standards in marketing might turn out to be a tactic of short-term value. The need for repeat business might be a guard against unethical behaviour, but the best protection lies in the company's overall ethical stance, reflected throughout its policies on internal standards and organisation, and its commitment to its external stakeholders.

████████ QUESTIONS AND TASKS ████████

1 Can tobacco be marketed ethically?

2 Why should the marketing of infant formula feed in less developed countries be ethically problematic?

3 Would the fact that a high percentage of those involved in marketing have expressed high moral standards mean that marketing would be unlikely to be conducted in an unethical way?

4 How would you market the practice and profession of marketing itself? What might an ethical advertising campaign for the marketing profession look like?

5 What the ethical difference between an ordinary franchise operation and pyramid selling?

CHAPTER 14

The Ethical Organisation and Human Resource Management

After reading this chapter you will:

- Be aware that human resource management is an area of work with many potential ethical issues

- Have a deeper understanding of the causes of ethical dilemmas in human resource management

- Be able to develop ways of thinking through and managing these ethical dilemmas.

14.1 Introduction

There is little mention of ethics in the current literature in the UK relating either to human resource management (HRM) or to personnel management. The term 'ethics' is hardly referred to in the most popular HRM/Personnel Management texts (Sisson 1989 and 1994; Torrington and Hall 1987; and Towers 2003): the word does not appear in any of the indexes. A recent UK text by Beardwell and Holden (1994), *Human Resource Management: A Contemporary Perspective*, does explicitly refer to ethics in relation to management, learning and development, and job design, but devotes no more than part of four pages (out of 687) to the issue. As far as business ethics textbooks are concerned, HRM is treated only narrowly (see Donaldson 1989; Chryssides and Kaler 1993). There is the occasional chapter on the workplace but, where this is the case, the discussion usually focuses on employee rights in general or on some novel situation, such as an employer's use of polygraph tests to access employee honesty (Beauchamp 1989).

A different picture emerges when textbooks from the US are surveyed, and where ethics and ethical issues feature prominently (Schuler and Huber, 1993; Mathis and Jackson 1994). Schuler and Huber state that: 'increasingly, human resource management professionals are becoming involved in more ethical issues.

Some of the most serious involve differences in the way people are treated based on favoritism or relationship to top management'.

As supporting evidence, they quote a survey carried out in 1991 (see Appendix 14.1) by the Society for Human Resource Management (SHRM) and the Commerce Case Clearing House (CCCH). The survey involved over 1000 human resource professionals who 'identified more than forty ethical incidents, events, and situations relevant to HR activities' (Schuler and Huber: 24).

Providing some answers to the question as to why interest in ethics among management and business academics would seem to be more developed in the US than in the UK is not the main purpose of this chapter, but the political context within which business operates in each of the two countries concerned might have some bearing on the matter. In the UK, the political context can be summed up by what Colin Crouch (1990) calls 'the rejection of compromise'. There are three aspects to this. First, there has been a rejection by the government of the search for compromise in industrial relations. Second, there has been the installation of a tough legal framework for trade union action. Third, the company has emerged as the most important level for industrial relations activity 'replacing the branch, shop-floor and state levels that had previously competed for importance within the British system' (Crouch: 327). The combination of economic, political and legal changes in the UK over the past fifteen years inspired by the 'rejection of compromise' has led to line managers becoming more influential than personnel managers. Increased competition has resulted in managers having to control labour costs tightly on the one hand, and to maximise employees' contributions on the other, thus finding themselves able to take more initiatives in the management of their organisation, and increasingly carrying out responsibilities traditionally undertaken by personnel managers.

Whether one holds the view that personnel management is more concerned with mediation and problem solving and is short-term and reactive, whilst HRM driven by line management is long-term and integrated into business policy and planning, there is a case to be made that suggests personnel management is likely to be more ethical than HRM. This is, quite simply, because line managers, who are nearer to the 'coal face', tend to be motivated by the need to achieve operational targets and are less concerned with the 'soft' moral issues. Personnel managers see themselves as personnel specialists first and as company managers second. Furthermore, many personnel managers are members of the Institute of Personnel Management. According to Keith Sisson (1989: 3) personnel management activities: 'have come to be associated with a group of specialist managers, above all in Britain, where they have had their own professional organisation, the Institute of Personnel Management (IPM), an examination scheme covering membership, and codes of practice.

The Institute of Management, a general professional body that is more attractive to line managers, also has its own Code of Conduct and Guides to Professional Management Practice. This states that one of the manager's duties: 'involves the acceptance and habitual exercise of ethical values, among which a high place should be accorded to integrity, honesty, loyalty and fairness'.

Added to such abstract and potentially meaningless notions, the Institute falls short of describing an external code of ethics. It does this on the grounds that: 'it is usual for managers to encounter circumstances or situations in which various values, principles, rules and interests appear to conflict', and, therefore, no ready answer can be provided.

In contrast to the Institute of Management Code and Guides, the IPM Codes of Practice address what constitutes ethical approaches to precise areas such as continuous development, employee data, equal opportunities, employee involvement and participation, redundancy, psychological testing, harassment and counselling. Although there is no compulsion, legal or otherwise, for IPM members to adhere to the guidelines laid down, they are supposed to represent good practice. These codes provide guidelines for more than mere minimum legal standards. For example, the IPM Code on Equal Opportunities includes recommendations to overcome discrimination in the areas of age and disability that go beyond legislative requirements. In the case of age discrimination, it recommends that 'as a general rule age should not be used as a primary discriminator in recruitment, selection, promotion and training decisions'. It is ironical that the IPM journal, *Personnel Management*, frequently contains job advertisements that discriminate on grounds of age.

In the US, the professional organisation for human resource specialists, the Society for Human Resource Management (SHRM) has a code of practice that emphasises 'a high standard of personal honesty and integrity at every phase of daily practice', 'thoughtful consideration to the personal interest, welfare and dignity of all employees', a 'high regard and respect for the public interest', and that human resource professionals must never 'overlook the importance of the personal interests and dignity of employees' (Schuler and Huber, 1993). It is in this 'respect for individuals' as the basis of policies, codes of conduct and practices that companies in the US might claim to be ethical in their relationships with their employees and potential employees. This is in marked contrast to the legalistic and formal approach adopted by the British IPM and the highly abstract notions coupled with an abdication of responsibility demonstrated by the Institute of Management. It is also to be noted that neither of these British institutions emphasise the notion of 'public interest', thus clearly reflecting the absence of the notion of social responsibility or accountability on the part of companies towards society or the community at large.

And yet, almost every human resource decision and issue can pose ethical questions. To what degree should managers consult with employees over issues that affect their everyday lives? What support should organisations give to employees who are now excess to requirements or who no longer can carry out their job? What degree of assistance should an employer offer to an employee who is suffering a personal crisis? Should employees be forced to work overtime? How should employers deal with job applicants? Should organisations operate affirmative action policies with regard to selection, training and promotion? To what degree should jobs be made safe? How much information should be given to employees regarding the organisation? Each of these questions, if one were to adopt the concept of 'respect for individuals' as the founding principle of an ethical code of conduct for HRM, would demand far clearer policies and practical answers than those outlined by the Institute of Management or the IPM.

Human resource management

Psychometric testing and personality profiling are often used in the private sector as a tool in selection and recruitment procedures, but, it seems, they are increasingly being considered in the public sector.

The *Nursing Standard* (18 April 2007) says that personality inventories remain rare in nursing. But Stephen Wright and Jean Sayre-Adams of the Sacred Space Foundation, which helps those suffering from stress and burn-out, suggest a more in-depth and complete understanding of their personality type and way of working can help nurses deal with problems at work.

But academics are concerned that personality testing is being used for less wholesome purposes. *The Times Higher Education Supplement* (20 April 2007) says that staff are concerned about being subjected to such controversial tests before being approved for jobs or promotion.

Experts say that 'corporate-style' psychometric testing is likely to be used increasingly to check for initiative, team-working and social skills. But teaching unions are concerned and describe the tests as 'highly subjective'.

The more reputable tests are, obviously, supported by valid psychological theory and evidence. But it is not possible to read straight off from the results someone's suitability for recruitment or promotion. Too often a professional analysis can be reduced to crude headlines and simple categories for the purposes of conveying the information to the selection panel. The risk is that this will result in unfairness to candidates and unsafe selection procedures for organisations.

14.2   Towards ethical recruitment and selection

One of the most problematic aspects of HRM concerns recruitment and selection. The following part of this chapter will discuss two case studies that will enable us to focus on some of the ethical issues encountered in this area. Although simple cases, they are typical of the type of recruitment and selection situations that occur in the UK today. According to Maclagan (1993: 3), most ethical situations faced by managers 'are not the headline-hitting issues one reads about in the press; research has shown that most managers never face such dramatic situations, but do continually experience small, everyday, matters which nevertheless have an ethical dimension'. The cases of Smallhouse School (Case Study 14.1) and Tiphill County Council (TCC) (Case Study 14.2) are real, but the names are fictitious. They demonstrate different issues and it is, therefore, not the intention that they can be directly compared.

Looking more closely, what does the advertisement tell us about the job? We know that it entails assisting with the teaching of French to children in the age range of 4 to 11 and that a French native speaker is preferred. We do not know how many hours are required or what the rate of pay is. Neither is there any information relating to qualifications and experience. The phrase 'assist with the teaching of' is not explained. It is not clear whether this person would be a

CASE STUDY 14.1

Smallhouse School

Smallhouse School is a private girls' grammar school that takes in pupils from the age of four and which provides education up to and including A-levels. It is a fairly large school and has a good reputation in the area of examination success. The following advertisement appeared in a national newspaper:

SMALLHOUSE SCHOOL – GIRLS' DIVISION
Small Lane, Small Town, OP3 5RT
Tel 002-245-555
Required to assist with the teaching of
FRENCH
in the Junior School age range 4/11 years. This is a part-time appointment.
Applications from native speakers preferred.
A letter of application with full curriculum vitae
and names of two referees should be sent to the Headmistress immediately.

teacher or merely 'an assistant'. The method of application, which seeks a letter of application as well as a full curriculum vitae together with the names of two referees, is quite clear. There is, however, no closing date for applications. Even though the job does not commence for another four months applicants are asked to apply 'immediately'.

The advertisement does not encourage candidates to telephone and seek more information. Those who did telephone to seek extra information were told 'you must be a qualified teacher', 'it will be for approximately 4 or 5 hours per week' and 'we have not decided what the rate of pay will be'. So, what Smallhouse School actually want is a qualified French native teacher for four or five hours per week.

Smallhouse School can certainly be accused of being inefficient. Key aspects of the personnel specification are missing from the advertisement. They have still not decided what the rate of pay will be and this has created some degree of inconvenience to some applicants. There are several ways, therefore, in which this advertisement falls short of what one would expect if respect for individuals had been demonstrated.

Since anyone seeing the advertisement would have inadequate information to decide whether to apply or not, many who telephoned to seek clarification would realise the job was not suitable and they would feel they had wasted their time as well the price of a telephone call. There could be others who would have completed the application process ignorant of the fact that they would fail at the first hurdle by not being qualified teachers. These people would have spent a considerable amount of time in completing their application. There would be others for whom the four or five hours would have been totally inadequate. The manner in which the School handled this stage of the recruitment process can be described as being incompetent and failing to show respect for individuals.

The failure to disclose an accurate description of the job and the qualities required for the position, as well as the absence of information relating to the hours required and pay, would almost certainly result in many applicants merely wasting time and effort applying for a job for which they do not qualify or which is unsuitable for them. It is probably not the case that the School deliberately demonstrated a lack of respect for potential applicants but, rather, more likely that they just did not think of the effect of their actions. Had the School followed good recruitment practice, for example as laid down in the IPM Code, then not only would it have been more ethical in its dealings with potential and actual applicants, but it would also have been more efficient to themselves. The School would have received fewer telephone queries and the applications would have been more likely to be from suitable candidates. In this case, it could be claimed, therefore, that the School was not only inefficient but that, in showing a lack of respect for individuals, they were also unethical.

Compared with Smallhouse School, TCC is well organised with regard to recruitment and selection. It has a clear recruitment and selection policy, which includes the requirement for a clear job description and personnel specification to be sent to all potential candidates. The personnel specification itemises those aspects that are essential and those that are desirable. The job advertisement describes the job adequately, clarifies the closing date for applications, provides full details of salary and makes it clear how candidates can seek additional information and how they can apply for the position. The personnel specification, which was drawn up by the members of the interviewing panel, is given in Case study 14.2.

TCC also organises its interviews well and keeps all candidates informed. All members of the interview panel are involved in the preparation of the short-list. Candidates who are not short-listed are informed of this. Some, but not all, of the interview panel members are trained. At the interview, the questions are free from bias and appear to be fair. Indeed, TCC take considerable pride in the fact that the selection process is fair. 'All questions relate directly to the person specification. Any other questions would break equal opportunities policies and allow the interviewee the right of appeal', stated the interview chairman. The questions are generally open-ended and candidates are given opportunities to explain their strengths. The interview organiser is prepared to spend time with unsuccessful candidates to explain why they did not obtain the job. So, is this an ethical company as far as recruitment and selection is concerned? It would be, had it not been for several aspects of their policy.

TCC's recruitment and selection policy requires that all jobs must be advertised and that at least three candidates must be short-listed and interviewed for each vacancy. This is based on a notion of fair competition. For example, if there were only one candidate, then the selection panel would have nothing to which to compare the candidate. This aspect will be discussed later. Given all of the apparent concern and effort paid to recruitment and selection at TCC, can it be described as ethical? In order to answer, it is necessary to examine what happens in practice. Case study 14.2 refers to a vacancy for a community worker.

The job was advertised in a local newspaper. Three candidates were short-listed: one was an 'internal candidate' already doing the job in a part-time

CASE STUDY 14.2

Tiphill County Council: vacancy for a community worker – person specification
Essential:
The person appointed to this post must:

(a) Have some experience in educationally based group work with adults and/or young people.

(b) Have a range of effective communication and listening skills as well as the ability to work with a range of people on their terms

(c) Have an understanding of the current issues affecting women's lives.

(d) Have experience of working with groups of people in a personal/collective development context.

(e) Have a clean driving licence and be prepared to drive the District minibus (after taking the appropriate preparation and test).

(f) Have an ability to plan and work in a systematic way.

There was also a list of desirable criteria but this will not be presented here because it is not central to the case.

capacity with the same authority; one was an ex-teacher who had considerable experience with working in the community but not in an official capacity, and certainly not as a community worker; the other, who eventually was offered the position, was an experienced community worker who was currently working for another authority. As stated in TCC's policy, the interview panel carried out the short-listing. The interview panel comprised a trained chairman and five people representing the community, of whom two had received formal interview training. The training involved mainly matters relating to the avoidance of discrimination. All three candidates were said to meet the criteria laid down in the person specification.

The selection event, which lasted all day, was organised as follows: an informal tour of the premises, with the opportunity to meet existing staff; lunch; a thirty-minute period where the three candidates could talk among themselves; and a forty-five minute individual interview. The interview was described by the candidates as a 'grilling'. The overall impression given to the candidates was that the interview panel was fairly well organised, although the interview concerning the ex-teacher did give rise to one problem. This candidate had made it clear on her application that she did not have direct experience of doing this type of work but had made out a case that she possessed the necessary skills to do it. During the interview, the candidate was asked 'What experience do you actually have in doing this type of work'? The candidate replied that she did not have any direct experience of community work in an official capacity and that she had made this clear on the application form. She then proceeded to explain that she had dealt with community matters on a voluntary basis and proceeded to give examples. Several members of the panel returned to this question later and persisted in drawing attention to this. The candidate felt irritated by this since she had made her position clear right at the start. Later, on the same day, the candidate was told during a telephone call from the chairman that although she had interviewed well she did not get the job because of her lack of experience in this area. So, the panel had decided that the candidate's lack of professional experience was the deciding factor despite the fact that they were fully aware of this before the interview and still decided to short-list this person.

Furthermore, this factor was not a requirement listed in either the essential or desirable criteria. During the session where the three candidates were left on their own, it became obvious to all of them that the ultimately successful candidate was the best person for the job. What was irritating for the others – particularly the ex-teacher – was that she felt that she had been invited to the interview to make up the numbers.

For an appointment to be made, the organisation's policy stated that at least three candidates were required. In this case, the ideal candidate was obvious from the application forms. On the basis of this case, one may ask how ethical is it to invite people for a full day's interview when they have virtually no chance of being successful?

The organisation's policy of insisting on at least three candidates should be questioned. The policy, aimed at ensuring 'fair competition' could be seen as flawed because what the panel ought to be doing is comparing candidates with the person specification and not against each other. If candidates had been rated against the person specification, then not only would the interviews have been more likely to be fair, but also the information obtained would have led to better decision-making. If only one applicant meets the initial selection criteria, would it have been less ethical or more ethical to interview that one candidate and appoint her rather than to interview the two other candidates under false pretences? I would submit that although the TCC policy in this case was fair, it remained unethical because it was based on formal notions of fairness and not 'respect for individuals'.

The two cases discussed in Case Studies 14.1 and 14.2 focused on matters of recruitment and selection, and demonstrated how a lack of care and respect for the individual can lead to unethical behaviours on the part of the employer, whether it be in not providing enough information or in misleading interviewees as to the actual job specification in order to be seen to adhere to company procedures that are 'seen to be fair'.

In the UK, selection is usually considered as being a one-way process where the applicants' needs are almost ignored. In discussing selection practice, Anderson (1992: 183) claimed that 'there may still be a tendency to focus exclusively on the organisation's perspective in making decisions and to neglect the increasingly important aspects of how candidates make decisions, in deciding whether to accept job offers or not'. He also identified the absence of candidates' rights in the UK, whilst giving an example from Sweden where employee representatives are present when psychologists' reports are considered and candidates are informed of the results before the potential employing organisation. The candidate can also have the results destroyed if he or she wishes to withdraw.

Other countries have practices that protect applicants in various, and sometimes novel, ways. In France, for example, 'candidates have the right to withhold information or give *incorrect* answers, if they feel that an employer is asking inappropriate questions, without prejudice to their subsequent employment rights' (Income Data Services, 1990). In the UK, the only safeguards that exist for applicants regarding interview questioning relate to discrimination on sex and race. If a successful candidate gives false information and the employer discovers this at some point in the future, then this may result in the employee's dismissal. An example of this could be where the applicant had previously left their employment because of ill health but had subsequently fully recovered. In a subsequent application, they might be expected to disclose reasons for leaving the previous job. The candidate may be unwilling to disclose the real reasons for leaving because their experience tells them that it would end their chances of being selected. Equally, if they give incorrect information, they are then vulnerable should this be ultimately discovered. Irrelevant and inappropriate questions can sometimes, therefore, lead the candidates to resort to being 'economical with the truth' so as not to disqualify themselves from the selection. A recruitment and selection policy that is very much one-way, and where the needs and rights of candidates are not respected (in this case, invasion of personal privacy and confidentiality), can leave the door wide open for abuse of power, disrespect and generally unethical behaviour on the part of recruitment and selection personnel.

In the UK, ethical recruitment and selection as key aspects of HRM will start to materialise if respect for individuals becomes a priority. However, for this to come about, a change in the political climate generally will be required, as ethical behaviour and attitudes towards individuals do not sit comfortably with notions of 'rejection of compromise', a market driven economy, and the idea that there is no such thing as society or communities. If works councils, along the lines that operate in West Germany or France, could be legislated for and given 'rights' to oversee recruitment and selection practices, then some improvements are likely. The notion of 'candidates' rights' could materialise, which would result in organisations having to adopt practices along the lines expressed in the next paragraph.

Ethical recruitment and selection practice might include the following: job descriptions and personnel specifications to be drawn up for all positions; these should accurately reflect the realities of the job; advertisements should contain all essential information including pay, conditions, job details, and qualities and experience required; no candidate should be invited to an interview unless they meet the essential qualities laid down in the personnel specification; unsuccessful applicants should have their applications returned to them along with the selectors' reasons for their decision; and applicants should be given the results of any assessment made about them, including referees' comments. This list is not exhaustive but could provide a starting point for ethical recruitment and selection. If companies adopt such practices and extend this type of thinking to other workplace issues, such as communication and consultation, then we will see the start of real ethical HRM.

There is much written about trust, commitment, cooperation and loyalty in current management literature. Most of the impetus for this comes from capital, not labour. It is claimed that some success has already been achieved in this direction but much of this is due to high levels of unemployment, the recession and the government's anti-union laws. Given these factors, employees are, in general, settling for a quiet time and making little in terms of demands. What is likely is that those companies who adopt ethical HRM will reap higher rewards in terms of the ideals of employee commitment, trust and loyalty than those organisations that merely adopt a strong line in rhetoric. For this to happen, British business must undergo a substantial shift in structure, finance and attitudes.

▮▮▮▮▮▮ QUESTIONS AND TASKS ▮▮▮▮▮▮

1 Write down the criteria that you would apply to an organisation if it wanted to be described as a 'good employer'

2 Find out 3 organisations that have reputations as 'good employers'

3 Compare their characteristics with your criteria and decide which ones are 'good employers' according to you.

4 Review your list of criteria and make any amendments you consider to be necessary.

APPENDIX A14. 1

Ethical issues

Situation	Percentage*
Hiring, training or promotion based on favouritism (friendships or relationships)	30.7
Allowing differences in pay, discipline, promotion, and so on because of friendships with top management	30.7
Sexual harassment	28.4
Sex discrimination in promotion	26.9
Using discipline for managerial and non-managerial personnel inconsistently	26.9
Not maintaining confidentiality	26.4
Sex discrimination in compensation	25.8
Non-performance factors used in appraisals	23.5
Arrangements with vendors or consulting agencies leading to personal gain	23.1
Sex discrimination in recruitment or hiring	22.6

* These percentages refer to those who responded with a 4 or 5 on a five-point scale measuring 'degree of seriousness'. Number of respondents = 1078.
Source: 1991 SHRM/CCH Survey, quoted in Schuler and Huber (1993).

CHAPTER 15

The Ethical Organisation and Accounting

After reading this chapter you will:

- Have a good understanding of some of the ethical dilemmas facing people who work in the accounting field

- Be aware of a range of approaches in dealing with ethical dilemmas

- Be aware of the professional body requirements for ethical conduct to which accountants are subject.

15.1 Introduction

Accountants are employed in many types of organisations – public, private and charitable. All the ethical issues faced by accountants resulting from the type of organisation by which they are employed cannot be examined in this chapter. From here onwards, therefore, the relevant issues will be examined in the context, primarily, of limited liability companies in the United Kingdom (UK).

The chapter is divided into two sections. The first section begins by providing an overview of the UK accounting profession, considering its role and distinguishing between professional accountants employed by business organisations (preparers of accounting information) and independent professional accountants (auditors). This distinction is used to facilitate the discussion of the rules governing the professional conduct of accountants.

The chapter then goes on to present three case studies to illustrate the kind of ethical dilemmas commonly facing accountants in the different facets of their working lives. Each case study is followed by an analysis of the influences prevailing upon the individual practitioner attempting to make ethical decisions.

15.2 The accounting profession

The modern accounting profession originated as a result of the creation of the limited liability company during the Industrial Revolution. The accounting profession grew out of the statutory accounting and auditing requirements of the various Companies Acts, culminating in the Companies Act 1967, which gave the accounting profession an exclusive right to audit the accounts of limited companies in the UK. These requirements were developed to protect the interests of the large number of new investors, who had no knowledge of, or influence on, the day-to-day management of the companies in which they had invested. In addition, the accounting profession itself gradually developed a consensus on the treatment of transactions, to avoid inconsistencies between the financial statements of different companies.

The accounting profession continues to influence both the framing and interpretation of legislation, and remains strong and independent. Currently, the profession is made up of six accounting bodies[1] that have formed a joint representative body, the Consultative Committee of Accounting Bodies (CCAB). The CCAB has provided an effective mechanism for producing a coordinated approach from these bodies.

15.3 Accountants: a variety of roles

It is useful to distinguish between the role of a professional accountant employed by a business organisation and an independent professional accountant.

Accountants employed within organisations

The role of the accountant within organisations has developed in two broad directions:

The management accountant

According to CIMA (1991), the role of management accounting is to provide: 'information required by management for such purposes as: formulation of policies; planning and controlling the activities of the enterprise; decision-taking on alternative courses of action; disclosures to those external to the entity (shareholders and others); disclosure to employees; and safeguarding assets'. If a business chooses to employ a management accountant, their role is to provide financial information that can be used by managers to help them achieve the objectives of the enterprise.

The financial accountant

The role of the financial accountant is to provide economic information (in the form of financial statements) about the performance and financial adaptability of an organisation to users in the 'outside world'. The Accounting Standards Board's Statement of Principles (1991) defines the users of financial statements as: investors; employees; lenders; suppliers and other trade creditors; customers; government agencies; and the public.

The directors of a company are responsible for preparing financial statements that comply with statutory requirements (embodied in the Companies Act 1985), and which give a 'true and fair view' of the company's position and performance. The financial accountant, acting on behalf of the directors, advises on which items should be selected for inclusion in the financial statements, and how they should be measured and presented.

Torex Retail

In January 2007, till software group Torex Retail issued a surprise warning about its likely profits – just eight days after its chief executive, Neil Mitchell, announced a series of big contract wins and pronounced the firm to be in rude health. Following the warning, Mitchell, who had joined the company four months previously, turned whistleblower and sent the Serious Fraud Office a dossier outlining accounting irregularities that allegedly explained the discrepancy between Mitchell's first announcement and the profits warning.

Following the profits warning in January, the home of the former Chairman of Torex Retail, Chris Moore, together with that of another former Chairman, Rob Loosemore, were searched by fraud investigators. In March 2007, Mr Moore resigned from the board as the SFO carried out a second wave of raids on homes and offices as part of its inquiries. Homes in Gloucestershire and Warwickshire were searched, as well as business premises in Banbury, Oxfordshire, which were understood to include neither Torex Retail's head office nor a second company unit in the town.

After the profits warning, the company had emergency talks with its lending banks. The business will need to be refinanced if it is to survive.

McAlpine

In February 2007, Alfred McAlpine revealed that the senior managers at Slate, its Penrhyn based slate quarry in North Wales, had systematically misrepresented the volume of the quarry's production and sales, and then sought to conceal this by extensive pre-selling of slate at substantially discounted prices. McAlpine believes that the misrepresentation was deliberate, and possibly fraudulent. The serious accounting irregularities were uncovered by internal audit, but McAlpine cannot rule out the involvement of the police.

Slate's net assets for 2005 were restated by about £11 m and there will be a reduction in the expected pre-tax profit for the year to the end of December 2006 of about £13 m. Two senior managers have been suspended, though there is apparently no evidence of any personal gain. McAlpine warned that the historic actions of those involved would continue to have repercussions on the company's profitability through into 2007/8.

Penrhyn has been producing slate since the thirteenth century.

Accountants in professional practice

Accountants in professional practice offer a variety of accounting services, which fall into two categories:

The auditor

Audits are undertaken by independent professional accountants appointed by the shareholders. Under the Companies Act 1985 (as amended by the Companies Act 1989), the auditor has three main duties: to report to the members whether, in the auditor's opinion, the financial statements give a true and fair view of the state of affairs of the company and comply with the Companies Act 1985; to fulfil their obligations under the Companies Acts and under the Articles of Association of the company; and to exercise reasonable care and skill.

The auditors' role, therefore, is to express an independent opinion on the fairness and reliability of the company's financial statements and, thus, on the directors' stewardship of the owners' funds.

Related services

Accountants in professional practice offer a variety of accounting services including tax services, management consultancy, insolvency services, advice on acquisitions and mergers, and, recently, environmental audits.

15.4 The rules regulating the professional conduct of accountants

Rules and standards, both technical and ethical, govern the professional conduct of members of the accounting bodies:

Technical rules (accounting regulations)

Governing the preparation of management accounting information.   An 'official terminology' of management accounting has been issued by CIMA (ibid.) that attempts to standardise the definitions of a range of commonly used concepts, techniques and methods. Its application, however, is not mandatory. Information that is to be made available outside the organisation should comply with the technical rules governing the preparation of financial statements.

Governing the preparation of financial statements.   In the UK[2] the predominant sources of accounting regulations are to be found in the form of legislation and accounting standards. Broadly speaking, the Companies Acts 1985 regulates the preparation, form and content of company financial statements, while accounting standards support the legal requirements by giving detailed guidance.

Accounting standards are formulated by a private sector, self-regulatory body, the Financial Reporting Council (FRC)[3]. The FRC is responsible for setting and issuing accounting standards, through the FRC's two main subsidiary organisations – the Accounting Standards Board and the Review Panel. The FRC has a chairman appointed jointly by the Secretary of State for Trade and Industry and the Governor of the Bank of England. Membership of the FRC is comprised of members of the accounting profession, together with others who are concerned with the use, audit or preparation of accounting information – for example, representatives from industry and commerce, stockbrokers and analysts, banks, trade unions and the Department of Trade and Industry. Finance comes from the government, the professional bodies and private sector contributions.

Some legal recognition, though not enforceability, was given to accounting standards by the amended Companies Act 1985, which required large companies to comply with accounting standards to explain departures in the notes to the accounts.

Governing the conduct of audits.   The conduct of audits is regulated by the Auditing Standards and Guidelines published by the Auditing Practices Board, which was established by the CCAB in 1991.

Professional ethics.   In its Guide to Professional Ethics, the ICAEW[4] states that: 'In addition to the duties owed to the public and to his or her client or employer a member of the Institute is bound to observe high standards of conduct which may sometimes be contrary to his personal self-interest.'

Guidance, which applies to members both in practice and business, is given in the form of fundamental principles and statements. The fundamental principles are framed in broad and general terms, and give basic advice on professional behaviour. Statements elaborate on what is expected of members in particular circumstances.

The fundamental principles are:

- A member should behave with integrity in all professional and business relationships. Integrity implies not merely honesty but, rather, fair dealing and truthfulness.

- A member should strive for objectivity in all professional and business judgements. Objectivity is the state of mind that has regard to all considerations relevant to the task in hand but no other.

- A member should not accept or perform work that he or she is not competent to undertake unless he obtains such advice and assistance as will enable him competently to carry out the work.

- A member should carry out his or her professional work with due skill, care, diligence and expedition and with proper regard for the technical and professional standards expected of him as a member.

- A member should conduct himself or herself with courtesy and consideration towards all with whom he comes into contact during the course of producing his work.

The statements identify areas of risk that may bring into question the independence of members. For members in practice, the areas of risk identified are: undue dependence on an audit client; significant overdue fees from a client; actual or threatened litigation; influences outside the practice; family and other personal relationships; interests in shares and other investments; beneficial interests in trusts; trustee investments; voting on audit appointments; loans; goods, services and hospitality; and the provision of other services to audit clients.

The code of professional ethics (and accounting regulations) is enforced through the Joint Disciplinary Scheme (JDS), which was formed in 1979, and is run jointly by the ICAW, the ICAS and the ACCA. These professional bodies can discipline members for misconduct, incompetence and inefficiency. The punishments available range from suspension from membership, fines, reprimands, serious reprimands and withdrawal of practising certificates.

15.5   Case studies

Background information

All the facts of this case study are fictitious, and they are not intended to resemble any companies, persons or ships.

RBSC Ltd is a company registered in the UK, and is a wholly owned subsidiary of the UK Shipping Consortium Ltd. RBSC Ltd's ultimate holding company is registered overseas, and is owned by a family with worldwide shipping interests. The principal activity of RBSC Ltd is the chartering of the supertanker *RBII*, which carries a cargo of crude oil. The ship is registered in Hong Kong and employs a British crew.

The *RBII* is due to sail to Portsmouth in March 2009 for dry-docking and a five-yearly overhaul of the hull. The company's next financial year end is 31 December 2008.

CASE STUDY 15.1

Management accountant

The Management Accountant, Angela, has been employed by RBSC Ltd for several years and now holds a senior position in the company.

In March 20×4, the management team identified four possible ports (in different parts of the world) with dry-docking facilities that could carry out the overhaul of the hull. Angela was asked to quantify each alternative, in order to determine the most cost-effective port. The costs relevant to the decision included estimates for each port of: the costs of sailing to the port; charter fees lost due to the ship being out of service; dry-docking fees; and repair costs. Where possible, Angela obtained estimates from suppliers, however a number of assumptions had to be made about the future exchange rates and the number of days the ship would be out of service.

At the end of the exercise, it was clear that the highest cost port, at an estimated £7m, would be Portsmouth. The Managing Director (MD), who has a financial interest in the Portsmouth shipyard, persuaded Angela to change a number of the assumptions on which the calculations were based in order to make Portsmouth appear to be the lowest cost port at an estimated £6m.

CASE STUDY 15.2

Financial accountant

The Financial Accountant, Frank, who was appointed in June 2008, has experience of auditing and is recently qualified. Being a relatively high profile, high-risk business, Frank had been pleased to be able to negotiate a salary substantially above the market rate for an equivalent position in other sectors, together with an annual bonus based on performance.

Frank is currently preparing the financial statements for the year ended 31 December 2008. The published, audited accounts for the year ended 31 December 2007 included a cumulative provision for dry-docking charges of £1 m. Frank is aware that a costing exercise has been carried out, but is unable to obtain a copy, and is being stonewalled by Angela and the MD. The receptionist, who opens the post, has informed him that 'everyone knows' that the dry-docking charge is likely to be in the region of £6 m.

The MD is putting Frank under considerable pressure to include a cumulative provision of only £3 m, and has suggested that any concerns about the likely level of dry-docking charges need not be disclosed to the auditors. The MD is currently negotiating a substantial loan from the bank.

CASE STUDY 15.3

Auditor

The Audit Manager After reviewing the financial statements (prepared by the Financial Accountant) for the year ended 31 December 20×4, the Audit Manager, Clare, identified the provision of £3 m for dry-docking charges as an item carrying significant audit risk. On investigation, the audit team was unable to obtain documentary evidence to substantiate the provision and has also been made aware of the rumour that the actual figure is likely to be £6 m.

The Managing Director is refusing to discuss the subject and threatening to appoint alternative auditors, unless the accounts are finalised before the meeting with the bank.

The Audit Partner The audit partner, Mike, is a junior partner in a medium-sized firm of chartered accountants. The audit fee from RBSC Ltd represents a significant proportion of his fee income, but a small proportion of the fee income of the partnership as a whole. Mike has also advised RBSC Ltd on the appointment of the Financial Accountant, and has given general advice on various sources of finance.

The Managing Director and Mike eventually compromised, and agreed on a provision of £4 m for dry-docking charges. The accounts were duly signed by the partnership as presenting a true and fair view, and were used by the company to obtain a bank loan. In March 20×5, the actual dry-docking charges amounted to £7 m.

███████ QUESTIONS AND TASKS ███████

Discussion

Case Study 15.1

In order to behave ethically, Angela must strive for objectivity and behave with integrity: in this situation, Angela must make a judgement as to whom exactly she owes these duties. Although the MD is her immediate superior, the primary duty is owed to the company itself, which is managed by the board of directors as a whole. Angela is, therefore, under a duty to ensure that the board has accurate information on which to base its decisions – for example, in relation to dry-docking. Further, as the Managing Director is seeking to influence Angela in this decision, she must take a decision as to whether or not she should inform the board of his attempts to 'persuade' her to alter her assumptions. In other words, does her ethical duty only extend to ensuring accurate information is provided or does it extend to reporting the surrounding circumstances?

Question:

If the board decide to go along with the MD's decision after the assumptions in favour of Portsmouth, does Angela's duty extend to trying to inform the company's shareholders/auditors of her misgivings?

Case Study 15.2

Frank is clearly a well-paid, highly valued member of the management team. However, he must not allow these factors to affect his professional judgement.

Frank has a clear duty to 'users' of financial information, which group includes lenders. Therefore, if the dry-docking costs would be a relevant factor in the bank's decision to lend, the Financial Accountant should ensure that accurate information is available. As in Case study 15.1, the Financial Accountant should report his findings direct to the board, whom he should also remind that they have a duty to ensure that the company's audited accounts present a 'true and fair view' of the company's affairs.

Question:

If the board take the same position as the MD, should the Frank inform the auditors of his concerns?

Case Study 15.3

The audit firm has a statutory duty to ensure that the company's accounts give a 'true and fair view' of the company's affairs. In a situation such as this, Clare should have insisted that documentary evidence of the dry-docking estimates be made available.

However, had this request been denied, Clare's ethical position becomes less clear. She clearly has a duty to the company's shareholders, but would she be fulfilling her duty by simply passing the problem on to the Audit Partner. The answer to the question is probably 'yes'. The Audit Partner is working within the same code of ethics as Clare but has greater experience on which to make the appropriate decision and, with his partners, will have the ultimate responsibility for signing off the accounts as presenting a 'true and fair view'.

Question:

What if the Audit Partner comes to a decision that Clare believes to be unethical, and one that potentially breaches the Auditor's statutory duties?

It seems that Mike put himself in a difficult position, even before this situation arose. Clearly, from a personal perspective, he may be relying too heavily on the fees from one audit client, even though the relevant provision of the professional code refers to the audit fee income of the practice as a whole. In addition, by providing related services, other than auditing, he has placed a further strain on his independence, or at least his apparent independence. In relation to these matters, he should consider his position for the future, following discussions with his partners.

None of these factors should have affected Mike's judgement in this situation; his duties here are both statutory and ethical. If he could not justify the relevant dry-docking provision in the accounts, and felt the item was material, he should not have signed the accounts; he should, indeed, have sought the advice of his partners. This is particularly important as his partners will be jointly and severally liable with Mike should action be taken against the firm in relation to the inaccurate accounts.

Question:

Would the partner's position be any different if the actual dry-docking charges amounted to £4.2 m?

CHAPTER 16

The Ethical Organisation and Production

After you have read this chapter you will:

- Understand what the role of production manager involves

- Appreciate the range and nature of the ethical issues this role raises

- Have engaged with some examples of those issues and considered one in some detail

- Be familiar with some frameworks and guidelines that can help clarify and resolve the issues.

16.1　Production management

Production management is concerned with making the best use of the resources of an organisation in order to produce the outcomes (which might be goods and/or services) that it has been set up to provide. In considering how ethical issues can arise in this area, we will need to examine ethical behaviour on the part of managers in both the production and service sectors. In order to do that, first, we need to specify the range of roles and activities relevant here. Such managers often carry between them a wide range of job titles. In order to identify whether they are production managers, we need to look at what they actually do and are described as doing – that is, as someone who is continually dealing with the efficient balancing of input resources to achieve planned output levels of goods and/or services with the right timing, quantity and quality levels.

The following model job specifications are useful. Model 1 is associated with the manufacturing sector and Model 2 with the service sector.

Model 1

The job specification for this type of manager includes ongoing responsibility for the:

- Reception of incoming raw materials and bought-out components

- Safe and secure storage of materials

- Movement of materials within the plant
- Production scheduling of orders
- Maintenance of quality specifications
- Negotiations with suppliers/customers on just-in-time issues
- Packaging and palleting of product
- Distribution of product using in-house or contract carriers
- Direction of employees engaged in these operational areas
- Training and development of staff
- General manufacturing productivity levels
- Standard time values used for the manufacturing processes
- Employee suggestion schemes
- Layout and design of the work areas
- Health and safety at work for employees
- Staff reward systems including bonus schemes
- Efficient maintenance of the machinery or plant
- Record keeping, scheduling and control of orders
- Decision-making on operational issues
- Management of quality.

Model 2

The job specification for this type of manager includes on-going responsibility for the:

- Reception of incoming mail, faxes, e-mails, computer printouts, telephone calls and bought-out materials
- Secure storage of documents and computer files
- Movement of information/data within the work area
- Prioritising of jobs to be done
- Maintenance of a quality staff performance
- Negotiations with suppliers/customers
- Dealing with enquiries
- Decision-making on policies
- Despatch of information using appropriate modes of delivery

- Direction of staff

- General productivity levels

- Training and development of staff

- Layout and design of the work areas

- Health and safety at work for staff

- Staff work systems including flexible and part-time work methods

- Staff reward systems including bonus schemes

- Maintenance of the computers and office equipment

- Record keeping: scheduling and control

- Decision-making on operational issues

- Management of quality.

Comparison of the lists associated with each model shows both similarities and differences. Some of the responsibility of the Model 1 manager is associated with a tangible outcome from the process, which can be checked and verified by quantitative methods. The Model 2 manager will tend, to a greater extent, to work with operations where there is a greater need for qualitative judgement, and the associated potential for disagreement and problems in communication.

16.2 Delivering ethical practice

There is an inevitable tension (and, it must be said, sometimes an opposition) between the demand for a high standard of ethical behaviour, both in principle and in practice, and the need for a company to be competitive and profitable. It also needs to be remembered that the drawing up of a corporate ethical policy is a comparatively straightforward affair compared with the problems of implementing and delivering it in practice.

Research undertaken in the USA in 1990 led to the listing of 26 ethical issues in business:

Rank	Issue
1	Drug and alcohol abuse
2	Employee theft
3	Conflicts of interest
4	Quality control
5	Discrimination
6	Misuse of propriety information
7	Fiddling of expense accounts
8	Plant closures and lay-offs
9	Misuse of company assets
10	Environmental pollution
11	Misuse of others' information
12	Industrial espionage

13 Inaccuracies in documents and records
14 Receiving excessive gifts and entertainment
15 False or misleading advertising
16 Giving excessive gifts or entertainment
17 Receiving 'backhanders'
18 Insider (information) trading
19 Relations with local communities
20 Antitrust issues (for example, price rings)
21 Bribery
22 Political contributions and activities
23 Improper relationships with local government personnel
24 Improper relationships with national government personnel
25 Inaccurate charging to government bodies
26 Improper relationships with foreign government personnel.

Source: Adapted from *Ethics, Policies and Programs in American business: Report of a Landmark Survey of US Corporations*, Ethics Resource Center, cited in Hellriegel et al. (1993).

Many of these issues could face both Model 1 and Model 2 managers. They would, for example, need to take account of the effects of drug or alcohol abuse on his/her own work performance and the performance of their teams. They would also need to be concerned about the safety of staff at the workplace where either their own judgement or the judgement of colleagues was impaired by alcohol or drugs (though this could well be a greater problem for a production manager in manufacturing, where the work hazards could be greater). They might be faced with the problems of enforcing drug testing on employees in sensitive positions. The requirements of the law, job security, personal embarrassment, or the problems involved in confronting such abuse might all have to be traded off against the damage disclosure could do to the overall well-being and productivity of the firm. Equally, although significant employee theft levels from the premises can be controlled to some extent by the introduction of increasingly sophisticated security and budgetary control procedures, the cost could outweigh the loss itself and the intrusion cause annoyance to the decent and honest staff.

The Model 1 manager could face problems with employee theft or environmental pollution. The Model 2 manager might be concerned about financial fraud, which could ultimately, in the worst case, ruin the firm. Solving such problems involves not only specialised technical expertise – possibly having to be imported into the firm on a contract basis – but also much painstaking detective work. The ethical dilemma here is one of relationship and trust, and the possibility of a witch-hunt once any real evidence is unearthed. Commercial espionage and breaches of the Data Protection Act would raise very similar issues.

16.3 Quality

Quality control issues will continually present ethical difficulties for production managers. The prominence currently being given to quality assurance and enhancement, together with increasing pressure to cut costs, mean that production managers have continually to work with very little ethical margin for error or misjudgement. The production manager in a food company might think about cutting costs by putting a little less cocoa mass into each bar of chocolate. The company can probably get away with it, at least in the short term, because it will be hard to spot by taste alone. But the public is being short-changed, whether it realises it or not, and market share might fall in the medium or long term. (Similar examples would be: more water in pre-packed ham, less fabric in the seams of garments, cheaper wood in the less visible parts of furniture, and so on.) The administrator controlling hospital ward contract cleaning could be tempted to cut the level of service slightly. Again, it could be some time before this was noticeable but, in the meantime, hygiene is compromised and the health of patients put at risk.

Although writing primarily about supervisors employed in the automotive industry, Lowe (1993) explains how, from the 1920s, there was a proliferation of specialist departments being formed, which narrowed the width of the job. Since the 1980s however, the search for so-called 'lean production' systems has now greatly widened the manufacturing supervisor's role – probably to an even wider span than before. They have become the central focus for integrating strategic goals, such as total quality and continuous improvement, with concerns such as scheduling and manning levels, which were previously the domain of higher managers. In the drive to optimise resources and achieve targets, production managers will inevitably face unavoidable ethical dilemmas.

16.4 Managerial roles

With the widening range of responsibilities, planning has become rather more important than the more traditional decision-making process, which focused on outcomes. A well-recognised problem with planning, however, is the difficulty of harmonising sub-plans and reconciling different objectives; of achieving, in a well-known phrase, 'joined-up thinking'. A production manager has to produce a plan that ensures there is no discrimination, uses optimal work methods that ensure health and safety, generates high productivity levels, meets quality and quantity criteria, enables detailed scheduling and financial control procedures to operate, maintains privacy and confidentiality, and, ultimately, satisfies the customer. This is no mean feat – particularly under the severe time constraints imposed by the pace of modern business. It follows, as Stevenson (1993) argues, that the production or operations manager is the key figure in a system, with the ultimate responsibility for the creation of goods and services.

Clearly, managing a banking operation requires a different kind of expertise from managing a steel-making operation. Nevertheless, they both need an essentially similar skill-set – the ability to coordinate the use of resources by planning, organising, staffing, directing and controlling within an ethical framework.

The planning process involves future courses of action and responding to questions such as:

- What are we making?

- What will be the effects on staff, the environment, the customer?

- Where shall we make it?

- How shall we provide the service?

- What quantities and quality standards will apply?

- What will be the effects of growth/decline on the staff and locality?

- What profit will accrue if we exploit the market?'

Organising means the creation or adaptation of an administrative structure – a working system in itself. Typically. it requires answers to questions such as:

- Are lines of responsibility and authority clear?

- How is information disseminated or, if necessary, kept confidential?

- Who is responsible for health and safety, and how?

- Who keeps records of what, how and where?

Staffing deals with the most unpredictable and volatile resource issue:

- How are staff recruited and selected?

- What training and skills are really necessary?

- What working system is required?

- What kind of pay and reward systems are appropriate and fair?

- Which types of formal procedure are necessary?'

16.5 Ethical problems – an analytical framework

Examples 16.1, 16.2 and 16.3 cover a range of situations, which can be analysed using the following principles:

Magnitude of consequences

- A decision on food quality that causes illness to 1,000 diners is of greater magnitude than a decision causing the same illness to 10 people

- A decision regarding machine safety that causes death to an operator is of greater magnitude than one that causes a cut finger.

Probability of the effect

- Manufacturing a car that is dangerous to occupants during a normal driving routine has a greater probability of harm than the manufacture of a car that is dangerous only at speeds far in excess of the legal limit

- Selling a hunting knife to a known criminal has a greater probability of harm than selling it to a law-abiding citizen.

Temporal immediacy

- Producing a new pharmaceutical product that will give bad side effects immediately to 1 per cent of the people taking it has greater temporal immediacy than a product that might produce those side effects in people after 30 years

- Cutting the company retirement pensions for existing pensioners has a greater temporal immediacy than announcing changes that will affect employees with another possible 20 years of service.

Concentration of effect

- A change in acceptance of claims under a product quality guarantee that denies 10 people each claiming £10,000 compensation has more concentrated effect than a change that denies claims made by 10,000 people of £10 each

- Delayed payment to an individual or small business of £1,000 has a more concentrated effect than non-payment of the same sum to government tax inspectors.

Not all of the six factors are present in each ethical decision. Where there is more than one present, the ethical intensity increases. Ethical intensity is the degree of importance of an ethical issue.

CASE STUDY 16.1

Bias

The operations manager of a haulage company is considering placing a £400,000 order for new 38-tonne lorries with a European manufacturer after visiting their plant for a couple of hours. The manager, who was accompanied by his wife, stayed for several days; his company paid for the trip. The specifications of the equivalent British made truck are similar.

CASE STUDY 16.2

Poaching

The production director of a technology-based company in a fast moving industry is under pressure from his board to try to poach an employee of a rival company. This employee has advanced R&D information and could be expected to bring with him specialised manufacturing knowledge of product and materials. The board recognises that it has under-resourced its R&D effort for some years, and has fallen well behind its competitors. The future of the company has become uncertain.

Tendering

A production manager in the construction industry is being encouraged by his CEO to submit a seriously under-costed tender to refurbish school buildings in the local authority. The CEO is persuaded that the authority will accept a contract with no penalties and that a reasonable profit can therefore be made from deliberate budget over-runs. In the meantime, the tender will, naturally, undercut all the rival bids.

Unfavourable practices

Production workers at British Depa Crepes Ltd, nylon processors in Oldham, were required to submit a daily timesheet from which bonus payments were calculated on a weekly basis.

Many workers were simultaneously performing similar jobs in the same department on adjacent machinery. The pay system allowed workers to claim extra time allowances on the grounds of having to work with poor materials or in difficult circumstances. Individual workers often came under a lot of peer pressure to do this, especially just before the annual or Christmas holiday period, thus increasing bonuses at a time when domestic finances were stretched. However, some employees were well aware that all additional manufacturing costs had to be funded out of a very slim profit margin and the business was under severe pressure from imported rival products. They were, as a result, uneasy about doing it.

The manager concerned with the authorisation of submitted timesheets was faced with a range of considerations. She could sympathise with the need to maximise earnings at very expensive times of the year, and she knew that the employees were paid adequately rather than handsomely. She also knew that the practice was of long standing and was considered by some to be an entitlement rather than a bonus. But she had every reason for thinking that the company could ill-afford it and that most of the claims were at least disingenuous, if not straightforwardly fraudulent. However, there was no doubt that tackling this issue would be extremely unpopular and might lead to industrial action. The checks and controls needed to monitor and verify the claims would be expensive, cause resentment and threaten trust. On the other hand, it would not do her reputation as a manager any good if her manager thought she had not noticed, did not care or was too weak to address the situation. The auditors might not like it either.

Let us now consider Case Study 16.4.

Initial suggested questions

1 Does the manager need any further information or corroboration before she decides what to do? If so, what and how should she obtain it?

2 How far should others be involved in the decision? And who?

3 Look at the Code of Ethics for the Institute of Management Services (p. 235). Is what it says helpful, relevant or appropriate?

Ethically, we can analyse this situation in a number of ways. Two approaches are particularly useful: the first is advocated by Premeaux and Mondy (1993), the second is adapted from the work of Hellriegel et al. (1992).

Analysis 1: By rights

The entitlements of the employees:

To act as an individual

To act honestly

Not be discriminated against either by peers or management

The entitlements of the manager:

To authorise correct claims

To reject excessive claims

To amend erroneous claims

To manage without threats from above or below

To act professionally at all times

Analysis 2: Justice

The equity and distributive fairness of the situation for workers:

Is the bonus scheme itself fair?

Is the time sheet booking system for extra allowance fair?

Does it pay to be honest?

The equity and distributive fairness of the situation for the manager:

Can a really fair decision be made?

What is best for all parties?

Are there precedents, custom and practice?

How can I maintain credibility?

Analysis 3: By outcome

Act utilitarian: the decision giving the greatest social benefit to the greatest number:

The Operations Manager must weigh up the full range of short and long-term effects of the final decision. The likelihood is that most will find the temporal immediacy of the short-term implications rather more compelling than the longer-term considerations. The achievement of being a trusted manager leading a better paid, more stable, happier workforce is also an attractive objective, it could conceivably make the company more productive and allow it to compete with its rivals. It is quite possible that any overpayments will be lost in the morass of data produced by the company information system.

Rule utilitarian: the evaluation of the rules governing the decision:

Even if allowing the situation to continue would make more people better off, it is clearly against the rules and not enforcing these rules could well lead to other rules being broken or ignored. However, the rules can be changed. What rules, if followed, would bring about the best result for everyone.

Analysis 3: By principles

Hedonist principle

The worker wants as much reward as possible, for as little effort as possible, for as much of the working life as possible: the Operations Manager may be guided by his/her own interests and personal objectives, rather than what is best for the firm.

'Might equals right' principle

The workers may feel strong in the collective sense as trade unionists with the ability to use local, even national, muscle to achieve objectives. The operations manager could have considerable lassitude in terms of what his or her managerial authority allows them to do with timesheet claims.

Conventionalist principle

The workers might have come to believe that it is customary and acceptable to the firm for them to over-claim just before a holiday.

Intuition principle

In the absence of clear rules, the manager makes whatever decision feels to her to be right, even if different decisions had been made previously.

Organisational ethic principle

This would apply if the managers had been trained (or cajoled) into always automatically thinking of the company first. This was not the case at British Depa Crepes Ltd. Clearly, many (but not all) employees had a 'them and us' mindset. However, many people who work for charitable organisations might so believe in its aims that personal concerns always take second place.

Consequentialist principle

The manager will need to weigh up perceived good and bad effects of all of the possible decisions and their consequences.

Professional ethic principle

The workers, if unionised, will, in effect, be operating to the principles regarding industrial relations that are espoused by their union. The manager who belongs to a professional body will probably be a signatory to the guidelines of that professional body. In some professions, loss of professional membership, accreditation and qualifications, results in unemployment.

Disclosure principle

The manager has already built up a relationship with staff and must decide how much information on the actions taken and the underlying rationale should be communicated to those affected. The timing of disclosure might also be highly significant.

Distributive justice principle

The workers will want to feel that equal treatment is being given with no discrimination based on arbitrary criteria. This is one of the reasons that workers join trade unions.

Categorical imperative principle

The employees may believe that excessive extra allowance claims are, at times, justifiable and should be formalised (that they should, in effect, become holiday bonuses) on the grounds that they are earned and deserved, and everyone thinks they should be paid what they earn and deserve. The manager may refuse all unwarranted extra allowance claims and advise staff that the norm is to only pay warranted claims, on the grounds that to do otherwise is to pay someone more than they have earned and no one thinks it reasonable that they should pay more than they owe.

16.6 Guidelines for ethical decision making in production management

Pagano and Verdin (1988) offer a list of guidelines that you can apply to difficult social problems and ethical dilemmas. These guidelines will not tell you exactly what to do, but they will help you evaluate the situation more clearly by examining your own values and those of your organisation.

- Is the problem/dilemma really what it appears to be? If you are not sure, find out.

- Is the action you are considering legal? Ethical? If you are not sure, find out.

- Do you understand the position of those who oppose the action you are considering? Is it reasonable?

- Whom does this action benefit? Harm? How much? How long?

- Would you be willing to allow everyone to do what you are considering doing?

- Have you sought the opinion of others who are more knowledgeable on the subject, and who would be objective?

- Would your action be embarrassing to you if it were made known to your family, friends, co-workers or superiors? Would you be comfortable defending your actions to an investigative reporter on the evening news?

16.7 Code of professional ethics

The Institute of Management Services, a leading professional body in the field of production management, has produced a code of ethics for its members: Members shall:

1 Conduct themselves in a manner which will merit the respect of the community for persons engaged in the profession;

2 Uphold the reputation of the Institute and the dignity of the profession;

3 Carry out their professional duties responsibly and with integrity;

4 Collect and marshal facts without bias, and not allow their personal views or the views of others to influence their professional judgement, interpretation, analysis and presentation of those facts;

5 Not discuss with, or disclose to, any persons not authorised to receive such information by their employer or their employer's delegated representative, whether within or outside their employer's organisation, the data, results, reports or proposals arising from their work; nor shall they cause such confidential information to be misused or to be published without permission;

6 Not use information acquired during a previous employment in any way that could be detrimental to their former employer;

7 Not receive any undisclosed material benefits other than their normal emoluments consequent upon any recommendation they may make in the course of their duties.

In addition, there is a guide to good practice that stipulates that members 'must always attempt to use their professional skills with integrity and objectivity. In the event of commitments conflicting, they should stress their professional accountability . . . and that their skills be used impartially and responsibly.'

QUESTIONS AND TASKS

Read the latest Social Responsibility Report of British American Tobacco. This company manufactures cigarettes.

1 Does it manufacture them in an ethical manner?

2 Is it possible for a company to have ethical production management but still be an unethical company? (Use the list of criteria you developed at the end of Chapter 1 to help you to answer this question.)

CHAPTER 17

The Ethical Organisation and Individuals at Work

LEARNING OUTCOMES

After reading this chapter you will:

- Be aware of the range of ethical issues facing individual managers working in organisations

- Be able to identify and use different ways of approaching ethical dilemmas as an individual within an organisation.

17.1 The individual at work

How are the ethical problems facing the individual at work any different from those to be faced anywhere else? Surely here, if nowhere else, the argument that business ethics is no more than ethics applied to business has some application. Certainly, it is true that many of the difficult moral decisions faced in the workplace are raised by issues that are not peculiar to work but, rather, are to do with one's treatment of other people and theirs of you. Must one keep this promise? Was that indeed a promise or merely a vague statement of intent? How far should one go in taking decisions that affect others without consulting or, at least, informing them? But it is also true that an individual who works in or for an organisation is in a position that is complicated by factors that do not apply to a person acting in a private capacity.

We all have rights, duties, responsibilities, powers, interests, and so on that accrue to us as people within a society. We have the right to vote, to apply for a passport, to join a political party; we have a duty of care towards our dependent children and, perhaps, to others such as elderly relatives; we have ties of affection and obligation that bind us to friends and acquaintances; we might belong to churches, clubs, building societies and the like. All of these contribute to defining us as moral individuals surrounded by a network of reciprocal relationships with others to whom we owe, and from whom we expect, loyalty, respect, esteem, friendship, duty and obligation in different proportions and to a greater or lesser extent.

We do not lose these moral relationships once we enter the workplace: obviously we gain new ones. Some of these will arise, as before, because of our status as a private person, the moral individual whom we are. Some of them, however, will be contingent not on our being whom we are, but on our holding the post that we do within the organisation. We acquire new powers and responsibilities that, strictly speaking, are not ours at all, but those of the position we fill or the function we perform. And not only will these new powers, responsibilities, duties, interests, concerns, and so on be different from the ones we had before, they may even conflict with them.

17.2   Power, authority and trust

For example, in a private capacity it is accepted that, whatever we may feel to be the nature and extent of the care and concern we should owe to everyone, we owe a special degree of consideration to those closest to us. We should look after them and help them whenever we can, and to the best of our abilities. But should the personnel manager of a large industrial company show special consideration to friends and relatives who apply for jobs within that company? Should a financial journalist use knowledge gained from doing the job to tip off people he or she knows have risky investments? Should someone with a large investment in a company warn close relatives who also have shares that he is about to unload his and that the values of those shares is therefore likely to go down substantially? Should the head of purchasing manager give a lucrative contract to a cousin who is in the right line of business but happens to be in financial difficulties at the moment and needs the business badly?

The fact that, in such cases, the person is no longer acting solely on her or his own account clearly makes a difference. What would be permitted, even laudable, behaviour for a private person becomes suspect once that person is acting in trust for a third party, the organisation. It is even more suspect if what makes it *possible* for that person to act in that way is the power and authority that is loaned by the organisation itself. But, though this is clear enough in principle, in practice, drawing the lines between the private and the public is not easy. Consider the following:

Situation 1

An executive of a financial services company is also the treasurer of a local charity. She is punctilious about not using company stationery or reprographic facilities for this work, but she does use a company computer for the work, because the software is too expensive for the charity to fund for the very occasional use it would make of it.

Situation 2

The manager of a large city centre store uses personal influence to obtain a relatively low-paid job for an old friend who has been out of work for a very long time. The friend is more than adequately qualified for the job, but the competition for it was fierce.

Situation 3

An estate agent arranges to sell a house that the owners wish to put on the market at a ridiculously low price because they want to move quickly. Before making the details public, the agent rings his sister-in-law whom he knows is looking for just such a house as this, and the deal is concluded privately.

Situation 4
As in situation 3, except that the agent realises that the price suggested is lower than it need be even for a quick sale, but says nothing: 'The customer is always right'.

Situation 5
As in 4, except that the sister-in-law does not want the house at all, but sells it on immediately and splits her profit with the agent.

Situation 6
The purchasing manager of a medium-sized company receives quotations for office stationery from a number of suppliers, including one run by a cousin. In terms of cost, the differences between them are marginal. The decision is taken to place the order with the cousin.

In situation 5, the actions of the estate agent may not be illegal, but hardly anyone would have any problem in deciding that they were morally indefensible. In all the other cases, a moral conclusion is not so easy to draw. Situation 1 may well be defensible, even praiseworthy, provided only that the executive does what she does openly and with the consent, tacit or explicit, of the company for which she works. All the cases show, at the least, a potential for an abuse of power that can arise from a failure to distinguish what is appropriate behaviour in one role as opposed to another.

17.3 Secrecy, confidentiality and loyalty

Problems created by the protection of confidential information and the circumstances under which it may or should be disclosed are not peculiar to business ethics, neither are they generated solely by role conflict. They arise in all circumstances, both public and private.

The duty to tell the truth is always qualified by the need to ask whether the person you are telling it to is entitled to know it. The simplest, most widespread and, usually, most trivial example of this is gossip. The word has two meanings: its most familiar being idle or groundless rumour, tittle-tattle, malicious or spiteful untruth. But the second is related to its origin as godparent (OE *godsibb*, person related to one in God: *Concise Oxford Dictionary*), where it means the easy or unconstrained small talk that goes on between close friends and relations. Both senses matter, for gossip need not be a source for moral concern and, in the second sense, is important in building and maintaining the intimacy necessary between those who work or live closely together.

It also has a vital function in its role as grapevine, where it is an extremely efficient communications network and acts to preserve the common knowledge base without which concerted cooperative action (at any level, from that of the family, through the institutional to the cultural) would be all but impossible. It cannot, therefore, nor should it be proscribed. But in its first sense it is clearly dangerous. Those who engage in gossip must walk a thin line between passing on what justifiably is in the public domain (the weather, last night's episode of *Eastenders*, the new policy on allocating spaces in the company car park) and what one may know but ought not to casually and promiscuously disclose (X's marital problems, Y's alcoholism or the state of Z's health). It is not that such things always ought to be kept secret, but disclosing them risks harming others and that risk, together with its avoidability and defensibility must always be considered. (Perhaps the information is already public knowledge – Y is proud of having being an ex-alcoholic and boasts of it; or perhaps there is a public interest in disclosure – Z persists in driving a car despite dizzy spells and in the teeth of doctor's advice.)

It also matters how one came to be in possession of such information, and here issues of trust are raised again. Many social positions and occupations require one to be entrusted with information that one may not deal with as if one had learned it in a private capacity. One might, indeed, have strong contractual, professional or moral obligations not to disclose such information at all, or only to specific individuals in specific circumstances. The confidentiality of medical records, for example, if not absolute, is very nearly so. Without the consent of the patient, such records may only be disclosed to other health care professionals who might need to see them, or by Court order, or to the police in the investigation of serious crime (see Brazier 1987: ch. 3). The field of medicine is special, however, only in the fact that the law treats virtually all of what goes on between doctor and patient as confidential, not in the degree of protection it offers such confidential information. Disclosure of *any* information given in confidence is an offence (though a civil rather than a criminal one) when protecting that confidentiality is in the public interest and is recognised as grounds for dismissal in English law (Selwyn 1993: 6.64). This may apply even after an employee has left an organisation, which raises problems of its own.

An organisation clearly has a right to protect information whose disclosure – to competitors, say – would threaten its prosperity or survival. This might include client lists, industrial processes, management structures or procedures – any form of information that might plausibly be considered the intellectual property of the organisation rather than of individual employees and not in the public domain. It is normally held that a contract of employment creates a duty of fidelity – that is, an employee owes a loyalty to an employer that would be violated by divulging information likely to damage that employer (Smith and Wood 1993: 3.5). So, for example, someone who, just before he left a business in order to set up in competition with it, copied out a list of its clients for future use, would be in breach of contract (*Robb v Green* [1895-9] All ER 1053). Two areas are less clear than this, however. The first concerns the extent to which someone may use the skills and knowledge they gained in one employment when they take up a new job or, even, make those skills and that knowledge the basis on which they obtain the new job. The Inland Revenue has long had the problem that expensively trained tax inspectors frequently find employment with businesses of the kind they were trained to inspect – gamekeepers become poachers. In television, too, it is well known that BBC-trained technicians are highly valued by independent production companies, whose size means that they do very little training of their own and whose competitiveness often depends on just that fact. The law distinguishes between confidential information – which is, in effect, the property of the original employer and may not be passed on even when the employee is in a new job – and the skills and knowledge that form part of an employee's ability and which he or she is entitled to use in order to gain new employment (*Faccenda Chicken Ltd v. Fowler* [1986] ICR 297). The moral issue is not so straightforward – though even the law finds it easier to make the distinction than to apply it. Are you justified in allowing an organisation to spend a lot of money in training and developing your skills so that you can immediately leave and find a better job somewhere else?

The second area concerns whistle-blowing. This problem has been given extensive treatment elsewhere (see, for example, Bok 1982; Donaldson 1989: ch. 7; and Shaw and Barry 1989: ch. 7), and so we do not intend to discuss it in full. It does need to be mentioned, however, because it also poses the question of whether one may pass on material that would otherwise be confidential. The law is perfectly clear on this: the duty to respect confidentiality does not extend to cover breaches of the law or other wrongful actions: 'there is no confidence as to the disclosure of an iniquity' (Selwyn 1993: 11.8), nor does it release an employee from a legal obligation to disclose information; for example, to the Health and Safety Executive or FSO. The law in the UK does (as it does not in the US, or only imperfectly so) protect an employee against dismissal for justifiably blowing the whistle, both at common law and by statute. But it does not, and probably cannot, protect an employee against loss of promotion, non-renewal of contract or other forms of victimisation. Nor is it even clear how far the whistle-blower will be protected against dismissal to the extent that what is disclosed is not criminal but, merely, immoral or, in some other way, dubious. Certainly, Sarah Tisdall was not protected from the consequences of her breach in 1984 of the Official Secrets Act in virtue of her disclosure that a government minister allegedly misled the House of Commons about the placement of Trident missiles.

EXAMPLE 17.1

Organisations and individuals

Civil servant of twenty-five years' standing, David Keogh, was charged on 29 November 2005 with breaking the Official Secrets Act. The charges against him relate to the alleged leak of a document containing details of a discussion between Tony Blair and George W. Bush. This document allegedly shows that Blair had to dissuade Bush from bombing Al Jazeera, the Arabic news service, in Qatar.

On 10 January 2006, his defence lawyer was shown the secret Al Jazeera bombing memo and declared it posed no threat to national security and vowed to have it made public by the court. The trial was due to begin on 9 October 2006. However, on that date the judge ruled that the hearing should be in secret. It was then reported that the trial itself would begin on 18 April 2007.

In arguing for the trial to remain secret, the government claimed the memo 'could have a serious impact upon the international relations' of the UK and that the 'risk is of such magnitude to outweigh the interest of open public justice'.

> On 10 May 2007, Keogh was found guilty on two counts of making a 'damaging disclosure' by revealing he memo and was sentenced to six months in jail. He was also ordered to pay £50,000 in costs to the prosecution.
>
> Civil Service rules state that someone in Keogh's position should report his concerns to his superior.

17.4   Resolving dilemmas

How can managers cope with the ethical dilemmas that they face at work? Are there any useful guidelines that they can be given?

The answers to these questions are not straightforward and the first essential step is to look further into the questions themselves. In relation to the first question, would our answer differ if we rephrased the question to ask 'How can people cope with the ethical dilemmas they face?' Why do we use the label 'manager' when dealing with the sub-set of ethical dilemmas faced by people at work? Again, would our answer differ if we asked 'How can people cope with the ethical dilemmas they face as a supporter at a football match?' Does the context of the ethical dilemma make a difference?

The use of a special label to describe a person – manager, shop floor worker, football supporter – implies a role, as we have seen. As a manager, you are expected to carry out the role of manager, however that is defined in your particular context. Roles carry expectations. Your superiors at work will define their expectations of your behaviour in your role in formal ways (through a job description), or in informal ways (by demonstrating in their own behaviour how they expect managers to behave). Coping with the differences between formal and informal expectations is a skill that adults acquire, to varying levels of competence, through experience. However, life is made more complicated by fact that you probably have several roles at work. Managers may have to act as spokesperson for their section, chair of a selection panel, contributor to a discussion or policy paper, receiver of complaints, peacemaker, leader, coordinator, and so on. Informally, they may organise the five-a-side football team or collect in the tea money.

Switching from role to role with skill and aplomb is a difficult art. However, assuming you can do it, would you expect your ethical standards to differ between these roles? There is a widespread acceptance that differing roles demand differing ethical standards. This general acceptance lays beneath the first question. Is it legitimate to ask this question? Some commentators argue that it is not. Carmichael and Drummond (1989), for example, state: 'It is time to stop feeling helpless and to see that there are ways in which you can bring together the kind of citizen you want to be in your private life and the kind of citizen you want your company to be in its public life.'

They argue that the ethical standards of a person should not be changed or ignored just because the context changes. However, it is the case that many managers do indeed make unethical decisions in their work role with a readiness that they may find unacceptable in their private lives. Why is this case?

Gellerman (1986) argues that there are four major rationalisations used by managers to justify unethical behaviour. These are:

- A belief that the activity is within reasonable ethical and legal limits – that it is not really illegal or immoral

- A belief that the activity is in the individual's or corporation's best interests – that the individual would somehow be expected to undertake the activity

- A belief that the activity is 'safe' because it will never be found out or publicised – the classic crime and punishment issue of discovery

- A belief that, because the activity helps the company, the company will condone it and, even, protect the person who engages in it.

The use of the term 'rationalisations' implies that there may be other more fundamental reasons that lay behind the manager's unethical behaviour. What is it about organisational life that provides the fertile ground for such rationalisations? In choosing not to behave ethically, and consequently using a rationalisation to justify their behaviour, are managers telling us more about their personal moral development than about their organisation?

When people enter into work for an organisation, they usually sign a contract and there is often a job description that indicates their tasks. They receive payment, and possibly other rewards, in return for their fulfilment of their tasks. No contract or job description will require the person to act illegally or unethically. However, the sale of one's labour power to another often carries with it implicit assumptions and expectations. People quickly get to know what is really expected of them. Organisational culture has a deep influence on employees.

The strength of the organisational culture is reinforced at times when jobs are scarce. When unemployment is high, people are more willing to bend the rules in order to keep their job. Social and organisational influences, therefore, do have a significant influence on behaviour at work and, consequently, on ethical behaviour.

17.5   Advising managers

Several influential management books end with a paean to ethics – for example, Tom Peters in *Thriving on Chaos*: 'Set absurdly high standards for integrity – and then live with them with no fuzzy margins'. Nash's (1981) view is that 'Such advice fails to help the already well-minded manager who nevertheless finds the ethical aspects of business sometimes painful frequently confusing and occasionally a matter for personal disappointment in oneself or in one's company.'

It is also the case that such advice will not be well received by those managers who have decided to act unethically, even if they are able to offer a rationalisation for their action. Preaching will do no good in this context, for either the well-minded manager or for those who have decided to act unethically.

Trying to understand the reasons why normal moral values of private life seem to break down or become ineffectual in a business context is the challenge. Nash offers five reasons:

- The analytical frameworks that managers use
- The goals they set
- The organisational structures they adopt
- The language they use to motivate others
- Their personal assumptions about the intrinsic worth of other people.

If ethical issues and concerns do not figure in any of these areas, then it is unlikely that the organisation will be fostering a climate in which ethical behaviour becomes the norm. The need to produce rationalisations to justify unethical behaviour is diminished in organisations that pay attention to the ethical dimension of its corporate life.

Assuming that managers do not wish to behave unethically and that the ethical dilemmas they face might sometimes not be amenable to simplistic, formulaic solutions, then managers need to develop skill and experience in coping with ethical dilemmas. Nash (1981) offers a list of questions to act as guidance for managers. Such an approach is helpful for managers who are predisposed to behave ethically and who work within organisations that require or encourage ethical behaviour. The questions are:

1 Have you defined the problem accurately?

2 How would you define the problem if you stood on the other side of the fence?

3 How did the situation occur in the first place?

4 To whom and to what do you give your loyalty as a person and as a member of the corporation?

5 What is your intention in making this decision?

6 How does this intention compare with the probable result?

7 Whom would your decision or action injure?

8 Can you discuss the problem with the affected parties before you make your decision?

9 Are you confident that your decision will be as valid over a long period of time as it is now?

10 Could you discuss without qualm your decision with your boss, your chief executive officer, the board of directors, your family, society as a whole?

11 What is the symbolic potential of your action if understood, if misunderstood?

12 Under what circumstances would you allow exception to your stand?

This modelling of an approach to ethical dilemmas might appear cumbersome at first sight and, for managers who have not been able to clarify their own values or who work in an unsympathetic climate, it might seem to be quite irksome. However, this kind of approach has been found to be useful in practice and it does become easier with practice – as does any other skill.

Behaving ethically is based partly on the strength of commitment to a value system, fortitude in adversity and skill in analysing ethical issues – and the skill level can be improved with practice (see, for example, Delaney and Sockell 1992; and Kavathatzopoulos, 1993)

QUESTIONS AND TASKS

Think of an ethical issue you have faced at work.

1 Describe this issue, using one of the models identified in this chapter.

2 Decide how you would deal with this now, and compare this with how you dealt with it when it first arose.

3 Identify any differences between your original approach and your approach now.

Notes

1 The Ethical Organisation

1 The exceptions are those who cannot be agents because they lack, have lost or have still to acquire the relevant capabilities. This might include infants, those in a coma, with dementia or with very severe learning difficulties.

2 'Arguably', because the interpretation of Smith as a champion of untrammelled free enterprise is contested. See *The Wealth of Nations*, Cannan (1961). Amartya Sen, in *On Ethics and Economics* (1987), argues that Smith's doctrine of the 'invisible hand' has, and was meant to have, a much more limited application than twentieth-century economic liberalism has supposed.

3 A phrase from Peters and Waterman (1982).

4 Those who profit from a situation without incurring the costs of maintaining it, (those who ride for free on a transport system maintained by those who buy tickets); in this case those who dishonestly exploit an honest market. (They could not, of course, continue to exploit the market once it became dishonest any more than a transport system could continue if everyone managed to avoid buying a ticket.)

2 The Use of Cases in the Study of Business Ethics

1 This is a rather informal paraphrase of Kant's 'I ought never to act except in such a way *that I can also will that my maxim should become a universal law*' (which is, admittedly, somewhat stronger than my version) (Kant 1948: 67).

2 For an extended discussion of Aristotelian virtue theory as applied to business ethics, see Robert Soloman (1992 and 1993).

3 The best known of these, and probably the most interesting, is still Peters and Waterman (1982), but even this apparently falls into the trap of supposing that there are rules or maxims for success that can be generalised from one case to another.

3 Turner & Newall: The Case of the Asbestos Industry

This was kindly supplied by Richard C. Warren, who is HRM&OB group subject leader in the Manchester Metropolitan University Business School. He holds degrees from the Polytechnics of Wolverhampton and Plymouth, and the University of Manchester. He was a merchant seaman for five years before working in the Commercial Department of the ship owners A.P. Moller-Mearsk. His research interests are business ethics, corporate governance and industrial relations, and he has published articles in a variety of journals and a book entitled *Corporate Governance and Accountability* (Liverpool Academic Press, 2000).

4 Virgin Atlantic and British Airways

1 *Guardian* 18.1.93.

2 *Guardian* 12.1.93.

3 *Independent on Sunday* 17.1.93.

4 Ibid.

5 D. Young (1989), *British Airways – Putting the Customer First*, for Ashridge Strategic Management Centre.

6 British Airways *Report & Accounts*, 1991–92.

7 Young, op. cit.: 13.

8 M. Bruce, 'Managing People First – Bringing the Service Concept to British Airways', *Industrial & Commercial Training*, March/April 1987.

9 Höpfl et al. (1992).

10 Op. cit. pp 14–15.

11 *Guardian* 15.1.93.

12 *Independent on Sunday* 17.1.93.

13 *Guardian* 15.1.93.

14 *Guardian* 16.2.93.

15 *Guardian* 8.2.93.

16 *Guardian* 12.1.93.

17 *Independent* 6.2.93.

18 *Guardian* 18.1.93.

19 Ibid.

20 *Independent* 20.3.93.

21 *Financial Times* 20.3.93.

6 Queens Moat Houses

1 Jeff Randall, 'Queens Moat: now you see it, now you don't', *Sunday Times*, 31.10.93.

2 Jeff Randall and Rufus Olins, 'Queens Moat: City anger turns on Howell as new horrors emerge', *Sunday Times*, 31.10.93.

3 Micro View Plus Report, *Results and 14 August 1991 Interim Results*, 10.4.91.

4 Micro View Plus Report, *Results*, 8.4.92.

5 Ibid.

6 Kirstie Hamilton, 'Queens calls in valuers again', *The Times*, 27.11.93.

7 Anon, 'Corporate governance reform hit by QMH affair', *Accounting Age*, 11.11.93.

8 Melvyn Marckus, 'Time for QMH to publish Assets in Wonderland', *The Times*, 6.11.93.

9 Ibid.

10 Micro View Plus Report, *AGM*, 29.11.93.

11 Micro View Plus, *Capital Reorganisation*, 2.2.94.

12 Micro View Plus, Balance *Sheet*, 19.1.94,

13 Philip Pangalos, 'QMH investor issue petition', *Sunday Times*, 28.11.93.

14 Michael Skapinker, 'Queens moat shareholders establish fighting fund', *Financial Times*, 16.11.93.

15 Melvyn Marckus, 'QMH chiefs face a gale of criticism', *The Times*, 29.11.93.

7 Codes of Ethics

1 Though this is a distinction more easily made than defended.

2 A good example of this is the somewhat inspirational Charter of The Body Shop and the role it plays in staff development.

8 Corporate Social Responsibility

1 Research published by Cambridge Business School, April 2003, see www.cus. cam.ac.uk/~akob2/ReputationsSurvey.html/

2 The Department of Trade and Industry, UK, website has a list that includes several of these bodies (www.societyandbusiness.gov.uk/about/business.htm).

3 See www.businessandsociety.gov.uk

4 Taken from the CSR Europe website, www.csreurope.org

5 See, for example, reports from Shell, BP, British American Tobacco (BAT) and MacDonald's, which are available on their websites.

6 See, for example, AA1000, developed by the Institute for Social and Ethical Accountability, UK.

7 From Community Affairs Briefing, December 2001.

I I Strategic Management

1 The Co-operative Bank has now been in existence for over 120 years. Scott-Bader (a 'common-ownership' company) has a turnover of about £50 m and has been in its present form since 1951 (Bader, 1986). Traidcraft (an 'alternative trading company') has a turnover of about £5 m and has been in existence since 1979 (Evans, 1991).

2 Lord Laing, Chairman of United Biscuits, in the forward to the company's Ethics and Operating Principles states: 'United Biscuits' business ethics are not negotiable – a well-founded reputation for scrupulous dealing is itself a priceless company asset and the most important single factor in our success is faithful adherence to our beliefs ... To meet the challenges of a changing world, we are prepared to change everything about ourselves except our values.'

3 Scott-Bader did just this and was the recipient the first certificate of the new legally recognised 'common-ownership' companies after the passing of the Industrial Common Ownership Act in 1976; the owners had in fact transferred ownership to the 'Commonwealth' in 1951 (Bader, 1986).

4 The UK use of the term 'Management Buyout' (MBO) differs from the American. MBOs in the UK sense refer to the purchase of part of a business by its managers – the equivalent American term is 'Leveraged Buyout'. MBOs in the American sense refer to the purchase of a whole company from the shareholders by its management (Williams 1993: i).

5 'Greenmail' is an analogy to 'blackmail'.

6 For example, the benefits of the 1969 merger between Cadburys and Schweppes remain mainly elusive even thirty odd years later; (see case study by Tony Eccles and Martin Stoll; originally published in Hendry and Eccles (1993). See also a newspaper article by William Gleeson, 'Accountants Add Up Cultural Differences', *The Independent on Sunday*, Business Section, 17 July 1994: 4.

7 These details are taken from an article by Jack Schofield entitled 'Mission Impossible', *The Guardian*, Thursday 14 April 1994: 19.

8 These details are taken from an article by Jane Simms entitled 'When a Corporate Resolution becomes Mission Impossible', *The Independent on Sunday*, Business Section, 6 February 1994: 15.

9 Under German law, companies can get the tax back on bribe payments to foreign countries.

10 This was proposed at the Amnesty International British Section Business Group inaugural meeting held at London Business School on 28 April 1994.

15 Accounting

1 The six accounting bodies are:

- The Institute of Chartered Accountants of England and Wales (ICAEW)

- The Institute of Chartered Accountants in Ireland (ICAS)

- The Institute of Chartered Accountants of Scotland (ICAS)

- The Chartered Association of Certified Accountants (ACCA)

- The Chartered Association of Management Accountants (CIMA)

- The Chartered Institute of Public Finance and Accountancy (CIPFA).

2 The extent to which accounting requirements are embodied in legislation or private sector regulations varies between countries.

3 The FRC replaced the Accounting Standards Committee (ASC) in 1990. Prior to 1990, the accounting bodies had direct responsibility for setting and issuing accounting standards, through the ASC.

4 The ICAEW's *Guide to Professional Ethics* is used to illustrate the fundamental principles guiding professional conduct, on which there is broad consensus among the six accounting bodies.

References

Accounting Standard Board (1991) *The Objective of Financial Statements and the Qualitative Characteristics of Financial Information* (Peterborough: ASB).

ACM Code of Ethics and Professional Conduct (adopted by ACM Council 16 November 1992).

Adams, R., Carruthers, J. and Hamil, S. (1991) *Changing Corporate Values* (London: Kogan Page).

Anderson, G. (1992) 'Selection', in B. Towers (ed.), *The Handbook of Human Resource Management* (Oxford: Blackwell).

Andrews, K. (1989) 'Ethics in Practice', *Harvard Business Review*, 67 (5): 99–104.

Ang, J.S. (1993) 'On Financial Ethics', *Financial Management*, Autumn: 32–59.

Aristotle (1947) *Metaphysics*, W.D. Ross (trans.), in T.L. Beauchamp, (1989), *Case Studies in Business Society & Ethics* (Englewood Cliffs, NJ: Prentice Hall).

Audit Commission (1991) *Opportunity Makes a Thief: An Analysis of Computer Abuse* (London: Audit Commission).

Audit Commission (1994) *Survey of Computer Fraud and Abuse* (London: Audit Commission).

Audit Commission (1998) *Survey of Computer Fraud and Abuse* (London: Audit Commission).

B&Q (1999) *Being a Better Trading Neighbour* (Eastleigh: B&Q).

Bader, G.E.S. (1988) 'New Frontiers in Planning – Strategic Issues for the 1990s', *Long Range Planning*, 19 (6): 66–74.

Baily, P. and Farmer, D. (1990) *Purchasing Principles and Management*, 6th edn (London: Pitman).

Baron, M. (1991) 'The Moral Status of Loyalty', in D.G. Johnson (ed.), (1991), *Ethical Issued in Engineering* (Englewood Cliffs, NJ: Prentice Hall): 225–40.

Barr, C. (1993) 'A Code of Ethics: Good, Bad or Indifferent?', Proceedings of 2nd PSERG Conference, University of Bath: 19–26.

Barry, A. (1992) 'Days of Wine and Roses', *Purchasing and Supply Management*, October: 22–25.

Bass, B.M. (1990) *Bass and Stodgill's Handbook of Leadership Theory, Research and Managerial Applications*, 3rd edn (New York: Free Press).

Baumol, W.J. and Batey Blackman, S.A. (1991) *Perfect Markets and Easy Virtue* (Oxford: Blackwell).

Beardwell, I. and Holden, L. (eds) *Human Resource Management: A Contemporary Perspective* (London: Pitman).

Beauchamp, T. and Childress, J. (1989) *Principles of Biomedical Ethics* (Oxford University Press).

Beauchamp, T.L. (1989) *Case Studies in Business, Society, and Ethics* (Englewood Cliffs, NJ: Prentice-Hall).

Bedeian, A.G. (1993) *Management* (New York: Harcourt Brace Jovanovich).

Bennis, W. (1993) *An Invented Life: Reflections on Leadership and Change* (Reading, MA: Addison-Wesley).

Bennis, W.G. (1959) 'Leadership Theory and Administrative Behaviour: The Problem of Authority', *Administrative Science Quarterly*, 4: 259–301.

Bentham, J. (1789) 'Introduction to the Principles of Morals and Legislation', in M. Warnock (ed.), (1962) *Utilitarianism* (London: Fontana).

Blanchfield, C. (1994) 'Consumer Market Responses to Perceived Business Ethics of Financial Institutions', Unpublished MPhil. thesis, University of Huddersfield.

Blanchfield, C., Lea, E.C. and Richards, G. (1994) 'Business Ethics, Do Consumers Care?', Marketing Education Group, Annual Conference, University of Ulster, Coleraine, 4–6 July.

Block, P. (1987) *The Empowered Manager* (San Francisco: Jossey-Bass).

Blyton, P. and Morris, J. (1992) 'HRM and the Limits of Flexibility', in P. Blyton and P. Turnbull (eds), (1992) *Reassessing Human Resource Management* (London: Sage).

Blyton, P. and Turnbull, P. (eds) (1992) *Reassessing Human Resource Management* (London: Sage).

Bok, S. (1983) *Secrets* (New York: Vintage).

Booms, B.H. and Bitner, M.J. (1981) 'Marketing Strategies and Organization Structures for Service Firms', in J.H. Donnelly and W.R. George (eds), (1981), *Marketing of Services* (Chicago, IL: American Marketing Association): 47–51.

Bowie, N. (1990) 'Business Ethics and Cultural Relativism', in P. Madsen and J.M. Shafritz (eds), (1990), *Essentials of Business Ethics* (New York, Meridian): 366–82.

Boyatzis, R.E. (1973), 'Affiliation Motivation', in D. McClelland (ed.), *Human Motivation: A Book of Readings*, (Morristown, NJ: General Learning Press): 252–78.

Bradley, I.C. (1987) *Enlightened Entrepreneurs* (London: Weidenfeld & Nicolson).

Bradley, P. (1989) 'Purchasing Ethics? The Rest of Business Should Be So Strict', *Purchasing*, 4 May: 24–5.

Brazier, M. (1987) *Medicine, Patients and the Law* (London: Penguin).

Brech, E.F.L. (1953) *The Principles and Practice of Management* (London: Longmans).

Brodeur, P. (1972) *Asbestos and Enzymes* (New York: Ballantine Books).

Brown, K.M. (1994) 'Using Role Play to Integrate Ethics into the Curriculum: A Financial Management Example', *Journal of Business Ethics*, February: 105–110.

Browning, J.M. and Zabriskie, N.B. (1980) 'Professionalism in Purchasing: A Status Report', *Journal of Purchasing and Materials Management*, Fall: 2–10.

Browning, J.M. and Zabriskie, N.B. (1983) 'How Ethical are Industrial Buyers?', *Industrial Marketing Management*, 12: 219–24.

Buchholz, R.A. (1989) *Fundamental Concepts and Problems in Business Ethics* (Englewood Cliffs, NJ: Prentice-Hall).

Burke, T., Maddock, S. and Rose, A. (1993) 'How Ethical is British Business?', *Research Working Paper Series 2*, 1, University of Westminster, January.

Business in the Community (2000) *Winning with Integrity – A Guide to Social Responsibility* (Business in the Community).

Cadbury, A. (1992) *The Financial Aspects of Corporate Governance* (London: Stock Exchange).

Caelli, W., Longley, D. and Shain, M. (1989) *Information Security for Managers* (New York: Stockton Press).

Cambridge Business School (2003) April, see www.cus.cam.ac.uk/~akob2/Reputations Survey.html/

Campbell, A. and Tawadey, K. (1992) *Mission and Business Philosophy* (Oxford: Butterworth Heinemann).

Campbell, A. and Yeung, S. (1994) 'Creating a Sense of Mission', in B. Dewit and R. Meyer (eds), (1994), *Strategy: Process, Content, Context* (*An International Perspective*) (St Paul, MN: West Publishing): 147–56.

Cannan, E. (ed.) (1961) *The Wealth of Nations* (Edn first published 1904; first edition 1776), (London: Methuen).

Cannon, T. (1992) *Corporate Responsibility* (London: Pitman).

Cannon, T. (1994) *Corporate Responsibility: A Textbook on Business Ethics, Governance, Environment: Roles and Responsibilities* (London: Pitman).

Carmen, R. and Lubelski, M. (1997) 'Whose Business Is It Anyway? The Question of Sustainability', in P.W.F. Davies (ed.), (1997), *Current Issues in Business Ethics* (London: Routledge).

Carmichael, S. and Drummond, J. (1989) *Good Business* (London: Business Books).

Cartwright, D. and Zander, A. (eds) (1968) *Group Dynamics: Research and Theory* (New York: Harper & Row).

Chadwick, R. (1993) 'Codes and Ethics – An Unhappy Alliance?', Conference on Professional and Business Ethics, Unpublished paper, University of Central Lancashire.

Chartered Institute of Management Accountants (1991) *Management Accounting: Official Terminology* (London: CIMA).

Chonko, L.B. and Hunt, S.D. (1985) 'Ethics and Marketing Management: An Empirical Examination', *Journal of Business Research*, 13 (August), 339–59.

Chryssides, G.D. and Kaler, J.H. (1993) *An Introduction to Business Ethics* (London: Chapman & Hall).

CIPS (1977) *The Ethical Code of the Chartered Institute of Purchasing and Supply* (Stamford: CIPS).

Claypool, G.A., Fetyko, D.F. and Pearson, A. (1990) 'Reactions to Ethical Dilemmas: A Study Pertaining to Certified Public Accountants', *Journal of Business Ethics*, September: 699–706.

Clutterbuck, D., Dearlove, D. and Snow, D. (1992) *Actions Speak Louder: A Management Guide to Corporate Social Responsibility* (London: Kogan Page/Kingfisher).

Cohen, J., Pant, L. and Sharp, D. (1993) 'A Validation and Extension of a Multi-dimensional Ethics Scale', *Journal of Business Ethics* 1: 13–26.

Cohen, J.R. and Pant, L.W. (1991) 'Beyond Bean Counting: Establishing High Ethical Standards', *Journal of Business Ethics*, January: 45–56.

Collins, J.C. and Porras, J.I. (1994) *Built to Last: Successful Habits of Visionary Companies* (London: Century/Random House).

Cooke, R.A. and Young, E. (1990) 'The Ethical Side of Takeovers and Mergers', in Madsen and J.M. Shafritz (eds), (1990), *Essentials of Business Ethics* (New York, Meridian): 254–69.

Co-operative Bank plc (1993) *Performance Management Appraisal*

Co-operative Bank plc. (1992) *Annual Report and Accounts.*

Cottee, P. (1994) 'Report of The Food Commission', in K. Knight, 'Healthy Profits on Low-fat Foods', in *The Times*, Wednesday 19 October 1994.

Croft, R. (1994) 'Multi-level Marketing: Claims to Respectability Under Scrutiny', Marketing Education Group, Proceedings of the 1994 Annual Conference, University of Ulster.

Crouch, C. (1990) 'United Kingdom: The Rejection of Compromise', in G. Baglioni and C. Crouch, *European Industrial Relations: The Challenge of Flexibility* (London: Sage).

Currie, R.M. (1977) *Work Study*, 4th edn (London: Pitman): 4.

Dainty, P.H. and Anderson, M. (1996) *The Capable Executive – Effective Performance in Senior Management* (London: Macmillan).

Danley, J.R. (1993) 'Corporate Moral Agency: The Case for Anthropological Bigotry', in T. Deal and A. Kennedy, (1982), *Corporate Cultures* (Reading, MA: Addison-Wesley).

Dart, R.L. (1991) *Management*, 2nd edn (London: Dryden Press).

David, F.R. (1991) *Strategic Management*, 3rd edn (Basingstoke: Macmillan).

Davies, P.W.F. (1992) *The Contribution of the Philosophy of Technology to the Management of Technology*, PhD Thesis, Brunel University with Henley Management College.

Davis, P. and Worthington, S. (1993) 'Cooperative Values: Change and Continuity in Capital Accumulation. The Case of the British Cooperative Bank', *Journal of Business Ethics*, 12: 849–59.

Deal, T. and Kennedy, A. (1982) *Corporate Cultures* (Reading, MA: Addison-Wesley).

Delaney, J.T. and Sockell, D. (1992) 'Do Company Ethics Training Programmes Make a Difference? An Empirical Analysis', *Journal of Business Ethics*, 11, 719–27.

Department for Trade and Industry (2000) *Modern Company Law Review for a Competitive Economy, Consultation Documents*, March and November.

Dewit, B. and Meyer, R. (eds) (1994) *Strategy: Process, Content, Context* (*An International Perspective*) (St Paul, MN: West Publishing Company).

Donaldson, J. (1989) *Key Issues in Business Ethics* (London: Academic Press)

Donaldson, J. (1992) *Business Ethics – A European Casebook* (London: Academic Press).

Donaldson, J. (1999) 'Codes, Stakeholders and Business Philosophy', *International Journal of Value Based Management*, 12: 241–57.

Donaldson, J. and Davis, P. (1990) 'Business Ethics? Yes, But What Can It Do for the Bottom Line?', *Management Decision*, 28 (6): 29–33.

Donaldson, T. (1989) *The Ethics of International Business* (New York: Oxford University Press).

Drucker, P.F. (1981) 'What is Business Ethics?', *The Public Interest*, Spring.

Dubinsky, A.J. and Gwin, J.M. (1981) 'Business Ethics: Buyers and Sellers', *Journal of Purchasing and Materials Management*, Winter: 9–16.

Engel, J.F., Blackwell, R.D. and Miniard, P.W. (1993) *Consumer Behaviour* (London: Dryden Press).

Ennew, C., McGregor, A. and Diacon, S. (1993) 'Ethical Aspects of Savings and Investment Products', MEG, Proceedings of Annual Conference, 1: 297–307.

Evans, R. (1991) 'Business Ethics and Changes in Society', *Journal of Business Ethics*, 10 (11): 871–6.

Evers, S. (1994) 'The Manager as a Professional', Institute of Management reviewed in *Management Services*, March 1994, 38 (3).

Fearnley, M. (1993) 'Corporate Reputation: The Wasted Asset', *Marketing Intelligence and Planning*, 11 (11): 4–8.

Felch, R.I. (1985) 'Standards of Conduct: The Key to Supplier Relations', *Journal of Purchasing and Materials Management*, Fall: 16–18.

Ferrell, O.C. and Fraedrich, J. (1994) *Business Ethics* (Boston, MA: Houghton Mifflin).

Ferrell, O.C. and Gresham, L.G. (1985) 'A Contingency Framework for Understanding Ethical Decision Making in Marketing', *Journal of Marketing*, 49, Summer: 87–96.

Financial Services Authority (1998) *The Combined Code on Corporate Governance* (London: Financial Services Authority).

Financial Times, 28 October 1995.

Forker, L.B. and Janson, R.L. (1990) 'Ethical Practices in Purchasing', *Journal of Purchasing and Materials Management*, Winter: 19–26.

Forsyth, D.R. (1992) 'Judging the Morality of Business Practice: The Influence of Personal Moral Philosophies', *Journal of Business Ethics*, 11.

Freeman, R.E. (1984) *Strategic Management – A Stakeholder Approach* (London: Pitman).

French, P. (1984) 'The Hester Prynne Sanction', *Business and Professional Ethics Journal*, 4 (2): 19–32.

Friedman, M. (1970) 'The Social Responsibility of Business is to Increase its Profits', *New York Times Magazine*, 13 September, reprinted in G.D. Chryssides and J.H. Kaler (eds), (1993), *An Introduction to Business Ethics* (London: Chapman & Hall) 249–54.

Friedman, M. and Friedman, R. (1980) *Free To Choose* (New York: Harcourt Brace Jovanovich).

Fritzsche, D.J. and Becker, H. (1984) 'Linking Management Behaviour to Ethical Philosophy – An Empirical Investigation', *Journal of Business Ethics*, 27 (1): 166–75.

Fusaro, Peter C. and Miller, Ross M. (2002) *What Went Wrong at Enron? Everyone's Guide to the Largest Bankruptcy in US History* (New York: Wiley).

Gaither, N. (1992) *Production and Operations Management*, 5th edn (Chicago, IL: Dryden Press).

Garrett, T. (1966) *Business Ethics* (Englewood Cliffs, NJ: Prentice-Hall).

Gellerman, S.W. (1986) 'Why Good Managers Make Bad Ethical Choices', *Harvard Business Review*, July/August.

Gibbs, P.T. (1993) 'Customer Care and Service: A Case for Business Ethics', *International Journal of Bank Marketing*, 11 (1): 26–33.

Gilligan, C. (1982) *In a Different Voice: Psychological Theory and Women's Development* (Cambridge, MA: Harvard University Press).

Goodpaster, K.E. (1983a), 'The Concept of Corporate Responsibility', *Journal of Business Ethics*, (2): 1–22.

Goodpaster, K.E. (1983b) *Some Avenues for Ethical Analysis in General Management*, Harvard Business School, Case 9-383-007.

Gordon, K. and Miyake, M. (2001) 'Business Approaches to Combating Bribery: A Study of Codes of Conduct,' *Journal of Business Ethics*, 34: 161–73,

Goyder, G. (1961) *The Responsible Company* (Oxford: Blackwell).

Goyder, G. (1993) *The Just Enterprise* (London: Adamantine Press) (first published in 1987 by André Deutsch).

Greenbury Report (1995) *Study Group on Directors' Remuneration* (London: Confederation of British Industry).

Gunz, S. and McCutcheon, J. (1991) 'Some Unresolved Ethical Issues in Auditing', *Journal of Business Ethics*, October: 777–85.

Hakansson, H. (ed) (1983) *International Marketing and Purchasing of Industrial Goods: An Interaction Approach* (Chichester: Wiley).

Hampel Report (1988) *Committee on Corporate Governance Final Report* (London: Gee Publishing).

Handy, C. (1978) *Understanding Organisations* (London: Penguin).

Handy,C. (1992) 'Balancing Corporate Power: A New Federalist Paper', *Harvard Business Review*, 70 (6), November/December: 59–72.

Harness, D. and MacKay, S. (1994) 'Product Elimination Strategies of the Financial Services Sector', Marketing Education Group, Proceedings of the Annual Conference, University of Ulster.

Harris, N. (1989) *Professional Codes of Conduct in the UK: A Directory* London: Mansell).

Hawken, P. (1993) *The Ecology of Commerce* (New York: HarperCollins).

Hawley, D. (1991) 'Business Ethics and Social Responsibility in Finance', *Journal of Business Ethics*, September: 711–21.

Hay, R.D., Gray, E.R. and Gates, J.E. (1976) Business and Society (Cincinatti, OH: Southwestern.

Hayek, F. (1982) *Law, Legislation and Liberty* (London: Routledge & Kegan Paul).

Hayek, F.A. von (1982) 'The Mirage of Social Justice', *Law, Legislation and Liberty, Vol. 2*, (First published 1976), (London: Routledge & Kegan Paul).

Healey, M. and Iles, J. (2001) 'The Establishment and Enforcement of Codes', Paper presented at the 14th Annual Congress of EBEN, Valencia, September 2001

Hellriegel, D., Slocum, J.W. and Woodman, R.W. (1993) *Organisational Behaviour*, 6th edn (St Paul, MN: West Publishing).

Hendry, J. and Eccles, T. (eds) (1993) *European Cases in Strategic Management: A Resource Pack* (London: Chapman & Hall).

Higgs, D. (2003) *Review of the Role and Effectiveness of Non-Executive Directors*, (London: DTI).

Hiltebeitel, K.M. and Jones, S.K. (1992) 'An Assessment of Ethics Instruction in Accounting Education', *Journal of Business Ethics*: January: 37–46.

Höpfl, H., Mith, S. and Spencer, S. (1992) 'Values and Valuations: The Conflicts between Culture Change & Job Cuts', *Personnel Review*, 21 (1): 24–38.

Hoffman, W,M, (1986) 'What is Necessary for Corporate Moral Excellence', *Journal of Business Ethics*, 5: 233–42.

Hoffman, W.M. (1986) 'What is Necessary for Corporate Moral Excellence', *Journal of Business Ethics*, 5: 232–42.

Hosmer, L.T. (1987) *The Ethics of Management* (New York: Irwin).

Hosmer, L.T. (1991) 'Managerial Responsibilities on the Micro Level', *Business Horizons*, July/August: 49–55.

Hunt, S.D., Chonko, L.B. and Wilcox, J.B. (1984) 'Ethical Problems of Marketing Researchers,' *Journal of Marketing Research*, 21, August: 304–24.

Huss, H.F. and Patterson, D.M. (1993) 'Ethics in Accounting: Values Education Without Indoctrination', *Journal of Business Ethics*, March: 235–43.

Iaccoca, L and Novak, W. (1984) *Iaccoca: An Autobiography* (New York: Bantam Books).

Income Data Services (1990) *European Management Guides: Recruitment* (London: Income Data Services/Institute of Personnel Management).

Institute of Social and Ethical Accountability (2003) Annual Report (London: ISEA).

IPM (1994) *The IPM Code of Professional Conduct: The IPM Codes of Practice* (London: IPM).

IRS (1991) *IRS Recruitment and Development Report*, 'The State of Selection 2', May.

Jago, A. (1982) 'Leadership: Perspectives in Theory and Research', *Management Science*, 28: 315–36.

Jay, A. (1967) *Management and Machiavelli* (London: Penguin).

Jennings, M. (1991) 'Ethics, Excellence and Accountants', *Accountancy*, January: 23–4.

Jeremy, D. (1995) 'Corporate Responses to the Emergent Recognition of a Health Hazard in the UK Asbestos Industry: The Case of Turner & Newall, 1920–1960', *Business and Economic History*, 24 (1): 254–65.

Johnson, D.G. (ed) (1991) *Ethical Issues in Engineering* (Englewood Cliffs, NJ: Prentice-Hall).

Kant, I. (1948) *Groundwork to the Metaphysics of Morals* (trans H.J. Paton), (London: Hutchinson).

Kanungo, R.N. and Mendonca, M. (1996) *Ethical Dimensions of Leadership* (London: Sage).

Kavathatzopoulos, I. (1993) 'Development of a Cognitive Skill in Solving Business Ethics Problems: The Effect of Instruction', *Journal of Business Ethics*, 12: 379–86.

Kitson, A. (1994) *Managing Ethics: The Case of the Cooperative Bank*, European Case Clearing House, no. 494-009-01

Kohlberg, L. (1981) *Essays on Moral Development, Vol. 1: The Philosophy of Moral Development* (San Francisco: Harper & Row).

KPMG (1999) *Most Admired Businesses, 1998* (London: KPMG).

Kullberg, D.R. (1990) 'Business Ethics: Not a Luxury; Standards of Ethical Conduct for Management Accountants', *Management Accounting*, February: 20–1.

Kurschner, D. (1995) 'The 1995 Business Ethics Awards', *Business Ethics Magazine* (online), November/December.

Ladd, J. (1982) 'Collective and Individual Moral Responsibility in Engineering: Some Questions', *IEEE Technology & Society Magazine*, June, 1 (2): 3–10.

Langlois, C.C. and Schlegelmilch, B.B. (1990) 'Do Corporate Codes of Ethics Reflect National Characteristics: Evidence from Europe and the United States', *Journal of International Business Studies*, 519–39.

Langtry, R. (1994) 'Selection', in I. Beardwell and L. Holden (eds), (1997), *Human Resource Management* (London: Pitman).

Lazcniak, G.R. (1983) 'Business Ethics: A Manager's Primer' *Business*, 33, January–March: 23–9.

Lee, S.M. and Schnieder, M.J. (1994) *Operations Management* (Boston, MA: Houghton Mifflin).

Lewis, B.R. (1991) 'Service Quality: An International Comparison of Bank Customers' Expectations and Perceptions', *Journal of Marketing Management*, 7: 47–62.

Lickona, T. (1987) 'What Does Moral Psychology Have to Say to the Teacher of Ethics?', in D. Callahan and S. Bok (eds), (1980), *Ethics Teaching in Higher Education* (New York: Plenum Press).

Loeb, S.E. and J. Rockness (1992) 'Accounting Ethics and Education: A Response', *Journal of Business Ethics*, July: 485–90.

Lowe, J. (1993) 'Manufacturing Reform and the Changing Role of the Production Supervisor', *Journal of Management Studies*, 30 (5), September.

Lynch, D. and Kordis, P.L. (1990) *Strategy of the Dolphin*: (*Winning Elegantly by Coping Powerfully in a World of Turbulent Change*), (First published by Hutchinson in 1989), (London: Arrow).

Lynn, M. (1993) 'Terry Thomas', *Management Today*, July: 44–6.

MacIntyre, A. (1977) 'Why are the Problems of Business Ethics Insoluble?', Conference proceedings from Bentley College, Massachusetts: 99–107.

MacIntyre, A. (1993) *A Short History of Ethics* (London: Routledge).

Maclagan, P. (1993) *Issues Concerning the Moral Development of People in Organisations*, Working Paper Series HUS/PWM/20, University of Hull.

Madsen, P. and Shafritz, J.M. (eds) (1990) *Essentials of Business Ethics* (New York: Meridian).

Malloy, D.C. and Lang, D.L. (1993) 'An Aristotelian Approach to Case Study Analysis', *Journal of Business Ethics*, 12: 511–16.

Manley, W.W. (1992) *The Handbook of Good Business Practice* (London: Routledge).

Martens, S. and Stevens, K. (1994) 'The FASB's Cost/Benefit Constraint in Theory and Practice', *Journal of Business Ethics*, March: 171–9.

Mathews, J.B., Goodpaster, K.E. and Nash, L.L. (1994) *Policies and Persons: A Casebook on Business Ethics* (2nd edn) (New York: McGraw-Hill).

Mathis, R.L. and Jackson, J.H. (1994) *Human Resource Management* (Cincinnati, OH: West Publishing).

McClelland, D.C. and Burnham, D.H. (1995) 'Retrospective Commentary', *Harvard Business Review* (January–February): 138–9.

McDonald, G.M. and Zepp, R.A. (1989) 'Business Ethics – Practical Proposals', *Journal of Management Development*, 8 (1): 55–66.

McIntyre, A. (1981) *After Virtue: A Study of Moral Theory* (London: Duckworth).

McKeon, R. (ed.) (1947) *Introduction to Aristotle* (New York: Modern Library).

McNair, F. and Milam, E.E. (1993) 'Ethics in Accounting Education: What Is Really Being Done', *Journal of Business Ethics*, October: 797–809.

Middleton, N. and O'Keefe, P. (2003) *Rio Plus Ten: Politics, Poverty and the Environment* (London: Pluto Press).

Mill, J.S. (1859) *On Liberty* (London: Longman).

Mill, J.S. (1861) 'Utilitarianism', in M. Warnock (ed.), (1962), *Utilitarianism* (London: Fontana).

Mintzberg, H. (1982) 'If You Are Not Serving Bill and Barbara Then You Are Not Serving Leadership', in J.G. Hunt, U. Sekaran and C.A. Schriesheim (eds), (1982), *Leadership Beyond Establishment Views* (Carbondale: Southern Illinois University Press).

Mintzberg, H. (1994) *The Rise and Fall of Strategic Planning* (Hemel Hempstead: Prentice-Hall International (UK) Ltd).

Mitchell, A., Puxty, T. and Sikka, P. (1994) 'Ethical Statements as Smokescreens for Sectional Interests: The Case of the UK Accountancy', *Journal of Business Ethics*, January: 39–51.

Moor, James H. (1985) 'What Is Computer Ethics?', *Metaphilosophy*, 16 (4): 266–75.

Moor, James H. (1988) 'Reason, Relativity and Responsibility in Computer Ethics', *Computers & Society*, 28 (1): 14–21.

Moor, James H. (1999) 'Just Consequentialism and Computing', *Ethics and Information Technology*, 1 (1): 65–9.

Morris, V.C. (1966) *Existentialism in Education* (New York: Harper & Row).

Murphy, P.E. and Laczniak, G.R. (1981) 'Marketing Ethics: A Review with Implications for Managers, Educators and Researchers', in B. Enis and K. Roering (eds), *Review of Marketing 1981* (Chicago, IL: American Marketing Association): 251–66.

Narayanam, D. (1992) 'The Right Stuff', *Purchasing and Supply Management*, October: 25–6.

Nash, L. (1981) 'Ethics without the Sermon', *Harvard Business Review*, November/December.

Nash, L. (1991) 'American and European Corporate Ethics Practices', in J. Mahoney and E. Vallance (eds), (1992) *Business Ethics in a New Europe* (Dordrecht: Kluwer).

Packard, V. (1969) *The Status Seekers* (New York: McKay).

Pagano, A.M and Verdin, J.A. (1988) *The External Environment of Business* (cited by R.L. Dart, 1991) (Chichester: Wiley): ch. 5.

Parasuraman, A., Zeithaml, V. and Berry, L.L. (1985) 'A Conceptual Model of Service Quality and its Implications for Future Research', *Journal of Marketing*, 49, Fall: 41–50.

Patten, D.M. (1990) 'The Differential Perception of Accountants to Maccoby's Head/Heart Traits', *Journal of Business Ethics*, October: 791–8.

Peek, L.E., Peek, G.S. and Horras, M. (1994) 'Enhancing Arthur Business Ethics Vignettes: Group', *Journal of Business Ethics*, March: 189–96.

Peters, T. (1987) *Thriving on Chaos* (New York: Alfred A. Knopf).

Peters, T.J. and Waterman, R.H. (1982) *In Search of Excellence* (New York: Harper & Row).

Petrella, R. *et al.* (2001) *The Water Manifesto: Arguments for a World Water Contract* (London: Zed Books).

Petrick, J.A. and Quinn, J.F. (1997) *Management Ethics: Integrity at Work* (Thousand Oaks, CA: Sage).

Porter, M.E. (1980) *Competitive Strategy* (New York: Free Press).

Premeaux, S.R. and Mondy, R.W. (1993) 'Linking Management Behaviour to Ethical Philosophy', *Journal of Business Ethics*, 12 (5), May.

Ramsey, J. (1989) 'No Bribes Please, We're Professionals', *Purchasing and Supply Management*, December: 31–3.

Raven, W. (1994) *Considering Stakeholders' Interests* (London: Corporate Social Responsibility Consultants).

Rawls, J. (1972) *A Theory of Justice* (Oxford: Oxford University Press).

Ricklefs, R. (1983) 'Executives and General Public Say Ethical Behaviour is Declining in US', *Wall Street Journal*, 31 October, 25.

Robinson, D. (2002) www.theglobeandmail.com, 12 December.

Robson, P. (1992) 'A Day at the Races, A Night at the Opera', *Purchasing and Supply Management*, October: 27–9.

Rogerson, S. (1998) 'The Ethics of Information and Communications Technologies (ICT) in Business', *IMIS Journal*, 8 (2), May).

Ross, W.D. (1938) *The Right and the Good* (Oxford: Clarendon Press).

Royal Society for the Encouragement of Arts, Manufacture and Commerce (RSA) (1995) *Tomorrow's Company: The Role of Business in a Changing World* (Aldershot: Gower).

Rudelius, W. and Buchholz, R.A. (1979) 'What Industrial Purchasers See as Key Ethical Dilemmas', *Journal of Purchasing and Materials Management*, Winter: 2–10.

Sager, I. Elgin, B., Elstrom, P., Keenan, F. and Gogoi, P. (2002) *The Underground Web Business Week Online*, (www.businessweek.com), 2 September.

Schlachter, P.J. (1990) 'Organisational Influences on Individual Ethical Behaviour', *Journal of Business Ethics*, November: 389–853.

Schroeder, Doris (2002) 'Ethics from the Top: Top Management and Ethical Business', *Journal of Business Ethics*, 11 (3), July : 260–7.

Schuler, R.S. and Huber, V.L. (1993) *Personnel and Human Resource Management* (St Paul, MN: West Publishing).

Selwyn, N.M. (1993) *Selwyn's Law of Employment* (London: Butterworth).

Sen, A. (1987) *On Ethics and Economics* (Oxford: Blackwell).

Senge, P.M. (1990) 'The Leader's New Work: Building Learning Organisations', *Sloan Management Review*, 32 (1), Fall: 7–23.

Senge, P.M. (1990) *The Fifth Discipline: The Art and Practice of the Learning Organisation* (New York: Doubleday/Currency).

Shaw, W. and Barry, V. (1989) *Moral Issues in Business* (Belmont, CA: Wadsworth).

Sibley, S.D. (1979) 'Images of the Purchasing Department', *Journal of Purchasing and Materials Management*, Fall: 19–23.

Simon, H.A. (1947) *Administrative Behaviour: A Study of Decision-making Processes in Administrative Organisations* (New York: Macmillan).

Sinclair, A. (1993) 'Approaches to Organisational Culture and Ethics', *Journal of Business Education*, 12: 63–73.

Singer, A.E. (1994) 'Strategy as Moral Philosophy', *Strategic Management Journal*, 15: 191–213.

Sisson K, 1994, *Personnel Management: A Comprehensive Guide to Theory and Practice in Britain* (Cambridge: Blackwell).

Sisson, K. (1989) *Personnel Management in Britain* (Oxford: Blackwell).

Skapinker, M. (2000) 'Diverse Qualities Vie for Attention', *Financial Times*, 13 December.

Smith, A. (1976) *An Inquiry into the Nature and Causes of the Wealth of Nations* (first published 1776) (Oxford: Oxford University Press).

Smith, A. (1982) *The Theory of Moral Sentiments* (first published 1759) (Indianapolis, IN: Liberty Fund).

Smith, I.T. and Wood, J.C. (1993) *Industrial Law* (London: Pitman).

Snoeyenbos, M. and Jewell, D. (1983), 'Morals, Management and Codes', in M. Snoeyenbos, R. Almeder and J. Humber (eds), (1983), *Business Ethics* (New York: Prometheus Books, New York.

Solomon, R. (1992) *Ethics and Excellence: Cooperation and Integrity in Business* (New York and Oxford: Oxford University Press).

Sorell, T. and Hendry, J. (1994) *Business Ethics* (Oxford: Butterworth Heinemann).

Sparkes, R. (2002) *Socially Responsible Investment: A Global Revolution* (London: John Wiley).

Stacey, R.D. (1993) *Strategic Management and Organisational Dynamics* (London: Pitman).

Stanga, K.G. and Turpen, R.A. (1991) 'Ethical Judgements on Selected Accounting Issues: An Empirical Study', *Journal of Business Ethics*, October: 739–47.

Stead, W.E., Worrel, D.L. and Stead, G.S. (1990) 'An Integrative Model for Understanding and Managing Ethical Behaviour in Organisations', *Journal of Business Ethics*, 9: 215–26.

Stevenson, W.J. (1993) *Production/Operations Management* (Chicago, IL: Irwin): 17.

Stone, B. (1997) *Confronting Company Politics* (London: Macmillan).

Tendler, S. (1994) 'A Nation of Robbers, Fiddlers and Thieves', *The Times*, 21 September.

The Register (2002) www.theregister.co.uk 26 September.

Times Higher Education Supplement, The (1995) 4 August.

Toffler, A. (1970) *Future Shock* (London: Bodley Head).

Tombs, The Lord (1995) 'Truth of "Substantial profits" at T&N', Business Letters in *The Times*, 17th November.

Tomlinson, Heather (2002) 'The Thing is: The Curse of Enron', *Independent on Sunday*, London, 25 August: 5.

Torrington, D. and Hall, L. (1987) *Personnel Management: A New Approach* (Englewood Cliffs, NJ: Prentice-Hall).

Towers, B. (2003) 'The Changing Employment Relationship', in B. Towers (ed.), (2003) (4th edn), *The Handbook of Employment Relations Law and Practice* (London: Kogan Page).

Turnbull Report, (1999) *Guidance for Directors on the Combined Code*, September, (London: ICAEW).

Tweedale, G. (2000) *Magic Mineral to Killer Dust: Turner & Newall and the Asbestos Hazard* (Oxford: Oxford University Press).

US Dept. Health, Education and Welfare, NIH 78-1594, 1978.

Unilever (1981) *Our Business Philosophy* (London: Unilever).

Waite, J. (1993a) 'The Shocking Story of Asbestos', *Face the Facts*, BBC Radio 4, 6 October.

Waite, J. (1993b) 'Asbestos in the Third World', *Face the Facts*, BBC Radio 4, 13 October.

Walzer, M. (1983) *Spheres of Justice* (New York: Basic Books).

Waples, E. and Shaub, M.K. (1991) 'Establishing an Ethic of Accounting: A Response to Westra's Call for Government Employment of Auditors', *Journal of Business Ethics*, May: 385–93.

Ward, S.P., Ward, D.R. and Deck, A.B. (1993) 'Certified Public Accountants: Ethical Perception Skills', *Journal of Business Ethics*, August: 601–10.

Warner, E. (2002) 'The Scandal is that a Parachute comes First', *The Guardian*, 5 January.

Warren, M.J. and Furnell, S.M. (1999) Australian Institute of Computer Ethics Conference, Lilidale.

Watson, T. (1994) 'Recruitment and Selection', in K. Sisson (ed.), (1994), *Personnel Management: A Comprehensive Guide to Theory and Practice in Britain* (Cambridge: Blackwell).

Weaver, G.R. (1993) 'Corporate Codes of Ethics: Purpose, Process and Content Issues', *Business and Society*, 33 (1): 46.

Webley, S. (1988) *Company Philosophies and Codes of Business Ethics: A Guide to their Drafting and Use* (London: Institute of Business Ethics).

Webley, S. (1992) *Business Ethics and Company Codes* (London: Institute of Business Ethics).

Webley, S. and Le Jeune, M. (2001) *Ethical Business – A Report on a Survey of Corporate Codes of Conduct* (London: Institute of Business Ethics).

Whittington, R. (1993) *What is Strategy – And Does It Matter?* (London: Routledge).

Williams, J.G. (1993) 'Management Buyouts: Technical Problems or Ethical Dilemmas', Conference on Professional & Business Ethics (unpublished paper), October, University of Central Lancashire.

Wittgenstein, L. (1980) *Culture and Value* (Oxford: Blackwell).

Wood, G. (1994) 'Ethical Issues at the Marketing/Purchasing Interface: The Practitioner's Experience', Proceedings of the British Academy of Management Conference, University of Lancaster.

World Bank (2007) *The Many Faces of Corruption* (Washington, DC: World Bank).

Zaleznik, A. (1977) 'Managers and Leaders: Are They Different?', *Harvard Business Review*, May–June: 67–78.

Websites

www.bbc.co.uk (2002) 'Fake Bank Website Cons Victims', 8 October.

www.businessweek.com

www.cauxroundtable.org

www.cepnyc.org

www.csreurope.org

www.cus.cam.ac.uk/~akob2/ReputationsSurvey.html/

www.ethical-junction.org

www.goodcorporation.com

www.salon.com (2002) 'Free Speech and the Internet: A Fish Story', 4 April.

www.uksif.org (UK Social Investment Forum)

Cambridge Business School, April 2003, see www.cus.cam.ac.uk/~akob2/ReputationsSurvey.html/

Index